5th Workshop on Technologies for MT of Low Resource Languages (LoResMT 2022)

Gyeongju, South Korea
12 – 17 October 2022

ISBN: 978-1-7138-6191-1

Printed from e-media with permission by:

Curran Associates, Inc.
57 Morehouse Lane
Red Hook, NY 12571

CURRAN ASSOCIATES INC. proceedings.com

Some format issues inherent in the e-media version may also appear in this print version.

Printed with permission by Curran Associates, Inc. (2023)

For permission requests, please contact the Association for Computational Linguistics at the address below.

Association for Computational Linguistics
209 N. Eighth Street
Stroudsburg, Pennsylvania 18360

Phone: 1-570-476-8006
Fax: 1-570-476-0860

acl@aclweb.org

Additional copies of this publication are available from:

Curran Associates, Inc.
57 Morehouse Lane
Red Hook, NY 12571 USA
Phone: 845-758-0400
Fax: 845-758-2633
Email: curran@proceedings.com
Web: www.proceedings.com

COLING

International Conference on Computational Linguistics

Proceedings of the Conference and Workshops

COLING

Volume 29 (2022), No. 2

Proceedings of The Fifth Workshop on Technologies for Machine Translation of Low-Resource Languages (LoResMT 2022)

The 29th International Conference on Computational Linguistics

October 12 - 17, 2022
Gyeongju, Republic of Korea

ISSN 2951-2093

Preface

Based on the success of past low-resource machine translation (MT) workshops at AMTA 2018 (https://amtaweb.org/), MT Summit 2019 (https://www.mtsummit2019.com), AACL-IJCNLP 2020 (http://aacl2020.org/), and AMTA 2021, we introduce the Fifth LoResMT workshop at COLING 2022. In the past few years, machine translation (MT) performance has improved significantly. With the development of new techniques such as multilingual translation and transfer learning, the use of MT is no longer a privilege for users of popular languages. Consequently, there has been an increasing interest in the community to expand the coverage to more languages with different geographical presences, degrees of diffusion and digitalization. However, the goal to increase MT coverage for more users speaking diverse languages is limited by the fact the MT methods demand vast amounts of data to train quality systems, which has posed a major obstacle to developing MT systems for low-resource languages. Therefore, developing comparable MT systems with relatively small datasets is still highly desirable.

Despite all these encouraging developments in MT technologies, creating an MT system for a new language from scratch or even improving an existing system still requires a considerable amount of work in collecting the pieces necessary for building such systems. Due to the data-hungry nature of NMT approaches, the need for parallel and monolingual corpora in different domains is never saturated. The development of MT systems requires reliable test sets and evaluation benchmarks. In addition, MT systems still rely on several NLP tools to pre-process human-generated texts in the forms that are required as input for MT systems and post-process the MT output in proper textual forms in the target language. These NLP tools include, but are not limited to, word tokenizers/de-tokenizers, word segmenters, and morphological analysers. The performance of these tools has a great impact on the quality of the resulting translation. There is only limited discussion on these NLP tools, their methods, their role in training different MT systems, and their coverage of support in the many languages of the world.

LoResMT provides a discussion panel for researchers working on MT systems/methods for low-resource, under-represented, ethnic and endangered languages in general. This year we received research papers covering a wide range of languages spoken in Asia, Latin America, Africa and Europe. These languages are Cebuano, English, Filipino, Gujarati, Haitian, Indonesian, Jamaican, Kannada, Lambani, Luhya, Malaysian, Marathi, Persian, Romanian, Spanish Sign and Swahili. We received both resource papers (monolingual, parallel corpora, formalisms) and methods papers, ranging from unsupervised, transfer-learning, and zero-shot to multilingual NMT. The workshop also received papers on Sign language and evaluation methods for MT. The acceptance rate of LoResMT this year is 53%. In addition to the research papers, the workshop hosts two invited talks. Vishrav Chaudhary gives the first invited talk from Microsoft Turing, who described the Mining Methods for Low Resource MT. In the second invited talk, Pushpak Bhattacharyya from the Indian Institute of Technology Bombay explains multilingual computation, focusing on Machine Translation, in a low-resource setting.

We would sincerely like to thank all of our program committee members for their valuable help in reviewing the submissions and providing their constructive feedback for improving the workshop: Alberto Poncelas, Alina Karakanta, Amirhossein Tebbifakhr, Anna Currey, Arturo Oncevay, Aswath Abhilash Dara, Barry Haddow, Beatrice Savoldi, Bogdan Babych, Constantine Lignos, Daan van Esch, Diptesh Kanojia, Ekaterina Vylomova, Eleni Metheniti, Eva Vanmassenhove, Jasper Kyle Catapang, Liangyou Li, Majid Latifi, Maria Art Antonette Clariño, Mathias Müller, Monojit Choudhury, Nathaniel Oco, Rico Sennrich, Saliha Muradoglu, Sangjee Dondrub, Santanu Pal, Sardana Ivanova, Shantipriya

Parida, Sunit Bhattacharya, Surafel M. Lakew, Thepchai Supnithi, Valentin Malykh, Vukosi Marivate, Wen Lai, Xiaobing Zhao. We are grateful to our invited speakers for their engaging presentations and the insights they brought to the workshop. We would further like to thank the workshop chairs, Sadao Kurohashi, Seung-Hoon Na, and Damira Mrsic, for their guidance and support in organising the workshop, as well as the remote presentation chair, for the hard work in preparing the workshop page. Finally, we are grateful to all the authors who submitted and presented their work to LoResMT.

Atul Kr. Ojha and Chao-Hong Liu
(On behalf of the workshop chairs)

Organizing Committee

Workshop Chairs

Atul Kr. Ojha, Data Science Institute, Insight Centre for Data Analytics, University of Galway & Panlingua Language Processing LLP
Chao-Hong Liu, Potamu Research Ltd
Ekaterina Vylomova, University of Melbourne, Australia
Jade Abbott, Retro Rabbit
Jonathan Washington, Swarthmore College
Nathaniel Oco, National University (Philippines)
Tommi A Pirinen, UiT The Arctic University of Norway, Tromsø
Valentin Malykh, Huawei Noah's Ark lab and Kazan Federal University
Varvara Logacheva Skolkovo, Institute of Science and Technology
Xiaobing Zhao, Minzu University of China

Program Committee

Alberto Poncelas, Rakuten, Singapore
Alina Karakanta, Fondazione Bruno Kessler
Amirhossein Tebbifakhr, Fondazione Bruno Kessler
Anna Currey, Amazon Web Services
Aswarth Abhilash Dara, Amazon
Arturo Oncevay, University of Edinburgh
Atul Kr. Ojha, Data Science Institute, Insight Centre for Data Analytics, University of Galway & Panlingua Language Processing LLP
Bharathi Raja Chakravarthi, University of Galway
Bogdan Babych, Heidelberg University
Chao-Hong Liu, Potamu Research Ltd
Constantine Lignos, Brandeis University, USA
Daan van Esch, Google
Diptesh Kanojia, University of Surrey, UK
Duygu Ataman, University of Zurich
Ekaterina Vylomova, University of Melbourne, Australia
Eleni Metheniti, CLLE-CNRS and IRIT-CNRS
Francis Tyers, Indiana University
Kalika Bali, MSRI Bangalore, India
Koel Dutta Chowdhury, Saarland University (Germany)
Jade Abbott, Retro Rabbit
Jasper Kyle Catapang, University of the Philippines
John P. McCrae, DSI, University of Galway
Liangyou Li, Noah's Ark Lab, Huawei Technologies
Majid Latifi, University of York, York, UK
Maria Art Antonette Clariño, University of the Philippines Los Baños
Mathias Müller, University of Zurich
Monojit Choudhury, Microsoft Turing
Nathaniel Oco, National University (Philippines)
Rico Sennrich, University of Zurich
Saliha Muradoglu, The Australian National University
Sangjee Dondrub, Qinghai Normal University
Santanu Pal, WIPRO AI
Sardana Ivanova, University of Helsinki

Shantipriya Parida, Silo AI
Sunit Bhattacharya, Charles University
Surafel Melaku Lakew, Amazon AI
Tommi A Pirinen, UiT The Arctic University of Norway, Tromsø
Wen Lai, Center for Information and Language Processing, LMU Munich
Valentin Malykh, Huawei Noah's Ark lab and Kazan Federal University

Invited Speakers

1. Pushpak Bhattacharya, IIT-Bomaby

   Title: Low Resource Machine Translation- A Perspective

   Abstract: This talk is on multilingual computation, focussing on Machine Translation, in low-resource settings. Tasks in this area have to grapple with the characteristic problem of disambiguation in the face of resource scarcity, which is the reality for most languages and also arguably for ANY language when it comes to very high-end NLP tasks like, say, 100% disambiguation as demanded by pure interlingua based MT. Starting with our early work on rule-based MT, we move to our research in Low Resource Machine Translation, covering SMT, NMT, segmenting, pivoting, and semi and unsupervised MT. The findings covered in this talk are based on contributions by many students and researchers over many years, reported in top conferences and journals.

   About the Speaker: Prof Pushpak Bhattacharyya (http://www.cse.iitb.ac.in/ pb) is a Professor of Computer Science and Engineering at IIT Bombay. He has done extensive research in Natural Language Processing and Machine Learning. Some of his noteworthy contributions are IndoWordnet, Eye Tracking assisted NLP, Low Resource MT and Knowledge Graph-Deep Learning Synergy in Information Extraction and Question Answering. He has published close to 400 research papers, has authored/co-authored 6 books including a textbook on machine translation, and has guided more than 350 students for their Ph.D., master's, and Undergraduate thesis. Prof. Bhattacharyya is a Fellow of the National Academy of Engineering, Abdul Kalam National Fellow, Distinguished Alumnus of IIT Kharagpur, and past President of ACL.

2. Vishrav Chaudhary, Microsoft Turing

   Title: Mining Methods for Low Resource MT

   Abstract: TBD

   About the Speaker: Vishrav Chaudhary, Senior Principal Researcher at Microsoft Turing, leading efforts around large-scale multilingual models. In the past, Vishrav's research has been focused on several aspects of Machine Translation including Low-Resource translation and Quality Estimation, Cross-lingual understanding, Transfer Learning, Efficient model architectures and Domain Adaptation.

Table of Contents

Conference Program

Sunday, October 16, 2022 (GMT+9)

09:00–10:05 **Inagural Session**
Chair: Atul Kr. Ojha

09:00–09:15 *Opening remarks*
Workshop Chairs

09:15–10:05 *Keynote talk: Mining Methods for Low Resource MT*
Vishrav Chaudhary, Microsoft Turing

10:00–10:30 **Q&A Session 1**
Chair: Ekaterina Vylomova

10:05–10:15 *Very Low Resource Sentence Alignment: Luhya and Swahili*
Everlyn Chimoto and Bruce Bassett

10:15–10:30 *Multiple Pivot Languages and Strategic Decoder Initialization Helps Neural Machine Translation*
Shivam Mhaskar and Pushpak Bhattacharyya

10:30–11:00 ***COFFEE/TEA BREAK***

11:00–12:30 **Q&A Session 2**
Chair: Jonathan Washington

11:00–11:30 *Known Words Will Do: Unknown Concept Translation via Lexical Relations*
Winston Wu and David Yarowsky

11:30–12:00 *The Only Chance to Understand: Machine Translation of the Severely Endangered Low-resource Languages of Eurasia*
Anna Mosolova and Kamel Smaili

12:00–12:30 *Data-adaptive Transfer Learning for Translation: A Case Study in Haitian and Jamaican*
Nathaniel Robinson, Cameron Hogan, Nancy Fulda and David R. Mortensen

12:30–14:00 ***LUNCH BREAK***

Sunday, October 16, 2022 (GMT+9) (continued)

14:00–14:55 Keynote talk
Chair: Chao-Hong Liu

14:00–14:55 *Low Resource Machine Translation- A Perspective*
Pushpak Bhattacharyya, Indian Institute of Technology Bombay

14:55–15:30 Q&A Session 3
Chair: Nathaniel Oco

14:55–15:05 *Augmented Bio-SBERT: Improving Performance for Pairwise Sentence Tasks in Biomedical Domain*
Sonam Pankaj and Amit Gautam

15:05–15:15 *Machine Translation for a Very Low-Resource Language - Layer Freezing Approach on Transfer Learning*
Amartya Chowdhury, Deepak K. T., Samudra Vijaya K and S. R. Mahadeva Prasanna

15:15–15:30 *HFT: High Frequency Tokens for Low-Resource NMT*
Edoardo Signoroni and Pavel Rychlý

15:30–16:00 *COFFEE/TEA BREAK*

16:00–17:00 Q&A Session 4
Chair: Valentin Malykh

16:00–16:30 *Romanian Language Translation in the RELATE Platform*
Vasile Pais, Maria Mitrofan and Andrei-Marius Avram

16:30–17:00 *Translating Spanish into Spanish Sign Language: Combining Rules and Data-driven Approaches*
Luis Chiruzzo, Euan McGill, Santiago Egea-Gómez and Horacio Saggion

Very Low Resource Sentence Alignment: Luhya and Swahili

Everlyn Asiko Chimoto
University of Cape Town, South Africa
African Institute for Mathematical Sciences
everlyn@aims.ac.za

Bruce A. Bassett
University of Cape Town, South Africa
African Institute for Mathematical Sciences, South Africa
South African Astronomical Observatory
bruce.a.bassett@gmail.com

Abstract

Language-agnostic sentence embeddings generated by pre-trained models such as LASER and LaBSE are attractive options for mining large datasets to produce parallel corpora for low-resource machine translation. We test LASER and LaBSE in extracting bitext for two related low-resource African languages: Luhya and Swahili. For this work, we created a new parallel set of nearly 8000 Luhya-English sentences which allows a new zero-shot test of LASER and LaBSE. We find that LaBSE significantly outperforms LASER on both languages. Both LASER and LaBSE however perform poorly at zero-shot alignment on Luhya, achieving just 1.5% and 22.0% successful alignments respectively (P@1 score). We fine-tune the embeddings on a small set of parallel Luhya sentences and show significant gains, improving the LaBSE alignment accuracy to 53.3%. Further, restricting the dataset to sentence embedding pairs with cosine similarity above 0.7 yielded alignments with over 85% accuracy.

1 Introduction

Sentence alignment is the creation of parallel corpora from monolingual data (Gale and Church, 1993; Kay and Roscheisen, 1993). This alignment can be done manually and/or automatically. Manual alignment is laborious and costly hence there has been a lot of work on automatic sentence alignment (Steingrímsson et al., 2021; Schwenk, 2018; Guo et al., 2018). Tasks such as Building Using Comparable Corpora (BUCC) focus on building parallel corpora using neural methods (Zweigenbaum et al., 2017, 2018). Essentially, sentences are aligned to the corresponding translation in another language using language agnostic sentence embeddings with the idea that sentences that are translations of each other will be close in the vector space (Huang et al., 2015; Zhang et al., 2015). These sentence embeddings are generated using pre-trained models such as Language Agnostic Sentence Representation (LASER) and Language Agnostic BERT Sentence Embeddings (LaBSE) (Schwenk and Douze, 2017; Artetxe and Schwenk, 2019; Feng et al., 2022). LASER and LaBSE have been used to effectively mine bitext from comparable corpora.

As these pre-trained models are effective in mining bitext, we investigate how they would perform on an unseen low-resource language: Luhya, Marama dialect, as well as Swahili. Our main contributions are:

1. We created a Luhya-English parallel corpus of nearly 8000 aligned Luhya[1] and English sentences.

2. An empirical evaluation of LASER and LaBSE on Luhya and Swahili datasets.

3. Fine-tuning Luhya embeddings to improve bitext mining for this unseen language to explore the value of small amounts of parallel sentences for improving zero-shot performance.

2 Multilingual Sentence Embeddings

In this section, we review LASER and LaBSE.

2.1 LASER

Language Agnostic SEntence Representation (LASER) is a framework used to obtain multilingual sentence embeddings (Schwenk and Douze, 2017). It borrows from neural machine translation by utilizing encoders and decoders to generate the sentence embeddings which are of a fixed size in this case 1024 (Kalchbrenner and Blunsom, 2013; Sutskever et al., 2014; Cho et al., 2014).

The encoder-decoder architecture is shown in Figure 1. The encoder consists of 1-5 stacked BiLSTM layers each of dimension size 512 Artetxe and Schwenk (2019). The output of the encoder is

[1] Also sometimes written as Luhyia.

Proceedings of the 29th International Conference on Computational Linguistic, pages 1–8
October 12–17, 2022.

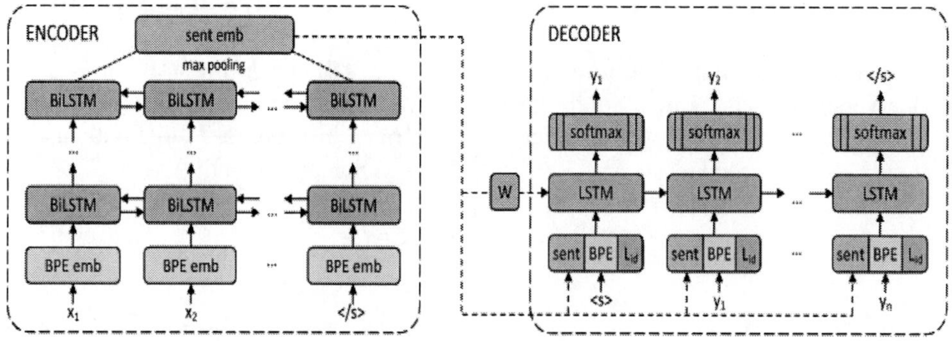

Figure 1: The LASER architecture as proposed by Artetxe and Schwenk (2019) consisting of a single encoder and a single decoder. The encoder has 1-5 stacked BiLSTM layers followed by a max pooling. The decoder is an auxiliary component.

max pooled to get the sentence embeddings. On the other hand, the decoder is an auxiliary component that consists of an LSTM layer of dimension 2048. LASER was trained by feeding 93 input languages to the system with a joint Byte Pair Encoding (BPE) with 50k merge operations. While the input to the encoder is just the BPE embedding, the input to the decoder consists of the sentence embedding generated by the encoder, the BPE embedding of the translation as well as the language ID. The encoder does not include the language ID since the goal is to allow the model to learn language-independent representations.

At the time of its release, LASER achieved state-of-the-art results in mining bitext in the BUCC task dataset (Zweigenbaum et al., 2017, 2018) for all language pairs except Chinese-English.

2.2 LaBSE

The Language Agnostic BERT Sentence Embeddings (LaBSE) framework is a cross-lingual approach that utilises a pre-trained BERT model to generate sentence embeddings (Feng et al., 2022; Yang et al., 2019a). The LaBSE model consists of 12-layer transformer dual encoders which share parameters (Guo et al., 2018). These encoders are initialized using pre-trained BERT weights (Devlin et al., 2019). Each encoder is fed source and target text respectively and embeddings are trained by minimizing the translation ranking loss with additive margin softmax (Yang et al., 2019b); see Figure 2 for further details. Each output embedding vector has dimension 768. The LaBSE model was trained on 109 languages and achieved state-of-the-art performance with bitext mining as shown in Feng et al. (2022); Heffernan et al. (2022).

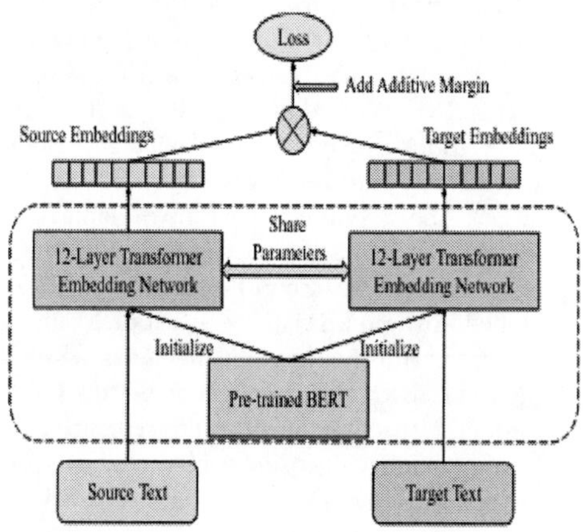

Figure 2: The LaBSE architecture as proposed by Feng et al. (2022) which uses a dual encoder, one taking in the source sentence while the other taking in the target sentence. The encoders are initialized using pre-trained BERT weights and the architecture is trained using the translation ranking loss with additive margin.

3 Languages

In this section, we provide a brief description of the low-resource languages experimented on: Luhya (Marama dialect) and Swahili. The Marama dialect of the Luhya language, also known as Olumarama, is spoken in Western Kenya in Kakamega and Vihiga region with about 43,000 speakers (Eberhard et al., 2021). The language status of Marama is educational as it is used vigorous both verbally and in broadcast media (Eberhard et al., 2021). On the other hand, Swahili is spoken in East and Central

Africa including countries such as Kenya, Tanzania, DRC, parts of Uganda & Rwanda and has approximately 100 million speakers (Eberhard et al., 2021). Its status is national as several countries use it as their national language (Eberhard et al., 2021). These two languages are both Bantu languages from the Niger-Congo language family (World Atlas of Language Structures, 2021). Being from the same language family, they have the same word order structure, namely sentences follow a Subject-Verb-Object (SVO) ordering. They are also both agglutinative. Since both LASER and LaBSE were trained on Swahili, Luhya makes a very interesting zero-shot example to see how much information is transferred from the raw embeddings.

4 Related work

With the proliferation of neural embedding techniques, there have been various efforts to align sentences in various low-resource languages. Thompson and Koehn (2019) introduce VecAlign which aligns sentences using LASER sentence embeddings (Artetxe and Schwenk, 2019) similarity as well as dynamic programming approximation. They experiment on low-resource language pairs namely: Sinhala-English and Nepali-English. They show that the sentences aligned using this method achieve improvement in machine translation models downstream.

On the other hand, Tien et al. (2021) proposed KC4Align that utilises a multilingual translation system to generate embeddings. The similarity in these embeddings is used to perform paragraph alignment. Sentences are aligned where the sentences appear in the paragraph alignment using similarity scores and sentence length ratio. This method was tested on the Vietnamese-Laos language pair. Focusing on African low-resource language, Schwenk et al. (2021) extracts parallel sentences from Wikipedia using multilingual sentences embeddings for Swahili among other languages.

Regarding Luhya, there has been work on building Luhya datasets. Steimel (2018) work focuses on parts of speech tagging for the Wanga Luhya dialect whereas Wanzare et al. (2022) focuses on producing parallel datasets for several Luhya dialects to English with the help of human translators. This is in contrast to our work which analyses automatic sentence alignment for Luhya.

5 Methodology

5.1 LASER and LaBSE evaluation

LASER and LaBSE were utilised to generate our raw embeddings. Following the embedding generation, we compute the cosine similarity and the Euclidean distance (L2) from each vector in the English embedding set and all the Luhya/Swahili embeddings. Sentences are aligned to the most similar or closest sentence. We took both the Top-1 and Top-3 best alignments to test the performance of the pre-trained models.

We use accuracy as our key metric. An important note is that we evaluate alignment performance by demanding exact matching of sentence indices on both sides. This means that if a sentence appears more than once in one of the languages, and the alignment chooses the "wrong" index, despite the sentence being identical to the "correct" sentence, then this is classified as a fail. This will apply primarily to the Top-1 results. As a consequence, our accuracy estimates should be taken as a lower bound on the true alignment performance.

5.2 Fine-tuning the embeddings

To fine-tune our Luhya embeddings, we added a fully-connected network with a single hidden layer to help learn new weights where the cosine similarity between the new embedding and the English embedding would be greatest. We defined the loss as:

$$\text{Loss}(\mathbf{x}, \mathbf{y}) = 1 - S_C(\tilde{\mathbf{x}}, \mathbf{y})$$

where $\mathbf{x}, \mathbf{y}$ are the raw Luhya and English embeddings, S_C is the cosine similarity and $\tilde{\mathbf{x}}$ are the fine-tuned Luhya embeddings which depend on $\mathbf{w}_{1,2}$, the vectors of new weights introduced by the fine-tuning architecture (Pal and Savvides, 2017). $\mathbf{w}_1$ representing weights to the hidden layer and $\mathbf{w}_2$ representing weights to the output layer. The bottleneck layer size is a hyper-parameter that we vary to explore its impact on performance; see Figure 3.

6 Experiments

6.1 Datasets and Alignment

We experiment on both Luhya-English and Swahili-English sentence alignment. The Luhya-English parallel set was created by aligning sentences from the New Testament Bible translations. This dataset consists of 7952 parallel sentences in the Marama dialect of Luhya. This bitext creation was achieved

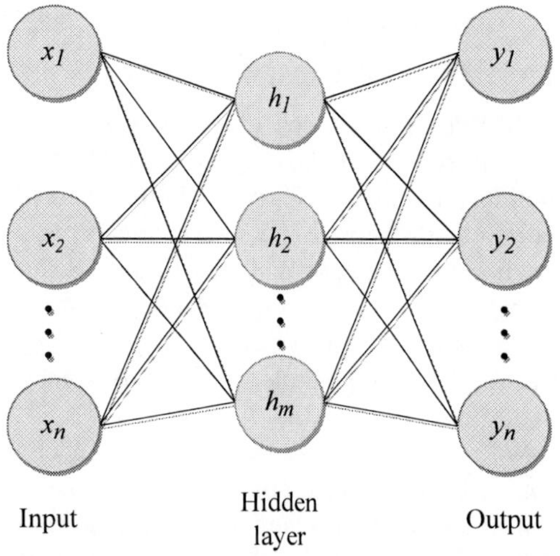

Figure 3: Fine-tuning architecture with one bottleneck layer that can vary in size. Hidden sizes of 32, 64, 96, 128 and 256 were tested. The network takes in the generated embeddings from LaBSE and outputs new vectors that maximize the similarity between the new Luhya embedding and English embedding.

by cleaning, curating and aligning the New Testament of the Bible in Luhya and English. After alignment, the dataset was assessed by three independent Native speakers to assess the quality of alignment. This dataset is the only known digital parallel corpus in Luhya-English for the Marama dialect. See examples of the aligned sentences on Table 1.

The Swahili-English dataset was sourced from the SAWA dataset which contains approximately $89k$ parallel sentences from various domains (De Pauw et al., 2009; Pauw et al., 2011). We sampled 10k parallel sentences from the Bible. This sampling allows comparison of automatic alignment specifically in the religious domain. Data cleaning involved getting rid of characters from different text encodings, removing both extra white spaces and verse numbers from all the datasets.

6.2 Results and Discussion

We utilize LASER and LaBSE to test out zero-shot bitext mining on Luhya-English dataset. Luhya is not included in the initial training of these models. We take both cosine similarity and Euclidian distance of the English embedding to the Luhya embedding. The results can be seen on table 2 where we can see we see LaBSE outperforming LASER on Luhya-English alignment by matching up to 22% of the sentences correctly whereas LASER only matched 0.02%. We also note that increasing the number of sentences that are match from 1 to 3 does not increase the performance of LASER in bitext mining while LaBSE performance increases by 10%. The top-3 result means we consider accurate alignment if the correct alignment was among the top 3 matched sentences.

The performance of LaBSE shows that there are great gains achieved by utilising a pre-trained model in the sentence embedding model. LaBSE model utilises BERT in its training offering cross-lingual benefit that results in up to 22% accurate alignment on a language it has not seen before. LASER on the other hand was trained from scratch and does not provide great results in aligning Luhya, an unseen language.

Considering the performance on Swahili, we see that prior knowledge of a language greatly helps in performance. Swahili performs better than Luhya in the alignment with LaBSE embeddings resulting in near perfect alignment (See table 2). The performance of LASER with Swahili does not correspond with the results by Artetxe and Schwenk (2019) where F1 scores of above 90% were recorded. In our case, the F1 score is equivalent to the accuracy as the number of extracted parallel sentences is equivalent to the number of gold standard alignments. Contrary to the LASER results, the results of LaBSE outperforming LASER corresponds with the results from Feng et al. (2022); Heffernan et al. (2022). We also observed that cosine similarity performs marginally better than Euclidean distance on average and hence is used for our fine-tuning experiments.

6.3 Fine-tuning LaBSE Luhya embeddings

Owing to the good performance of 22% on zero-shot alignment, we fine-tune the LaBSE Luhya embedding to evaluate the extent one needs to go to see improvements. Initially, we added one additional layer without the bottleneck and trained this network with 50% of the Luhya dataset while testing on the other 50%. This achieved an accuracy of 40.22%. However, we did not pursue this network further as the number of trained parameters was too large to offer value for a small data as the Luhya dataset. We added a bottleneck layer whose input was the 768-sized embedding and the output layer was of size 768. Our experimental setup aimed to investigate what amount of correctly aligned sentences are needed to fine-tune the embeddings and

Luhya	English
Nebutswa omukholi , womumukunda oyo namukalusia ari , ‘ Omwami , lekha , kubekhwoho omuyika kuno khandi , nasi ndalakwachila , nekurakhwo imbolela.	But he answered and said to him , ‘ Sir , let it alone this year also , until I dig around it and fertilize it.
Ne , nali emakombe nanyasibungwa muno , yahenga ikulu ne , nalola Aburahamu nende Lazaro nibali halala ehale.	And being in torments in Hades , he lifted up his eyes and saw Abraham afar off , and Lazarus in his bosom.
Saulo namenya ninabo nayaala muliira lia Yesu , mu Yerusalemu obularia likhuwa liosi liosi tawe.	So he was with them at Jerusalem , coming in and going out.

Table 1: Sample aligned sentences from our bible dataset.

		LASER		LaBSE	
		Top-1	*Top-3*	*Top-1*	*Top-3*
Luhya-English	Cos. Sim.	0.02	0.02	0.22	0.32
	L2	0.00	0.01	0.22	0.32
Swahili-English	Cos. Sim.	0.50	0.55	0.97	1.00
	L2	0.45	0.55	0.97	1.00

Table 2: Alignment accuracy for Luhya and Swahili using the raw LASER and LaBSE embeddings (no fine-tuning). The Top-1 (Top-3) columns represent the accuracy of correctly aligned sentences based on the sentences with the top 1 (3) most similar embeddings based either on cosine similarity ("Cos. Sim") or Euclidean distance ("L2"). LaBSE performs better than LASER on both languages, correctly aligning 22.0% of Luhya-English sentences and 97.1% of Swahili-English sentences. LASER performs poorly when aligning Luhya-English with only 1.5% being aligned correctly.

see improvement as well as what is the optimal hidden size to achieve improvement in alignment. We split the Luhya-English dataset into 5-folds. At each iteration of training, one fold of 1591 parallel sentences was used for testing while the other folds were used for training. To investigate how many sentences are required to see improvements, we used 10% of the training set to fine-tune the embeddings and evaluated the model with the test set and continuously added 10% until the whole training set was used up. The training set consisted of 6361 parallel sentences.

Figure 5 shows the results in which we see that regardless on the hidden size only 20% of the training data set, about 1272 sentence, is sufficient to result in the improvement of the alignment. Also, looking at the different hidden sizes 128 and 96 hidden sizes were the best with no distinct difference between the two. As much as the hidden size of 128 is comparable with 96, hidden size of 96 works with fewer parameters thus more efficient. Increasing the hidden size beyond 128 degraded the performance as evidence by the performance of hidden size 256. Also, smaller hidden sizes did not offer much gain.

Training Size	Threshold	Precision	Recall	F1 Score
At 10%	-0.2	0.22	0.22	0.22
	0.54	0.29	0.18	0.22
	0.68	0.54	0.03	0.06
At 20%	-0.2	0.34	0.34	0.34
	0.5	0.38	0.31	0.34
	0.69	0.72	0.05	0.09
At 40%	-0.2	0.44	0.44	0.44
	0.52	0.49	0.41	0.45
	0.72	0.83	0.06	0.11
At 60%	-0.2	0.48	0.48	0.48
	0.53	0.54	0.43	0.48
	0.73	0.88	0.06	0.11
At 80%	-0.2	0.51	0.51	0.51
	0.5	0.55	0.49	0.52
	0.75	0.9	0.05	0.09
At 100%	-0.2	0.53	0.53	0.53
	0.5	0.56	0.51	0.53
	0.75	0.92	0.05	0.09

Table 3: Precision, Recall and F1 score as the cosine similarity score threshold is increased with different training sizes. -0.2 threshold represents not setting a threshold at all, this results in all sentences being aligned however the precision is very low as some sentences are wrongly aligned. As the threshold increases fewer sentences are considered aligned, however there are more accurate alignment. Hence, the precision increases while the recall and F1 score decrease.

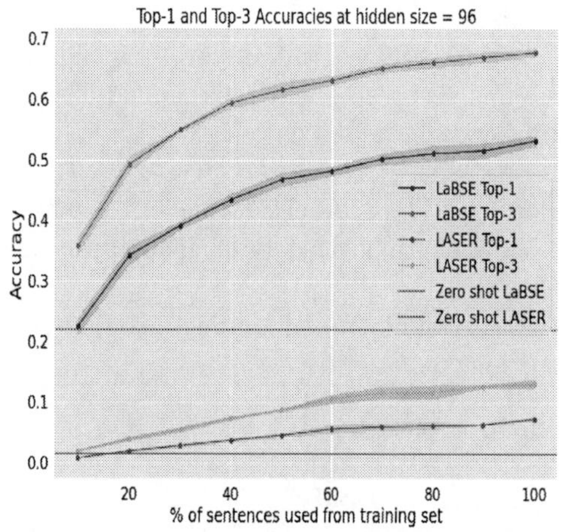

Figure 4: LaBSE outperforms LASER in both the Top-1 and Top-3 results from fine-tuning the respective embeddings (with a hidden layer dimension of 96) for Luhya. Results are shown as a function of the percentage of the full training set of 6361 sentences used for training. For LaBSE the Top-1 (Top-3) accuracy reaches 53% (68%). Error bars are standard deviations estimated from 5-fold cross-validation.

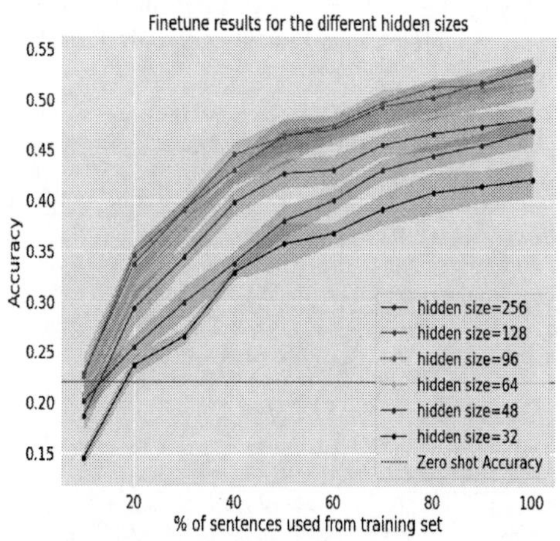

Figure 5: Top-1 results from fine-tuning the Luhya embeddings from LaBSE using different hidden layer sizes, as a function of the percentage of the full training set of 6361 sentences, together with the zero-shot result of 22.0%. Results are the mean of 5-fold cross validation with error bands given by $\pm 1\sigma$, where σ is the standard deviation of the 5 folds. The best hidden sizes are for hidden layers of dimensionality 96 and 128.

As we note good results with a hidden size of 96, we perform both the top-1 and the top-3 evaluation for both LASER and LaBSE Luhya embedding fine-tuning. Figure 4 shows that fine-tuning with hidden size 96 results in an accuracy of up to 68%. These results show that with little effort, LaBSE embeddings can be used to effectively mine bitext of languages not seen during training. This is practical for various very low-resource languages.

To assess the accuracy of aligned sentences after fine-tuning, we analyse the accuracy against different similarity score thresholds along with different training set size. Figure 6 shows that fine-tuning with 40% of the training dataset gets an accuracy of above 80% meaning with 2500 sentences one can get >80% accuracy in alignment past 0.65 threshold. Table 3 shows that setting a high similarity threshold results in higher precision but we see a significant drop in recall. Using the full training set, we see that without setting a threshold, the precision and recall are 53%. However, setting the threshold to 0.75 improves the precision to 92% while the recall drops to just 5%. Setting a higher threshold results in more accurate alignments but selects fewer sentence pairs. Choosing the optimal threshold to balance precision and recall will depend on the task being considered.

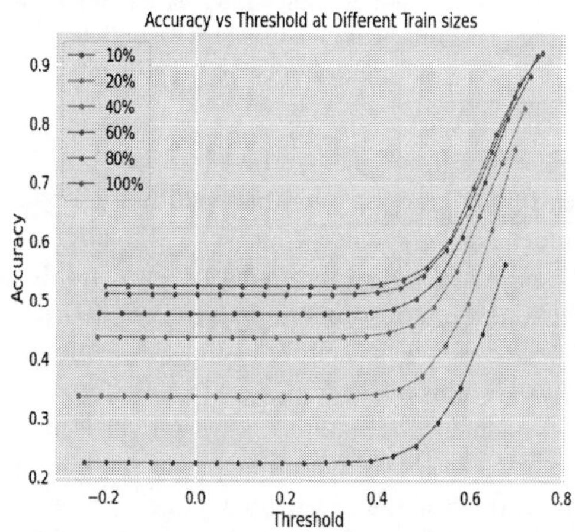

Figure 6: Top-1 accuracies as a function of cosine similarity threshold and training dataset percentage. We see that accuracy correlates with similarity, allowing the curation of high-accuracy datasets suitable for use in machine translation.

Conclusion

Low-resource languages lack digitized parallel data needed for developing machine translation models. Sentence embedding models offer a potential way to create parallel data cheaply for these low and very low-resource languages but themselves need parallel data for their training.

In this work we present a new dataset consisting of 7952 sentences translating the Luhya (Marama)

	10%	20%	30%	40%	50%	60%	70%	80%	90%	100%
Top-1	0.22	0.34	0.39	0.43	0.47	0.48	0.50	0.51	0.52	**0.53**
Top-3	0.36	0.49	0.55	0.59	0.62	0.63	0.65	0.66	0.67	**0.68**

Table 4: Fine-tuning results with a hidden layer size of 96 for the LaBSE embeddings. With 100% of the training data, (6362 sentences), the Top-1 accuracy is 53.2%, while the Top-3 accuracy is 67.8%.

dialect into English. We use this data, together with a similar Swahili dataset, to explore transfer learning and fine-tuning based on raw embeddings from the LASER and LaBSE algorithms for alignment on these languages.

We show that LaBSE significantly outperforms LASER on both Swahili and Luhya but that both struggle with zero-shot learning on Luhya, achieving alignment accuracies of 22.0% and 1.5% respectively.

We also show that fine-tuning with as little as 1200 correctly aligned Luhya sentences can result in models with significantly improved sentence alignments. In addition, setting a minimum similarity score threshold results in datasets with much more accurate alignments, useful for curating high-quality parallel corpora for machine translations. However, this comes at the cost of significantly reducing the number of aligned sentences. We leave it to future work to investigate active learning for the choice of sentences for fine-tuning that will result in the greatest gains in performance.

Acknowledgements

The authors gratefully acknowledge the contributions of Joy Nyende, Roger Nyende and Stephen Wakhu for their help in curating the Luhya Bible dataset. We thank Emmanuel Dufourq and the anonymous reviewers for comments and contributions to the draft. This publication was made possible by a grant from Carnegie Corporation of New York (provided through the African Institute for Mathematical Sciences). The statements made and views expressed are solely the responsibility of the authors.

References

Mikel Artetxe and Holger Schwenk. 2019. Massively multilingual sentence embeddings for zero-shot cross-lingual transfer and beyond. *Transactions of the Association for Computational Linguistics*, 7:597–610.

Kyunghyun Cho, Bart van Merriënboer, Caglar Gulcehre, Dzmitry Bahdanau, Fethi Bougares, Holger Schwenk, and Yoshua Bengio. 2014. Learning phrase representations using RNN encoder–decoder for statistical machine translation. In *Proceedings of the 2014 Conference on Empirical Methods in Natural Language Processing (EMNLP)*, pages 1724–1734, Doha, Qatar. Association for Computational Linguistics.

Guy De Pauw, Peter Waiganjo Wagacha, and Gilles-Maurice de Schryver. 2009. The SAWA corpus: A parallel corpus English - Swahili. In *Proceedings of the First Workshop on Language Technologies for African Languages*, pages 9–16, Athens, Greece. Association for Computational Linguistics.

Jacob Devlin, Ming-Wei Chang, Kenton Lee, and Kristina Toutanova. 2019. BERT: Pre-training of deep bidirectional transformers for language understanding. In *Proceedings of the 2019 Conference of the North American Chapter of the Association for Computational Linguistics: Human Language Technologies, Volume 1 (Long and Short Papers)*, pages 4171–4186, Minneapolis, Minnesota. Association for Computational Linguistics.

David M. Eberhard, Gary F. Simons, and Charles D. Fennig(eds.). 2021. Ethnologue: Languages of the world. twenty-fourth edition.

Fangxiaoyu Feng, Yinfei Yang, Daniel Cer, Naveen Arivazhagan, and Wei Wang. 2022. Language-agnostic BERT sentence embedding. In *Proceedings of the 60th Annual Meeting of the Association for Computational Linguistics (Volume 1: Long Papers)*, pages 878–891, Dublin, Ireland. Association for Computational Linguistics.

William A. Gale and Kenneth W. Church. 1993. A program for aligning sentences in bilingual corpora. *Computational Linguistics*, 19(1):75–102.

Mandy Guo, Qinlan Shen, Yinfei Yang, Heming Ge, Daniel Cer, Gustavo Hernandez Abrego, Keith Stevens, Noah Constant, Yun-Hsuan Sung, Brian Strope, and Ray Kurzweil. 2018. Effective parallel corpus mining using bilingual sentence embeddings. In *Proceedings of the Third Conference on Machine Translation: Research Papers*, pages 165–176, Brussels, Belgium. Association for Computational Linguistics.

Kevin Heffernan, Onur Çelebi, and Holger Schwenk. 2022. Bitext mining using distilled sentence representations for low-resource languages. *ArXiv*, abs/2205.12654.

Kejun Huang, Matt Gardner, Evangelos Papalexakis, Christos Faloutsos, Nikos Sidiropoulos, Tom Mitchell, Partha P. Talukdar, and Xiao Fu. 2015. Translation invariant word embeddings. In *Proceedings of the 2015 Conference on Empirical Methods in Natural Language Processing*, pages 1084–1088, Lisbon, Portugal. Association for Computational Linguistics.

Nal Kalchbrenner and Phil Blunsom. 2013. Recurrent continuous translation models. In *Proceedings of the 2013 Conference on Empirical Methods in Natural Language Processing*, pages 1700–1709, Seattle, Washington, USA. Association for Computational Linguistics.

Martin Kay and Martin Roscheisen. 1993. Text-translation alignment. *Computational Linguistics*, 19(1):121–142.

Dipan K. Pal and Marios Savvides. 2017. Copernican loss : Learning a discriminative cosine embedding.

Guy De Pauw, Peter Waiganjo Wagacha, and Gilles-Maurice de Schryver. 2011. Exploring the sawa corpus: collection and deployment of a parallel corpus english—swahili. *Language Resources and Evaluation*, 45:331–344.

Holger Schwenk. 2018. Filtering and mining parallel data in a joint multilingual space. In *Proceedings of the 56th Annual Meeting of the Association for Computational Linguistics (Volume 2: Short Papers)*, pages 228–234, Melbourne, Australia. Association for Computational Linguistics.

Holger Schwenk, Vishrav Chaudhary, Shuo Sun, Hongyu Gong, and Francisco Guzmán. 2021. WikiMatrix: Mining 135M parallel sentences in 1620 language pairs from Wikipedia. In *Proceedings of the 16th Conference of the European Chapter of the Association for Computational Linguistics: Main Volume*, pages 1351–1361, Online. Association for Computational Linguistics.

Holger Schwenk and Matthijs Douze. 2017. Learning joint multilingual sentence representations with neural machine translation. In *Proceedings of the 2nd Workshop on Representation Learning for NLP*, pages 157–167, Vancouver, Canada. Association for Computational Linguistics.

Kenneth Steimel. 2018. Part of speech tagging in Luyia: A Bantu macrolanguage. In *Proceedings of the Fifth Workshop on NLP for Similar Languages, Varieties and Dialects (VarDial 2018)*, pages 46–54, Santa Fe, New Mexico, USA. Association for Computational Linguistics.

Steinþór Steingrímsson, Pintu Lohar, Hrafn Loftsson, and Andy Way. 2021. Effective bitext extraction from comparable corpora using a combination of three different approaches. In *Proceedings of the 14th Workshop on Building and Using Comparable Corpora (BUCC 2021)*, pages 8–17, Online (Virtual Mode). INCOMA Ltd.

Ilya Sutskever, Oriol Vinyals, and Quoc V. Le. 2014. Sequence to sequence learning with neural networks. *CoRR*, abs/1409.3215.

Brian Thompson and Philipp Koehn. 2019. Vecalign: Improved sentence alignment in linear time and space. In *Proceedings of the 2019 Conference on Empirical Methods in Natural Language Processing and the 9th International Joint Conference on Natural Language Processing (EMNLP-IJCNLP)*, pages 1342–1348, Hong Kong, China. Association for Computational Linguistics.

Ha Nguyen Tien, Dat Nguyen Huu, Huong Le Thanh, Vinh Nguyen Van, and Minh Nguyen Quang. 2021. KC4Align: Improving sentence alignment method for low-resource language pairs. In *Proceedings of the 35th Pacific Asia Conference on Language, Information and Computation*, pages 354–363, Shanghai, China. Association for Computational Lingustics.

Lilian D.A Wanzare, Florence Indede, Owen McOnyango, Edward Ombui, Barack Wanjawa, and Lawrence Muchemi. 2022. KenTrans: A Parallel Corpora for Swahili and local Kenyan Languages.

World Atlas of Language Structures, 2021. Accessed July 2021. Languages. Wals, `https://wals.info/languoid`.

Yinfei Yang, Gustavo Hernández Ábrego, Steve Yuan, Mandy Guo, Qinlan Shen, Daniel Cer, Yun-Hsuan Sung, Brian Strope, and Ray Kurzweil. 2019a. Improving multilingual sentence embedding using bidirectional dual encoder with additive margin softmax. *CoRR*, abs/1902.08564.

Yinfei Yang, Gustavo Hernández Ábrego, Steve Yuan, Mandy Guo, Qinlan Shen, Daniel Matthew Cer, Yun-Hsuan Sung, Brian Strope, and Ray Kurzweil. 2019b. Improving multilingual sentence embedding using bi-directional dual encoder with additive margin softmax. *ArXiv*, abs/1902.08564.

Jiajun Zhang, Shujie Liu, Mu Li, Ming Zhou, and Chengqing Zong. 2015. Towards machine translation in semantic vector space. *ACM Trans. Asian Low-Resour. Lang. Inf. Process.*, 14(2).

Pierre Zweigenbaum, Serge Sharoff, and Reinhard Rapp. 2017. Overview of the second BUCC shared task: Spotting parallel sentences in comparable corpora. In *Proceedings of the 10th Workshop on Building and Using Comparable Corpora*, pages 60–67, Vancouver, Canada. Association for Computational Linguistics.

Pierre Zweigenbaum, Serge Sharoff, and Reinhard Rapp. 2018. Overview of the Third BUCC Shared Task: Spotting Parallel Sentences in Comparable Corpora. In *Workshop on Building and Using Comparable Corpora*, Miyazaki, Japan.

Multiple Pivot Languages and Strategic Decoder Initialization helps Neural Machine Translation

Shivam Mhaskar, Pushpak Bhattacharyya
Department of Computer Science and Engineering
Indian Institute of Technology Bombay
Mumbai, India
{shivammhaskar, pb}@cse.iitb.ac.in

Abstract

In machine translation, a pivot language can be used to assist the source to target translation model. In pivot-based transfer learning, the source to pivot and the pivot to target models are used to improve the performance of the source to target model. This technique works best when both source-pivot and pivot-target are high resource language pairs and the source-target is a low resource language pair. But in some cases, such as Indic languages, the pivot to target language pair is not a high resource one. To overcome this limitation, we use multiple related languages as pivot languages to assist the source to target model. We show that using multiple pivot languages gives 2.03 BLEU and 3.05 chrF score improvement over the baseline model. We show that strategic decoder initialization while performing pivot-based transfer learning with multiple pivot languages gives a 3.67 BLEU and 5.94 chrF score improvement over the baseline model.

1 Introduction

Neural Machine Translation (NMT) models have made huge improvements in the performance of machine translation systems. But NMT models are *data hungry*. NMT models require huge amounts of parallel corpus for training. To overcome this limitation and improve the performance of the source to target NMT model, the resources of a pivot language can be used. Zoph et al. (2016) used a parent model trained on a high resource language pair to initialize the parameters of the child model, which is then trained on a low resource language pair. Kim et al. (2019) introduced pivot-based transfer learning techniques to utilize the resources of the pivot language. In pivot-based transfer learning techniques, the source to pivot and the pivot to target models are used to initialize the source to target NMT model.

The pivot-based transfer learning techniques work best when both the source to pivot and the pivot to target language pairs are relatively high resource language pairs. It also helps if the pivot language is related to the source or target language, to utilize language relatedness (Kunchukuttan and Bhattacharyya, 2020). In the task of translation from English to an Indic language, another Indic language can be used as a pivot language, as Indic languages are related. But in such a setting, the pivot to target language pair may not be a high resource language pair. In the task of English to Marathi translation, Hindi can be used as a pivot language, as Hindi is a related language to Marathi. The English-Hindi language pair is a relatively high resource language pair, but the Hindi-Marathi language pair is not a high resource language pair. To overcome this shortcoming, we use multiple Indic languages as pivot languages to assist the source to target NMT model.

Transformer (Vaswani et al., 2017) model has shown state-of-the-art results for various natural language processing tasks, including machine translation. In a Transformer based NMT model, the decoder consists of two modules, self-attention, and cross attention. The self-attention layer works only with the target side language, but the cross attention layer works with the source and target side languages. We experiment with various techniques to initialize the modules of the decoder.

The major contributions of this work are as follows,

- We show that using multiple pivot languages to assist the source to target model helps improve the performance of NMT models.
- We show that strategic decoder initialization while performing pivot language-based transfer learning improves the performance of NMT models.

Proceedings of the 29th International Conference on Computational Linguistic, pages 9–14
October 12–17, 2022.

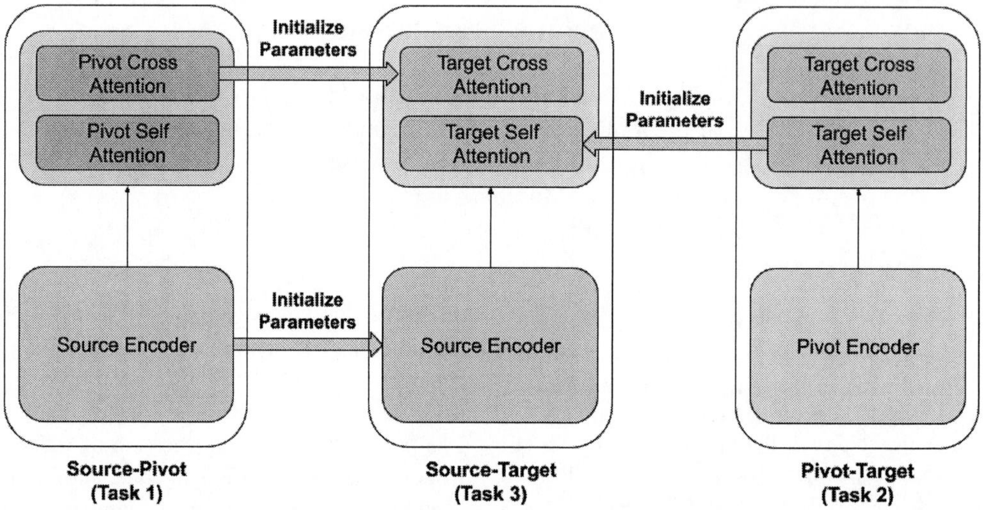

Figure 1: Initializing the *source* → *target* cross attention module with the cross attention module of the *source* → *pivot* model in pivot based transfer learning.

2 Approaches

We first discuss the approach to using multiple pivot languages to assist the source to target model. Then we discuss the various techniques to initialize the decoder of the source to target model in pivot-based transfer learning.

2.1 Multiple Pivot Languages

The task is to improve the performance of the English to Marathi NMT model. Initially, we use Hindi as a pivot language, which is related to Marathi and is a relatively high resource language among Indic languages. The English-Hindi language pair is a high resource language pair, but the Hindi-Marathi language pair is not a high resource. The amount of parallel corpus available for Hindi-Marathi is lower than English-Marathi. In order to bridge this gap, we introduce multiple Indic languages as pivot languages. We use Hindi, Bengali, Gujarati, and Tamil as pivot languages to assist the English-Marathi NMT model.

As we are using four pivot languages, the amount of parallel corpus for source-pivot and pivot-target language pairs increases significantly. This helps train better source-pivot and pivot-target models, which can be used to initialize the source-target model. In this technique, we first train an English to four Indic languages NMT model using the English to Hindi, Bengali, Gujarati, and Tamil parallel corpus. Then we train four Indic languages to the Marathi NMT model using the Hindi, Bengali, Gujarati, and Tamil to Marathi parallel corpora. We use these models to initialize the encoder and decoder modules of the source to target model and train it on the source-target parallel corpus.

2.2 Decoder Initialization

In direct pivot-based transfer learning, the decoder of the source to target model is initialized with the decoder of the pivot to target model. The decoder cross attention layer of the source to target works with the source-target language pair. The decoder cross attention layer of the pivot to target model works with the pivot-target language pair. In order to overcome this mismatch, we experiment with various initialization techniques for the decoder module.

2.2.1 Randomly Initialized Cross Attention Module

In this technique, we first initialize the encoder of the source to target model with the encoder of the source to pivot model. Then we only initialize the decoder self-attention layer of the source to target model with the decoder self-attention of the pivot to target model. The cross attention layer of the source to target model is randomly initialized. In the English-Marathi (source-target) model, the decoder self-attention layer is initialized with the decoder self-attention layer of the Hindi-Marathi (pivot-target) model.

2.2.2 Initializing the Cross Attention Module from *source to pivot* model

In this technique, the encoder of the source to target model is initialized with the encoder of the source to pivot model. The decoder self-attention layer of the source to target model is initialized with the decoder self-attention layer of the pivot to target model. The decoder cross attention layer of the source to target model is initialized with the decoder cross attention of the source to pivot model.

The cross attention layer of a Transformer decoder consists of three types of parameters, the query matrix, the key matrix, and the value matrix. The cross attention module is also called encoder-decoder attention, as it works with the source and target sequence. The query matrix is exposed to the target side sequence, and the key and value matrices are exposed to the source side sequence. The decoder cross attention of the Hindi-Marathi (pivot-target) model works with the Hindi and Marathi sequences. But in English-Marathi (source-target) model, we want the cross-attention module to work with the English and Marathi sequence. So there is a mismatch between, the sequence to which the key and value matrices are exposed during the training of, the pivot to target and the source to target model. During the training of the Hindi-Marathi model, the key and value matrices are exposed to the Hindi language but during the training of the English-Marathi (source-target) model, the key and value matrices are exposed to the English language.

In order to overcome this mismatch, we initialize the cross attention module of the English-Marathi (source-target) model with the cross attention module of the English-Hindi (source-pivot) model. Now there is no mismatch between the sequence exposed to the key and value matrices. But there is a mismatch between the sequence exposed to the query matrix. As in the English-Hindi model, the query matrix is exposed to the Hindi language but in the English-Marathi model, it is exposed to the Marathi language. But the effect of this mismatch is minimized because Hindi and Marathi are related languages.

3 Experimental Setup

In this section, we discuss the setup of the various experiments that we performed. We use byte pair encoding (BPE) (Sennrich et al., 2016) technique to split words into subwords. We use the fairseq (Ott et al., 2019) library to perform all the experiments.

Language Pair	# Sentence Pairs
English-Marathi	3.2M
English-Hindi	8.4M
English-Bengali	8.4M
English-Gujarati	3.0M
English-Tamil	5.0M
Hindi-Marathi	1.9M
Bengali-Marathi	1.8M
Gujarati-Marathi	1.7M
Tamil-Marathi	2.0M

Table 1: Dataset Statistics of Samanantar Parallel Corpus

3.1 Model

We used the Transformer model to implement all the NMT models. The model has 6 encoder layers and 6 decoder layers. The number of encoder attention heads is 8 and the number of decoder attention heads is 8. The Transformer feed-forward layer dimensions are 2048. The encoder and decoder embedding dimensions are 512. We used the same model architecture to implement the bidirectional NMT models and En-Indic multilingual NMT models.

For training the model we used label smoothed cross entropy criterion with label smoothing of 0.1. We used the Adam optimizer with beta values of 0.9 and 0.98. We used the inverse square root learning rate scheduler with 4000 warmup updates. We used a dropout value of 0.3. The batch size was 4096 tokens. We trained the model for 300,000 iterations and chose the model that gave the best loss value on the validation set.

3.2 Datasets

For all the experiments, we used the Samanantar (Ramesh et al., 2022) parallel corpus. We used the parallel corpora for the English to Hindi, Marathi, Gujarati, Bengali, and Tamil language pairs. We also used the Hindi, Gujarati, Bengali, and Tamil to Marathi parallel corpora. The dataset statistics of the parallel corpora used are mentioned in Table 1. We evaluate our models on the Facebook Low Resource (FLORES) MT Benchmark (Guzmán et al., 2019) which consists of 1012 sentence pairs from various domains.

Technique	English→Marathi			
	Pivot=Hi		Pivot=Hi,Bn,Gu,Ta	
	BLEU	chrF	BLEU	chrF
Baseline	9.02	38.58	9.02	38.58
Direct Pivoting	10.49	40.47	11.95	43.82
+ Randomly Initialized Cross Attention Module	10.82	40.90	11.99	43.69
+ Cross Attention Module Initialized from source → pivot model	**11.05**	**41.63**	**12.69**	**44.52**

Table 2: Results (BLEU and chrF Scores) of the English→Marathi NMT model. The table shows a comparison of models using only one pivot language, Hindi (Hi), and using multiple pivot languages, Hindi (Hi), Bengali (Bn), Gujarati (Gu), and Tamil (Ta). The table also shows the comparison between different decoder initialization techniques in pivot-based transfer learning. The Baseline model score is the score of the English-Marathi model trained on the English-Marathi parallel corpus

Pivot Language	English→Marathi
	BLEU
Hi	10.49
Bn	9.95
Gu	10.17
Ta	9.15
Hi, Bn, Gu, Ta	**11.95**

Table 3: Results (BLEU scores) of English→Marathi model trained by using different pivot languages as the single pivot language. The single pivot languages used are Hindi (Hi), Bengali (Bn), Gujarati (Gu), and Tamil (Ta). The last row shows the results of the English→Marathi model trained with multiple pivot languages.

3.3 Baseline

The baseline model is an English to Marathi NMT model which is trained on English-Marathi parallel corpus.

3.4 Direct Pivoting

In the Direct Pivoting model, we first train an English-Hindi and Hindi-Marathi NMT model. Then we initialize the encoder and decoder of the English-Marathi model using the encoder and decoder of the English-Hindi and Hindi-Marathi model, respectively. Finally, we train the English-Marathi model on English-Marathi parallel corpus.

3.5 Multiple Language Pivoting

In Multiple-Language Pivoting models, we use Hindi, Gujarati, Bengali, and Tamil as pivot languages. The source to pivot model is now an English to Indic NMT model, and the pivot to target model is an Indic to Marathi NMT model. For all the experiments with multiple pivoting languages, we use the four Indic languages as pivot languages instead of using only Hindi as the pivot language.

3.6 Randomly Initialized Cross Attention Module

In this experiment, we first train an English-Hindi and Hindi-Marathi NMT model. We initialize the encoder of the English-Marathi model with the encoder of the English-Hindi model. The decoder self-attention layer of the English-Marathi model is initialized with the decoder self-attention layer of the Hindi-Marathi model. The decoder cross attention layer of the English-Marathi model is randomly initialized. Finally, the model is trained on English-Marathi parallel corpus.

3.7 Initializing Cross Attention module from *source to pivot* model

In this experiment, an English-Hindi and a Hindi-Marathi model are trained. The encoder of the English-Marathi model is initialized using the encoder of the English-Hindi model. The decoder self-attention layer of the English-Hindi model is initialized using the decoder self-attention layer of the Hindi-Marathi model. The decoder cross attention layer of the English-Marathi model is initialized using the decoder cross attention layer of the English-Hindi model. Finally, the model is trained on English-Marathi parallel corpus.

English-Source	The smaller the Rossby number, the less active the star with respect to magnetic reversals.
Marathi-Reference	रॉस्बी संख्या जितकी लहान असेल तितकाच तो तारा चुंबकीय परावर्तनाच्या बाबतीत कमी सक्रिय असेल.
Marathi-Reference Gloss	Rossby number as-much small will-be that-much that star magnetic changes in-case less active will-be.
Marathi-Single	रॉसबी संख्या जितकी कमी असेल, तितकेच चुंबकीय मागे पडण्याच्या बाबतीत स्टार कमी सक्रिय आहे.
Marathi-Single Gloss	Rossby number as-much small will-be, that-much magnetic behind to-fall in-case star less active is.
Marathi-Multiple	रोस्बी संख्या जितकी लहान तितकीच चुंबकीय उलथापालथींच्या बाबतीत तारा कमी सक्रिय असतो.
Marathi-Multiple Gloss	Rossby number as-much small will-be magnetic of-upheavals in-case star less active is.

Table 4: Illustrative examples of improvement of the English→Marathi model trained with a multiple pivot language over the model trained with a single pivot language on a sentence from the test set. 'English-Source' is the input English sentence. 'Marathi-Reference' is the reference Marathi translation in the test set and 'Marathi-Reference-Gloss' is the word-to-word translation of the Marathi sentence in English which is done manually. 'Marathi-Single' is the output translation of the English→Marathi model trained with single pivot language Hindi and 'Marathi-Multiple' is the output translation of the English→Marathi model trained with multiple pivot languages. 'Marathi-Single Gloss' and 'Marathi-Multiple Gloss' are the word-to-word translations of the outputs 'Marathi-Single' and 'Marathi-Multiple', respectively, in English which is done manually.

4 Results And Analysis

We use BLEU (Papineni et al., 2002) and chrF (Popović, 2015) scores to evaluate the performance of all the models. We used the sacreblue[1] implementation for computing the BLEU scores and the NLTK[2] implementation for computing the chrF scores. Table 2 shows the results of various strategies to initialize the decoder module in pivot language-based transfer learning. The table also shows the results of experiments performed by using a single pivot language and using multiple pivot languages.

From the results, we can observe that models using multiple pivot languages outperform models using only Hindi as a pivot language. The best model using only a single pivot language achieves a BLEU score of 11.05 and chrF score of 41.63. The model using multiple pivot languages improves the BLEU score by 1.64 points to 12.69 and chrF score by 2.89 points to 44.52. This shows that using multiple pivot languages improves the performance of the source to target NMT models.

We can observe that randomly initializing the decoder cross attention module of the source to target model gives better or comparable performance over direct pivoting. Initializing the decoder cross attention module of the source to target model with the decoder cross attention module of the source to pivot model gives the best performance. In multi pivot languages setting, the direct pivoting technique achieves a BLEU score of 11.95 and chrF score of 43.82 and the strategic decoder initialization technique improves the BLEU score by 0.74 BLEU points to 12.69 and the chrF score by 0.7 points to 44.52.

Table 3 shows the results of the English-Marathi model trained using different pivot languages as the single pivot language and the model trained with multiple pivot languages. From the results, we can observe that using Hindi as single a pivot language performs better than using other languages such as Bengali, Gujarati, and Tamil as single pivot languages. We can also observe that a model trained using multiple pivot languages performs better than any model trained with only a single pivot language.

[1]https://github.com/mjpost/sacrebleu

[2]https://www.nltk.org

5 Illustrative examples of improvement

In this section, we show some examples of improvement in translation with the model with multiple pivot languages over the model with a single pivot language. Table 4 shows an English sentence, its reference Marathi translation (Marathi Reference), the output of the model trained with a single pivot language (Marathi-Single), and the output of the model trained with multiple pivot languages (Marathi-Multiple). The model with a single pivot language does not translate the word 'reversals' properly but the model with multiple pivot languages is able to translate the word properly. The model with single pivot language translated the word 'reversals' as 'मागे पडण्याच्या' which means 'to fall behind'. The model with multiple pivot languages correctly translated the word 'reversals as 'उलथापालथींच्या' which means 'of-upheavals'.

The model with a single pivot language transliterated the word 'star' to 'स्टार' whereas the model with multiple pivot languages correctly translated the word 'star' to 'तारा'.

6 Conclusion and Future Work

In this work, we show that using multiple pivot languages to assist the source-target NMT model improves its performance. We show using various metrics such as BLEU and chrF, that using multiple Indic languages as pivot languages and utilizing language relatedness improves the performance of the English-Marathi NMT model. We also show that strategic decoder initialization techniques while performing pivot language-based transfer learning improves the performance of the source-target NMT models. In the future, we plan to perform experiments by adding more pivot languages to assist the source to target the NMT model and see the performance of the system.

References

Francisco Guzmán, Peng-Jen Chen, Myle Ott, Juan Pino, Guillaume Lample, Philipp Koehn, Vishrav Chaudhary, and Marc'Aurelio Ranzato. 2019. The FLORES evaluation datasets for low-resource machine translation: Nepali–English and Sinhala–English. In *Proceedings of the 2019 Conference on Empirical Methods in Natural Language Processing and the 9th International Joint Conference on Natural Language Processing (EMNLP-IJCNLP)*, pages 6098–6111, Hong Kong, China. Association for Computational Linguistics.

Yunsu Kim, Petre Petrov, Pavel Petrushkov, Shahram Khadivi, and Hermann Ney. 2019. Pivot-based transfer learning for neural machine translation between non-English languages. In *Proceedings of the 2019 Conference on Empirical Methods in Natural Language Processing and the 9th International Joint Conference on Natural Language Processing (EMNLP-IJCNLP)*, pages 866–876, Hong Kong, China. Association for Computational Linguistics.

Anoop Kunchukuttan and Pushpak Bhattacharyya. 2020. Utilizing language relatedness to improve machine translation: A case study on languages of the indian subcontinent. *arXiv preprint arXiv:2003.08925*.

Myle Ott, Sergey Edunov, Alexei Baevski, Angela Fan, Sam Gross, Nathan Ng, David Grangier, and Michael Auli. 2019. fairseq: A fast, extensible toolkit for sequence modeling. *arXiv preprint arXiv:1904.01038*.

Kishore Papineni, Salim Roukos, Todd Ward, and Wei-Jing Zhu. 2002. Bleu: a method for automatic evaluation of machine translation. In *Proceedings of the 40th Annual Meeting of the Association for Computational Linguistics*, pages 311–318, Philadelphia, Pennsylvania, USA. Association for Computational Linguistics.

Maja Popović. 2015. chrF: character n-gram F-score for automatic MT evaluation. In *Proceedings of the Tenth Workshop on Statistical Machine Translation*, pages 392–395, Lisbon, Portugal. Association for Computational Linguistics.

Gowtham Ramesh, Sumanth Doddapaneni, Aravinth Bheemaraj, Mayank Jobanputra, Raghavan AK, Ajitesh Sharma, Sujit Sahoo, Harshita Diddee, Divyanshu Kakwani, Navneet Kumar, et al. 2022. Samanantar: The largest publicly available parallel corpora collection for 11 indic languages. *Transactions of the Association for Computational Linguistics*, 10:145–162.

Rico Sennrich, Barry Haddow, and Alexandra Birch. 2016. Neural machine translation of rare words with subword units. In *Proceedings of the 54th Annual Meeting of the Association for Computational Linguistics (Volume 1: Long Papers)*, pages 1715–1725, Berlin, Germany. Association for Computational Linguistics.

Ashish Vaswani, Noam Shazeer, Niki Parmar, Jakob Uszkoreit, Llion Jones, Aidan N Gomez, Łukasz Kaiser, and Illia Polosukhin. 2017. Attention is all you need. *Advances in neural information processing systems*, 30.

Barret Zoph, Deniz Yuret, Jonathan May, and Kevin Knight. 2016. Transfer learning for low-resource neural machine translation. In *Proceedings of the 2016 Conference on Empirical Methods in Natural Language Processing*, pages 1568–1575, Austin, Texas. Association for Computational Linguistics.

Known Words Will Do: Unknown Concept Translation via Lexical Relations

Winston Wu*
Computer Science and Engineering
University of Michigan
wuws@umich.edu

David Yarowsky
Center for Language and Speech Processing
Johns Hopkins University
yarowsky@jhu.edu

Abstract

Translating into low-resource languages is challenging due to the scarcity of training data. In this paper, we propose a probabilistic lexical translation method that bridges through lexical relations including synonyms, hypernyms, hyponyms, and co-hyponyms. This method, which only requires a dictionary like Wiktionary and a lexical database like WordNet, enables the translation of specialized terms into low-resource languages for which we may only know the translation of a related concept. Experiments on translating a core vocabulary set into 472 languages, most of them low-resource, show the effectiveness of our approach.

1 Introduction

When humans encounter lexical gaps in their speech, they may attempt to "talk around" it — a process known as circumlocution — or use another known, related word such as a synonym. Similarly, in machine translation (MT), one method for resolving out-of-vocabulary words (OOVs) involves replacing them with synonyms from the known lexicon. Synonym replacement is especially useful in a low-resource setting and has been recently investigated, for example in Vietnamese (Ngo et al., 2019) and Japanese (Tanaka and Baldwin, 2003). Some MT evaluation metrics also use synonyms as part of their computation (Banerjee and Lavie, 2005; Liu et al., 2010; He et al., 2010). Other applications of synonyms include improving robustness of MT systems (Cheng et al., 2018), finding translations in comparable corpora Andrade et al. (2013), and improving information retrieval systems (Collier et al., 1998).

However, synonyms are not the only lexical relation through which translations can be found. For example, the concept of watermelon can be translated in Serbo-Croatian as *бостан* 'melon' (a hypernym) and in Italian as *cocomero* 'cucumber' (a co-hyponym). These lexical relations have not been adequately studied in the literature as sources for translation. Translation via lexical relations are usually studied in the context of constructing multilingual WordNets (Huang et al., 2002, 2005; Nien et al., 2009), where researchers translate the English WordNet in order to bootstrap the construction of a new WordNet in their target language. In contrast, our work investigates the acceptability of a word's translation in a low-resource language based on lexically-related concepts across *multiple* languages. Our work is related to the idea of translation bridging (Tanaka and Umemura, 1994; Mann and Yarowsky, 2001; Schafer and Yarowsky, 2002), where a word in the source language is first translated into an intermediate bridge language, then translated into the target language. However, instead of bridging through a third language, we propose bridging through lexically-related words in the same language.

We specifically focus on four types of lexical semantic relations: synonymy, hypernymy, hyponymy, and co-hyponymy. Using the aggregation of these translations across hundreds of languages available in Wiktionary in Wiktionary, we develop and analyze a probabilistic model of lexical relation bridging to enable the translation of unknown concepts using existing known words in the target language's lexicon. Code and data for this paper are available at github.com/wswu/bridging-lexrel.

2 Translation Bridging via Lexical Relations

Suppose we wish to translate into a low-resource language a concept, such as *hound*, whose translation we do not know in said language. This is quite common in extremely low-resource scenar-

*This research was conducted while the first author was a PhD student at JHU.

Proceedings of the 29th International Conference on Computational Linguistic, pages 15–22
October 12–17, 2022.

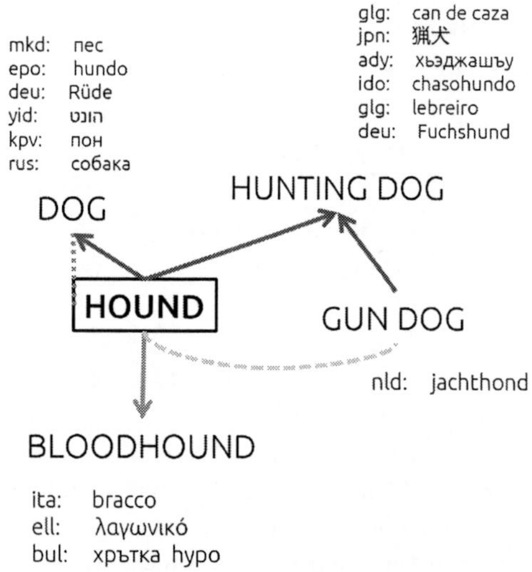

Figure 1: Concepts related to hound and their corresponding translations in various languages. Green indicates synonyms, blue indicates hypernyms, red indicates hyponyms, and orange indicates co-hyponyms.

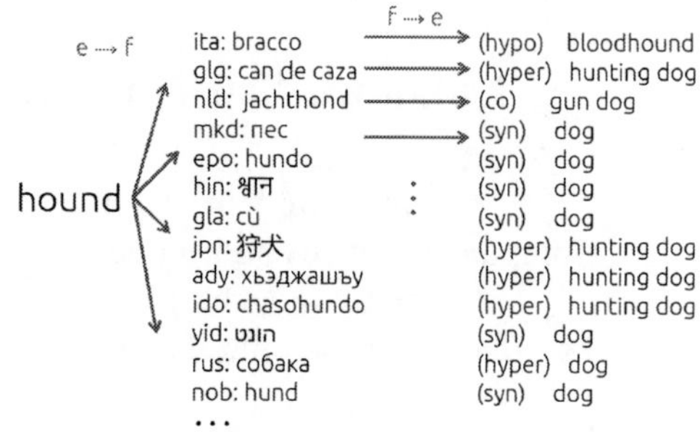

Figure 2: Process of computing the probability distribution for the concept hound. This involves aggregating the back-translations of the original concept filtered by the lexical relations in WordNet.

e_{rel}	$p(e_{rel} \mid e)$
dog	0.54
hunting dog	0.13
gun dog	0.07
bloodhound	0.06
greyhound	0.03
foxhound	0.02

Table 1: Most probable replacement translation of $e =$ *hound*, computed by bridging through lexical relations.

ios, where little to no bitext exists for training machine translation systems, nor is there even any monolingual text for applying unsupervised machine translation methods such as cross-lingual embeddings. This scenario is more common than one might imagine. The world has around 7,000 languages, but roughly 160 of them have readily available bitext or monolingual text, which might be acquired from the web using methods such as ParaCrawl (Bañón et al., 2020) or Common Crawl (Smith et al., 2013). Beyond this range, we enter the territory of low-resource languages, where the only significant source of text is likely to be the Bible, available for roughly 1,600 languages (McCarthy et al., 2020). Beyond this, the best one can hope for is a small bilingual dictionary perhaps manually constructed by a field linguist or a native informant.

What kind of translation is possible with no other bilingual resource but a small dictionary? In English, the word *hound* is usually used to indicate a hunting dog, so one might intuitively talk about their *dog* instead of their *hound*. Although *Dog* may not capture the full semantic nuances of *hound*, it at least conveys the notion that the word it replaces, *hound*, is a four-legged canine. Moreover, it is more likely that the word *dog* exists in any given dictionary than *hound*; *hound* is a more specialized word and thus ranks lower in terms of coreness (see Wu et al. (2020) for one definition of core vocabulary).

Thus we can replace a less core word with a more core word. The replacement word could be a hypernym, such as *dog* for *hound*,[1] but could also be a synonym, hyponym, or even a co-hyponym. These four lexical relations are illustrated in the lexical relation graph in Figure 1, using the concept of HOUND.[2] Synonyms share the same meaning. Hyperynms and hyponyms comprise the *is-a* relation, where the hypernym is the supertype (e.g. *melon*) and the hyponym is the subtype (e.g. *watermelon*). Co-hyponyms are words that share the same hypernym. In order to obtain lexically-related words, we use WordNet 3.0 (Fellbaum, 2010), a freely-available lexical database of English words and their relations. Because these relationships are stored in WordNet at the synset level, rather than at the word level, a pair of words may be linked by more than one relation. For example, *dog* is both a synonym and a hypernym of *hound*.

To develop a model of translations of related

[1]In WordNet, *hound* and *dog* are also synonyms. This is because *hound* and *dog* exist in multiple synsets.

[2]We distinguish between the semantic concept HOUND and the English word *hound*. The lexical relation graph constructed around concepts are valid in any language.

Relation	Count	%
Synonym	962K	39
Co-Hyponym	593K	23
Hyponym	468K	19
Hypernym	460K	19

Table 2: Lexical relations extracted from Wiktionary backtranslations.

Lang	Word	Relation	Related Word
ara	بطيخ	hyper	melon
bul	диня	hyper	melon
haw	ipu	hyper	melon
hbs	bostan	hyper	melon
hbs	бостан	hyper	melon
isl	vatnsmelóna	hyper	melon
ita	cocomero	co-hypo	cucumber
mkd	бостан	hyper	melon
mri	merengi	hyper	melon
por	melancia	hyper	melon
ron	pepene	co-hypo	cucumber
ron	pepene	hyper	melon
rup	peapini	hyper	melon
scn	miluni	hyper	melon
tsn	lekatane	hyper	melon
vie	dưa hấu	hyper	melon

Table 3: Words lexically related to *watermelon*, with their translations in various languages.

concepts across languages, we extract a translation dictionary from the English Wiktionary using Yawipa (Wu and Yarowsky, 2020a,b), a Wiktionary parsing and extraction tool. Using this dictionary, we translate every English word e in Wiktionary into all other available languages and then back into English to obtain a set of back-translations e_{rel}. We then look up each $e \rightarrow e_{rel}$ pair in WordNet to identify the lexical relation (synonym, hypernym, hyponym, and/or co-hyponym). From these pairs $e \rightarrow e_{rel}$, we compute a probability distribution $p(e_{rel}|e)$ that describes the likelihood that e_{rel} is an acceptable replacement translation of e. A diagram of this process is shown in Figure 2, with the resulting probability distribution in Table 1.

In total, this process learns translation distributions for over 42K concepts from 2.4 million relation pairs. As shown in Table 2, we find most of the relations are overwhelmingly synonyms, with the other three relations relatively close in scale. Some example lexical relations are shown for the words *watermelon* in Table 3 and *rodent* in Table 4.

Lang	Word	Relation	Related Word
bul	гризач	syn	gnawer
dan	gnaver	syn	gnawer
deu	Nager	syn	gnawer
fin	jyrsijä	syn	gnawer
hbs	glodar	syn	gnawer
hbs	глодар	syn	gnawer
hil	balabaw	hypo	mouse
hil	balabaw	hypo	rat
msa	tikus	hypo	mouse
msa	tikus	hypo	rat
nld	knaagdier	syn	gnawer
swe	gnagare	syn	gnawer
zho	鼠	hypo	mouse
zho	鼠	hypo	rat

Table 4: Concepts lexically related to *rodent*, with their translations in various languages.

3 Experiments

We evaluate our lexical relation translation bridging model on the task of generating translations from English into a foreign language. That is, in the $e \rightarrow f$ direction, the model translates $e \rightarrow e_{rel} \rightarrow f$, where $p(e_{rel} \mid e)$ is learned via Wiktionary and WordNet, and $e_{rel} \leftrightarrow f$ is a mapping that exists in Wiktionary. We evaluate our translation model on a test set of 1,000 concepts in the core vocabulary (Wu et al., 2020), a set of concepts ranked by their propensity to be included in any dictionary. We examine 472 languages with at least 100 word coverage over this test set.[3] Furthermore, we provide in-depth analysis on for four diverse test languages: Bulgarian, Irish, Galician, and Maltese. These languages are all of different language families and are medium- to low-resource languages based on their number of entries in Wiktionary (recall we assume no other data is available besides what is in Wiktionary). Note that because these are low-resource languages, their dictionaries may not contain all 1,000 test concepts. Ultimately, we can only test on available existing ground truth.

Results on languages with over 100 word coverage of the core vocabulary are presented in Figure 3. Because our translation model provides a probability for each hypothesis, we report 1-best accuracy (is the top hypothesis in the gold translations?) and 10-best accuracy (are any of the top 10

[3]Although we have Wiktionary translation data for over 4,300 languages, the majority of these are extremely low-resource. Evaluating translation via lexical relations requires that we have ground truth for the translation for the related word. Thus, for testing purposes, we limit our analysis to languages for which we have at least 100 words of ground truth.

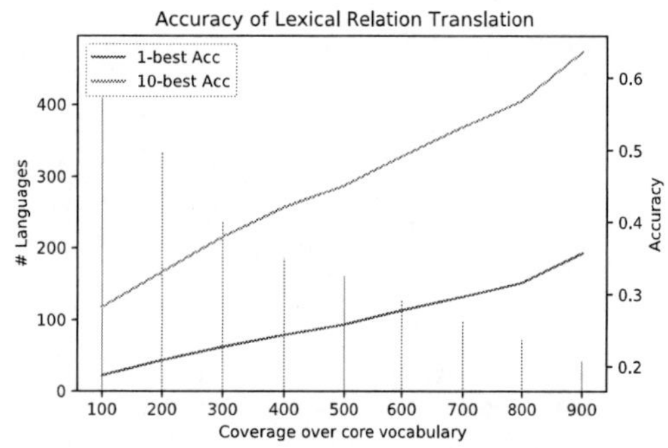

Figure 3: Accuracy of lexical relation translations, with languages grouped by their coverage of the 1,000 concept core vocabulary, a proxy for language resourceness. The gray bars plot a histogram of the number of languages containing at least x number of core vocabulary words. 43 languages cover over 900 core concepts, obtaining a 1-best accuracy of 36% and 10-best accuracy of 64%. On the low-resource end, 472 languages cover over 100 concepts, obtaining a 1-best accuracy of 19% and a 10-best accuracy of 28%.

hypotheses in the gold translations?). In addition, we evaluate groups of languages by their coverage of the core vocabulary to test the effectiveness of lexical relation translations at various levels of language resourceness.

Figure 3 presents a high-level summary of this translation approach's performance. We find that for 43 high resource languages (with over 900 word coverage of the core vocabulary), a 1-best accuracy of 36% and a 10-best accuracy of 64% shows that almost 2/3 of concepts can be translated using a lexically-related concept. For low-resource languages that cover at least 100 concepts of the core vocabulary, a respectable 1-best accuracy of 19% and a 10-best accuracy of 28% indicates that translation via lexical relations is still viable even when few known translations exist.

4 Analysis

To more deeply understand bridging through lexical relations, we analyze our translation approach in depth, focusing on four test languages, Bulgarian, Irish, Galician, and Maltese. Detailed results on these languages are shown in Table 5. We report 1-best, 10-best, and n-best accuracy (do any of the hypotheses appear in the gold translations?). Results on these languages follow from the overall results presented in Figure 3.

We first explain why one should consider

Lang	# Test	1-best	10-best	n-best
bul	739	.12	.30	.38
gle	502	.11	.25	.29
glg	617	.10	.22	.31
mlt	234	.14	.26	.27

Table 5: Lexical relation translation, all test concepts.

Lang	# Test	1-best	10-best	n-best
bul	412	.21	.54	.69
gle	239	.23	.53	.61
glg	333	.18	.41	.57
mlt	106	.30	.58	.60

Table 6: Lexical relation translation, only test concepts that exists in WordNet.

other metrics besides 1-best accuracy. In a low-resource generating-into-a-vacuum scenario, producing good 1-best results is often not a necessity; 10-best or even 100-best hypothesis lists generated by any dictionary induction method can be filtered using a language model once target language data is acquired. Thus, n-best accuracy provides an upper bound on the performance of this approach. We find that our translation model can correctly identify translations of over a third of test concepts as words already in the target language's translation dictionary. Considering the extremely impoverished size of low-resource languages' dictionaries, this is quite impressive and useful for low-resource languages and tasks.

One strength of our approach is our use of WordNet as a universal lexical relation database. Our model is language agnostic and does not rely on WordNet in any specific target language. Rather, we assume the relations in WordNet to hold across languages. As future improvements and additions are made to the English WordNet as well as WordNets in other languages, they can be easily incorporated into our model to potentially improve the quality of our translations. At present, we find that the English WordNet only covers roughly half the concepts in our test set. Thus, we also report performance on the subset of test concepts that exist in WordNet in Table 6. In this test scenario, our model achieves 2x improved performance, because all test concepts are guaranteed to occur in WordNet.

We now examine some model predictions in detail. Table 7 shows predictions when translating into Irish. For example, when the Irish words for *remedy* (*leigheas, neart, íoc*) were held out,

Concept	Gold	Hypotheses
single	aonartha, aonta, singil, aonarach, aonarúil	(syn) unmarried → singil 0.357
		(syn) one → aonta 0.310
remedy	leigheas, neart, íoc	(hyper) medicine → leigheas 0.363
		(co) medicine → leigheas 0.363
		(syn) cure → leigheas 0.171
		(syn) cure → íoc 0.171
		(hypo) antidote → leigheas 0.036
marsh	corcach, seascann, riasc, corrach, eanach	(co) swamp → eanach 0.480
		(co) swamp → corcach 0.480
		(syn) fen → eanach 0.085

Table 7: Translation hypotheses in Irish from lexical relations.

Concept	Gold	Hypotheses
she-goat	коза, козá	(hyper) goat → козá 0.917
liberty	свободá	(hyper) freedom → свободá 0.659
cumin	кимион	(co) caraway → кимион 0.667
gradient	склон, градиент, наклон	(syn) slope → склон 0.353
		(co) inclination → склон 0.216
		(co) inclination → наклон 0.216
		(hypo) pitch → наклон 0.098
		(hypo) grade → наклон 0.078
		(hypo) rake → наклон 0.059

Table 8: Translation hypotheses in Bulgarian from lexical relations.

Concept	Gold	Hypotheses
liberate	liberar, ceibar	(syn) free → liberar 0.427
		(hyper) free → liberar 0.427
		(syn) release → liberar 0.152
		(syn) release → ceibar 0.152
		(syn) loose → ceibar 0.026
		(co) open → ceibar 0.013
quarrel	rifar, cotifar	(hyper) argue → cotifar 0.093
		(hyper) argue → rifar 0.093
azure	blao, azul	(hyper) blue → azul 0.514
claw	garra, uña, coca, gadoupa	(co) nail → uña 0.284
		(co) hoof → uña 0.123

Table 9: Translation hypotheses in Galician from lexical relations.

Concept	Gold	Hypotheses
white	bojod, bajda, abjad	(co) pale → abjad 0.101
stick	ħatar, bastun	(hypo) staff → bastun 0.089
		(co) rod → ħatar 0.075
		(hypo) club → ħatar 0.052
deceive	lagħab, gidem, baram, qarraq	(hypo) cheat → qarraq 0.283
		(hypo) cheat → lagħab 0.283
		(co) cheat → qarraq 0.283
		(co) cheat → lagħab 0.283
		(hypo) betray → qarraq 0.103
		(syn) betray → qarraq 0.103

Table 10: Translation hypotheses in Maltese from lexical relations.

Concept	Gold	Hypotheses
die	éag, faigh bás, básaigh, caill	(co) decay → éag 0.007
moment	móimint, nóiméad	(syn) minute → nóiméad 0.087
now	anois, adrásta, anuas	(syn) at present → adrásta 0.150
resin	bí, roisín	(syn) rosin → roisín 0.800
empty	fásach	(co) desert → fásach 0.015
penance	aithrí	(syn) penitence → aithrí 0.233
		(syn) repentance → aithrí 0.233
accumulator	bailitheoir	(syn) collector → bailitheoir 0.750

Table 11: Irish translations which were correctly predicted when training on all languages, but could not be correctly predicted when training on only related languages.

the model was able to apply the lexical relations *remedy* → {*medicine, cure, antidote*}, for which we have known translations, allowing the model to produce an appropriate translation of *remedy*'s hypernyms, hyponyms, co-hyponyms, and synonyms.

For Bulgarian (Table 8), we see similar model behavior. *she-goat* is a rather specific term, but since our model has learned that *goat* is the hypernym of *she-goat* and is an acceptable translation, and that *goat* already exists in the dictionary, the model correctly predicts коза́, the translation of *goat*, as the translation for *she-goat*. *Caraway* translated as *cumin* is an interesting successful example. Although they are not the same herb, caraway and cumin are visually similar, and Bulgarian uses the same word for both: кимион (kimion). Indeed, caraway is also known as Persian cumin.

Galician (Table 9) also contains several examples of words with subtle meanings that can be expressed with a more general-purpose word. For example, *liberate* (*liberar, ceibar*) is adequately translated with *free* or *release*. To *quarrel* is essentially to *argue*, albeit in a heated manner, and *azure* is a specific shade of *blue*. These hypernym translations are successfully found by our model.

Finally, for Maltese (Table 10), the lowest-resourced language in the test set, we find that the translation with lexical relations approach provides the greatest benefits. For the word for *stick* (*ħatar, bastun*), our model finds that other more specialized sticks (staff, rod, club) are also translated as *stick*. Similarly, *deceive* can be translated as *cheat* or *betray*, hyponmys of *deceive*.

In addition to these experiments, we also examined the effects of training on only languages in the same language family as the test language, versus training on the entire test set. We find that performance is *worse* when trained on all languages, for Bulgarian, Galician, and Maltese. Only for Irish did the performance increase. Table 11 shows some Irish examples in which the model trained on all languages was able to outperform the model trained on only Irish-related languages. Thus, we find that training on more languages on average reduces performance on the translation task. While the reasons for this finding require more investigation, we suspect that training on more languages introduces more noise. For example, in word compounding, often it is not the word itself, but rather the compounding recipe (a calque) that gets borrowed (Wu and Yarowsky, 2018). For example, the English *brainwash* comes from Chinese 洗脑 'wash+brain', due to contact between different languages and cultures. In contrast, lexically related words are often language specific. Translating *watermelon* as *cucumber* is unusual and only occurs in Italian and Romanian; there is little reason to believe that any non-Romance language would share this translation. Indeed, other languages use compounds such as 西瓜 'west melon' (in Chinese) or görögdinnye 'Greek melon' (in Hungarian), which is a compositional formation recipe, but not a robust one.

5 Conclusion

Using only the existing lexical resources Wiktionary and WordNet, we develop a probabilistic method for accurately predicting the translation of unknown words by bridging through lexically related hypernyms, hyponyms, co-hyponyms, and synonyms. This simple but effective method that identifies existing known words as valid translations does not require any neural model nor intensive training, and is especially well-suited for extremely low-resource languages for which little resources are available. Future work will augment our lexical resources with other WordNets and dictionaries, and apply our method to complement existing low-resource translation systems.

References

Daniel Andrade, Masaaki Tsuchida, Takashi Onishi, and Kai Ishikawa. 2013. Translation acquisition using synonym sets. In *Proceedings of the 2013 Conference of the North American Chapter of the Association for Computational Linguistics: Human Language Technologies*, pages 655–660, Atlanta, Georgia. Association for Computational Linguistics.

Satanjeev Banerjee and Alon Lavie. 2005. METEOR: An automatic metric for MT evaluation with improved correlation with human judgments. In *Proceedings of the ACL Workshop on Intrinsic and Extrinsic Evaluation Measures for Machine Translation and/or Summarization*, pages 65–72, Ann Arbor, Michigan. Association for Computational Linguistics.

Marta Bañón, Pinzhen Chen, Barry Haddow, Kenneth Heafield, Hieu Hoang, Miquel Esplà-Gomis, Mikel L. Forcada, Amir Kamran, Faheem Kirefu, Philipp Koehn, Sergio Ortiz Rojas, Leopoldo Pla Sempere, Gema Ramírez-Sánchez, Elsa Sarrías, Marek Strelec, Brian Thompson, William Waites, Dion Wiggins, and Jaume Zaragoza. 2020. ParaCrawl: Web-scale acquisition of parallel corpora. In *Proceedings of the 58th Annual Meeting of the Association for Computational Linguistics*, pages 4555–4567, Online. Association for Computational Linguistics.

Yong Cheng, Zhaopeng Tu, Fandong Meng, Junjie Zhai, and Yang Liu. 2018. Towards robust neural machine translation. In *Proceedings of the 56th Annual Meeting of the Association for Computational Linguistics (Volume 1: Long Papers)*, pages 1756–1766, Melbourne, Australia. Association for Computational Linguistics.

Nigel Collier, Hideki Hirakawa, and Akira Kumano. 1998. Machine translation vs. dictionary term translation - a comparison for English-Japanese news article alignment. In *36th Annual Meeting of the Association for Computational Linguistics and 17th International Conference on Computational Linguistics, Volume 1*, pages 263–267, Montreal, Quebec, Canada. Association for Computational Linguistics.

Christiane Fellbaum. 2010. Wordnet. In *Theory and applications of ontology: computer applications*, pages 231–243. Springer.

Yifan He, Jinhua Du, Andy Way, and Josef van Genabith. 2010. The DCU dependency-based metric in WMT-MetricsMATR 2010. In *Proceedings of the Joint Fifth Workshop on Statistical Machine Translation and MetricsMATR*, pages 349–353, Uppsala, Sweden. Association for Computational Linguistics.

Chu-Ren Huang, I-Li Su, Jia-Fei Hong, and Xiang-Bing Li. 2005. Cross-lingual conversion of lexical semantic relations: Building parallel wordnets. In *Proceedings of the Fifth Workshop on Asian Language Resources (ALR-05) and First Symposium on Asian Language Resources Network (ALRN)*.

Chu-Ren Huang, I-Ju E. Tseng, and Dylan B.S. Tsai. 2002. Translating lexical semantic relations: The first step towards multilingual wordnets. In *COLING-02: SEMANET: Building and Using Semantic Networks*.

Chang Liu, Daniel Dahlmeier, and Hwee Tou Ng. 2010. TESLA: Translation evaluation of sentences with linear-programming-based analysis. In *Proceedings of the Joint Fifth Workshop on Statistical Machine Translation and MetricsMATR*, pages 354–359, Uppsala, Sweden. Association for Computational Linguistics.

Gideon S. Mann and David Yarowsky. 2001. Multipath translation lexicon induction via bridge languages. In *Second Meeting of the North American Chapter of the Association for Computational Linguistics*.

Arya D. McCarthy, Rachel Wicks, Dylan Lewis, Aaron Mueller, Winston Wu, Oliver Adams, Garrett Nicolai, Matt Post, and David Yarowsky. 2020. The Johns Hopkins University Bible corpus: 1600+ tongues for typological exploration. In *Proceedings of the 12th Language Resources and Evaluation Conference*, pages 2884–2892, Marseille, France. European Language Resources Association.

Thi-Vinh Ngo, Thanh-Le Ha, Phuong-Thai Nguyen, and Le-Minh Nguyen. 2019. Overcoming the rare word problem for low-resource language pairs in neural machine translation. In *Proceedings of the 6th Workshop on Asian Translation*, pages 207–214, Hong Kong, China. Association for Computational Linguistics.

Tzu-yi Nien, Tsun Ku, Chung-chi Huang, Mei-hua Chen, and Jason S. Chang. 2009. Extending bilingual WordNet via hierarchical word translation classification. In *Proceedings of the 23rd Pacific Asia Conference on Language, Information and Computation, Volume 1*, pages 375–384, Hong Kong. City University of Hong Kong.

Charles Schafer and David Yarowsky. 2002. Inducing translation lexicons via diverse similarity measures and bridge languages. In *COLING-02: The 6th Conference on Natural Language Learning 2002 (CoNLL-2002)*.

Jason R. Smith, Herve Saint-Amand, Magdalena Plamada, Philipp Koehn, Chris Callison-Burch, and Adam Lopez. 2013. Dirt cheap web-scale parallel text from the Common Crawl. In *Proceedings of the 51st Annual Meeting of the Association for Computational Linguistics (Volume 1: Long Papers)*, pages 1374–1383, Sofia, Bulgaria. Association for Computational Linguistics.

Kumiko Tanaka and Kyoji Umemura. 1994. Construction of a bilingual dictionary intermediated by a third language. In *COLING 1994 Volume 1: The 15th International Conference on Computational Linguistics*.

Takaaki Tanaka and Timothy Baldwin. 2003. Noun-noun compound machine translation a feasibility study on shallow processing. In *Proceedings of the ACL 2003 Workshop on Multiword Expressions: Analysis, Acquisition and Treatment*, pages 17–24, Sapporo, Japan. Association for Computational Linguistics.

Winston Wu, Garrett Nicolai, and David Yarowsky. 2020. Multilingual dictionary based construction of core vocabulary. In *Proceedings of the 12th Language Resources and Evaluation Conference*, pages 4211–4217, Marseille, France. European Language Resources Association.

Winston Wu and David Yarowsky. 2018. Massively translingual compound analysis and translation discovery. In *Proceedings of the Eleventh International Conference on Language Resources and Evaluation (LREC 2018)*, Miyazaki, Japan. European Language Resources Association (ELRA).

Winston Wu and David Yarowsky. 2020a. Computational etymology and word emergence. In *Proceedings of the 12th Language Resources and Evaluation Conference*, pages 3252–3259, Marseille, France. European Language Resources Association.

Winston Wu and David Yarowsky. 2020b. Wiktionary normalization of translations and morphological information. In *Proceedings of the 28th International Conference on Computational Linguistics*, pages 4683–4692, Barcelona, Spain (Online). International Committee on Computational Linguistics.

The only chance to understand: machine translation of the severely endangered low-resource languages of Eurasia

Anna Mosolova
Université de Lorraine
Nancy, France
a.mosolova333@gmail.com

Kamel Smaïli
Loria, Campus Scientifique
Vandoeuvre-Lès-Nancy, France
smaili@loria.fr

Abstract

Numerous machine translation systems have been proposed since the appearance of this task. Nowadays, new large language model-based algorithms show results that sometimes overcome human ones on the rich-resource languages. Nevertheless, it is still not the case for the low-resource languages, for which all these algorithms did not show equally impressive results. In this work, we want to compare 3 generations of machine translation models on 7 low-resource languages and make a step further by proposing a new way of automatic parallel data augmentation using the state-of-the-art generative model.

1 Introduction

Being one of the oldest tasks of natural language processing (NLP), machine translation changed many different state-of-the-art approaches over the past 70 years. Starting with old dictionary-based systems, then going forward with statistical algorithms, switching to neural approaches with sequence-to-sequence methods, currently, the best MT systems use language models (LM) with Transformer architecture inside.

All these new language models rely on huge data corpora from which they are able to extract general patterns about any language including grammar, vocabulary, discourse characteristics, etc. Their results are especially remarkable on the translation tasks from one rich-resource language to another, where they achieve results sometimes indistinguishable from the human ones.

However, when it comes to the low-resource languages, not all models can perform well. Recently, new large LMs were developed especially for few-shot learning, however, they are still evaluated on the datasets containing several tens of thousands of samples.

In this work, we want to evaluate the performance of the algorithms coming from 3 different generations of models: statistical, sequence-to-sequence and transformer-based. Additionally, we want to propose a new fully automatic parallel data augmentation method based on GPT model and compare the quality of the models fine-tuned with the generated data.

For our purposes, we will take 7 extremely low-resource languages of Eurasia coming from 4 different language families. All these languages will be the source languages of translation, while Russian will be the target one. These languages are mainly spoken in Russia, so linguists have already collected small corpora of linguistic data for these languages including the sentences translations to Russian. We extracted sentences from these corpora and composed 7 datasets of parallel sentences. The minimum size of the corpus used is 586 training pairs and the maximum size is equal to 8619.

In the following, we will start by presenting the related work that has been carried out so far (Section 2), then the languages used for this study (section 3). After this, we will describe the experiments (Section 4) and analyse the obtained results (Section 5). All the contributions made in this paper will be summed up in the conclusion (Section 6) as well as the direction of the future work.

2 Related work

Throughout the history of machine translation, numerous models have been proposed. During the era of statistical machine translation, one of the first models were word-based models such as IBM ones (Brown et al., 1993). These models were then followed by the phrase-based systems (Koehn et al., 2003) which became widely used for several years.

The next decade was marked by the appearance of neural network-based machine translation algorithms starting with a sequence-to-sequence model with LSTM layers (Sutskever et al., 2014) which was then modified with CNN (Gehring et al., 2017) and different types of attention mechanism (Luong

Proceedings of the 29th International Conference on Computational Linguistic, pages 23–34
October 12–17, 2022.

et al., 2015).

In the recent years, the Transformer architecture (Vaswani et al., 2017) appeared and it showed groundbreaking results in many NLP tasks. For machine translation, firstly, the original Transformer paper showed new state-of-the-art scores and then the metrics were improved by the T5 model (Raffel et al., 2020), the multilingual mBART-25 (Liu et al., 2020) and mBART-50 (Tang et al., 2020) models followed by the other transformer-based architectures.

These three generations of models have also been used in the low-resource settings. We can find adaptions of all kinds of algorithms for the under-resourced conditions. For example, the phrase-based statistical models have been used for the translation of the low-resource Arabic dialects (Meftouh et al., 2015).

As for the sequence-to-sequence models, an interesting approach to data processing and further Seq2Seq model training and tuning was shown in the paper by Goel et al. (2020). The authors transliterated all low-resource languages that they had into the common alphabet shared with a rich-resource language coming from the same language group. Then they pre-trained a sequence-to-sequence model using the corpus of a rich-resource language and fine-tuned it with small corpora of the low-resource languages. Another example of the successful application of the Seq2Seq model to the low-resource machine translation is the multi-task training using the translation task from and to several dialects at the same time (Moukafih et al., 2021).

The Transformer-based models have also been tested in the low-resource conditions. For example, Garcia et al. (2021) proposed a new 3-stage training approach with no data for the low-resource languages. The authors trained the Transformer model using the corpora of the close rich-resource languages. Additionally, they used the so-called synthetic corpora which contained the translations of the sentences from all zero-source languages which they generated using the model obtained after the first stage of training.

As we can see, the main approach that is used to improve the quality of the translation is transferring some knowledge from the languages that are coming from the same language group or family. Moreover, these language families have many daughter languages that are popular in the world. However, in our work, some of the languages either are the only remaining living languages of their family or come from the families which are not widely known, so we will try to exploit some approaches that do not rely on the languages similarities.

3 Study of several low-resource languages

3.1 Motivation

In this study, we want to evaluate the performance of 3 different types of models on a particularly difficult type of the machine translation task which is the translation of extremely low-resource languages. The target language for all our experiments is Russian, while the source sentences come from 7 low-resource languages.

Being a member of the *Indo-European language family*, Russian is considered to be a high-resource language with a common word order Subject-Verb-Object (SVO) and fusional type of inflection. Apart from many European languages, Russian uses Cyrillic alphabet which makes it difficult to transfer the knowledge of the pre-trained monolingual language models by fine-tuning them on a small Russian corpus. However, many popular language models were trained on huge Russian corpora (for example, Common Crawl (Eberius et al., 2015) or Taiga (Shavrina and Shapovalova, 2017)), such as BERT[1], T5[2] or GPT[3] and then applied on various down-stream tasks.

The low-resource languages that we use in this study are: Karelian, Ludic, Veps, Selkup, Evenki, Chukchi and Ket. They are spoken in Eurasia, mainly in Russia and adjacent countries, however, none of them belongs to the Indo-European language family. We chose these languages as they are the heritage of the nationalities that use these languages as the native one and of the countries to which these nationalities belong. Unfortunately, currently these languages are not widely spoken any more, as it becomes more and more popular to use Russian as a native language and learn English as a second one. In Russia, studying the language that represents the identity of a region is mandatory only during the first 4 years of education in school, so many students stop using their national language

[1]https://huggingface.co/DeepPavlov/rubert-base-cased

[2]https://huggingface.co/cointegrated/rut5-base-multitask

[3]https://github.com/ai-forever/ru-gpts

once they are 11 years old. With our work, we want to draw attention to these languages, as some of them are on the verge of extinction.

3.2 Languages description

In this section, we will give some linguistic facts about the studied languages such as their language family and which word order, word formation method and alphabet they use. We will also provide the examples of the translation of a Russian sentence *Ja ne ponimaj tebja* (I do not understand you), when possible.

Karelian, Ludic, Veps and Selkup[4] languages come from the *Uralic language family*. All of them have SVO word order, are agglutinative and are written with the Latin alphabet. Karelian phonetic system consists of 8 vowels and 19 consonants, Ludic has the same number of vowels and one more consonant, Selkup contains 25 vowels and 16 consonants, while Veps has 10 vowels and 34 consonants.

The difference between these languages can be seen from the examples. For instance, the sentence *I do not understand you* in Karelian is *en ymärrä teitä*, in Ludic is *en elgenda teid*, in Veps is *mina en el'genda teid* and in Selkup is *mat assa sintit tenimak* (all words are transliterated into Latin where necessary). Selkup's translation does not resemble others at all, while Ludic and Veps are almost similar except for the pronoun *minä* (En: I) in Veps.

Chukchi language[5] is a member of the *Chukotko-Kamchatkan language family* with Subject-Object-Verb (SOV) word order, agglutination and Latin alphabet which consists of 6 vowels and 14 consonants. The example of a sentence in this language is: *wanewan mesisewtek* (I do not understand you), where the first word expresses the negation and the tense and the second word expresses the verb's meaning, the subject (*me-*) and the object (*-tek*).

Evenki language[6] is a part of the *Tungusic language family*, it uses SOV word order, agglutination for word formation and inflection and Cyrillic alphabet for writing which contains 11 vowels and 18 consonants. The following phrase is an example of a sentence in the Evenki language: *bi sine ehim tylle* (I do not understand you), where *bi* is a subject, *sine* is an object, *ehim* expresses the negation (*e-*), the present tense (*-hi-*) as well as person and number (*-m*) and *tylle* is a verb which also carries the meaning of negation (*-le*).

Ket language[7] is the only living member of the *Yeniseian language family*. This language uses SVO word order and Cyrillic alphabet as well. Its phonetic system has 11 vowels and 20 consonants. It has fusional type of word formation and inflection. Here is an example of a sentence in the Ket language: *bu duoton kolet* (he sees the city), where *bu* is the subject, *kolet* is the object and *duoton* is a verb in which the grammatical information about the subject is expressed in the *du-* part and the grammatical information about the object is shown with the *-o-* part.

The summary of the sizes of the corpora available for our study is presented in the table 1.

Language	Training corpus size
Ket	586
Chukchi	806
Ludic	1100
Karelian	1571
Selkup	1932
Evenki	4524
Veps	8619

Table 1: Corpora sizes for 7 low-resource languages. The size is represented by the number of parallel sentences in an X language and Russian

4 Machine translation models for the languages of Eurasia

In this section, we will describe 4 different machine translation models that we trained on our datasets.

Before we started the experiments, we uniformly preprocessed the datasets. The following steps were applied: punctuation removal, lower-casing, deleting the sentences that are longer than a certain threshold. For each language, we determined the optimal maximum length of the sentences on the basis of the loss curve during the training. We noticed that loss values are abnormally big on the long sequences, so for each language we built the plots with the dependency between loss values and sentence's lengths and chose the maximum length by finding an optimal point, where we do not lose too many training samples and loss values are not

[4]The datasets are composed from the extracts of the corpus presented in Zaytseva N. G. (2017) and Brykina et al. (2018)

[5]The dataset is composed from the sentences extracted from the corpus of the Siberian Lang project

[6]The dataset is composed from the sentences extracted from the corpus of the Siberian Lang project

[7]The dataset is composed from the sentences extracted from the corpus of the Chucklang website

extremely high. In general, we deleted from 10 to 20 pairs from each dataset.

4.1 Statistical Machine Translation

Despite the existence of neural approaches to machine translation, statistical machine translation still remains a preferable solution in some cases. It is attractive due to the fact that it does not require as mush data as neural approaches and, additionally, the vocabulary used to translate the sentences is sometimes richer than the one of neural models, especially, in the low-resource settings. Another advantage of the statistical model is the speed of training. In our experiments, it took only a few minutes to fully train a model for one language.

We used the Moses system (Koehn et al., 2007) to evaluate the quality of statistical MT approaches. For our purposes, we took the phrase-based system with the trigram KenLM language model (Och and Ney, 2003) and the GIZA++ alignment model (Heafield et al., 2013). We trained the translation model on the training corpus of each language and tuned it on the validation part.

4.2 Sequence-to-Sequence

In this study, we used the sequence-to-sequence model with LSTM layers and attention (Luong et al., 2015) from the OpenNMT library (Klein et al., 2017). We used Adam as an optimizer and a batch size equal to 64 for our training. We also experimented different learning rate values and chose 1e-5 as a final one, because the model was overfitting with the bigger ones and underfitting otherwise.

4.3 mBART

A popular mBART architecture has shown SoTA results on many rich and medium-resource language, so we decided to check if it is possible to transfer some of its knowledge to the new, unseen languages. For these purposes, we took a large mBART-CC25 model from the Fairseq repository[8] and fine-tuned it using the parallel corpora of 7 low-resource languages. We preprocessed the corpora using the mBART SentencePiece model[9]. For the fine-tuning, we took the standard Adam optimizer and a learning rate equal to 3e-05 to prevent model from forgetting the knowledge about the language it extracted from the corpora during the pre-training. We also set the early stopping to 10 epochs without validation loss improvement.

4.4 GPT

The model from the GPT family are known for their generative abilities, that is why we decided to check if a decoder Transformer-based model is able to learn the translation task. To train a model for this task, we tried several prompts and ended up with a form *"<Source language name>: <Sentence in a source language>. Russian: <Translation of the sentence into Russian> <|endoftext|>"*.First, we tried using the mGPT model (Shliazhko et al., 2022) which is said to be a GPT-3 model based on GPT-2. This model was trained on 60 different languages including Russian.

However, this model kept producing the translations on other languages, so we switched to the ruGPT-3 model[10] which was trained only on the Russian corpus. For this model, we translated the prompt so it became: *"<Source language name in Russian>: <Sentence in a source language>. <Word 'translation' written in Russian>: <Translation of the sentence into Russian> <|endoftext|>"*.

4.5 Augmentation with GPT

As GPT-3 is a generative model, we tried to use it to generate new samples of the data. After training the model to translate from one of the source languages to Russian, we prompted it with a name of a source language (for example, *"Evenki: "*, but written in Cyrillic) to check if it can generate the source sentence and its translation. For these purposes, we used the Beam search with the following parameters: maximum length = 40, repetition penalty = 1.2, top-k = 50, top-p = 0.95, temperature = 0.7.

This combination produced examples that sometimes were a real translation pair. However, many pairs were wrong due to the fact that the model continued generating the Russian translation up to the maximum length, so we filtered all examples that had more then twice words in the translation than in the source sentence. Additionally, we checked if all words from the source part were present in the training dataset. Hypothetically, the model could have learnt how to conjugate verbs or decline nouns. Nevertheless, none of the authors is a native speaker of any source language from this study, so we decided to stick to the definitely

[8] `https://github.com/facebookresearch/fairseq/tree/main/examples/mbart`

[9] `https://github.com/google/sentencepiece`

[10] `https://github.com/ai-forever/ru-gpts`

existing words to avoid fine-tuning a model with the fake data.

We augmented all the datasets with 10% of the newly generated translation pairs and fine-tuned the mBART models using these new datasets.

5 Results

In this section, we will show and discuss the performance of all machine translation models that we implemented. The figures with the comparison of all results for every language are presented in the Appendix A.

5.1 Phrase-based statistical model

BLEU scores that we obtained with the Moses model are shown in the table 2.

We analysed the translations and noticed that the model leaves all words for which it cannot find the corresponding translation unchanged in the translation. Comparing the SMT results to the other models, we can see that this behaviour allowed it to achieve the highest BLEU scores among other models for 3 languages with the smallest training corpora (Chukchi, Ket, Ludic). Neural network-based models were not able to understand the structure of the language with such a small number of sentences, while statistical approach not only retained all possible correct translations, but also copied the words from the input to the output instead of repeating or generating random words. It was especially helpful in the case of Ket, where native speakers sometimes included Russian words in the Ket sentences.

5.2 Seq2Seq

Table 3 presents the results of the Seq2Seq model. We can see that these results are the worst ones among other models, as this model needed to learn the grammar and the vocabulary from scratch using only our small training corpora which were not sufficient for the network. In the original Seq2Seq paper(Sutskever et al., 2014), the authors showed BLEU scores of 34.81 after training on the corpus of 12M parallel sentences which can explain close to 0 results of our models which did not have that much training data. During the analysis of the results, we have noticed that Seq2Seq models tend to repeat simple words or replace some words with the *<unk>* token which also affected the final results.

An additional reason of the low scores for some languages is the fact that the models needed to learn to translate from the Latin alphabet to Cyrillic and from the languages with a completely different grammatical structure. For example, the Chukchi language has the SOV word order and tends to incorporate the information about the subject and the object into a verb (see Section 3.2 for an example).

5.3 mBART

In the table 4, the performance of the mBART models is shown.

During the evaluation of the translations produced by the model, we noticed that sometimes it replaces some words with their synonyms, so the BLEU score may show lower results, despite the fact that the translations were still understandable.

One can see that the Ket language performance is again better than for almost all other languages which is related to the sentences size, small vocabulary size and the fact that some sentences already contained words in Russian which did not need any translation.

We can also see that the mBART model achieves the highest result for the Karelian language and almost highest results for the other Uralic languages. This is related to the fact that mBART was trained on Finnish and Estonian languages, so the knowledge transfer was made not only for the target translations in Russian, but also for the source sentences in our low-resource languages.

The low results of the Veps model are caused by the tendency of the model to overfit and predict the same token instead of translations. For this reason, we stopped the training before the repeating token started occurring in the translations which led to worse results. We suppose this behavior is related to the bigger corpus size compared to the other languages.

5.4 ruGPT-3

BLEU scores we obtained with the ruGPT-3 model are shown in the table 5.

We can see that the results are comparable with the mBART model when the alphabet used by the language is Cyrillic, while for other languages the BLEU values are smaller. The only exception is Veps language which shows better results then the mBART model due to the problems with the mBART model.

When analysing the results, we have also noticed that the GPT model sometimes is not able to trans-

Language	BLEU-1	BLEU-2	BLEU-3	BLEU-4
Evenki	33.2	23.1	16.5	12.1
Chukchi	19.9	12.8	8.4	5.6
Ket	53.2	42.3	34.5	27.4
Selkup	27.6	16.8	10.5	6.8
Ludic	30.5	17.7	11.4	7.8
Veps	43.6	28.7	19.9	14.5
Karelian	49.3	34.3	24.8	18.3

Table 2: Phrase-based model results on translation task from 7 low-resource languages to Russian

Language	BLEU-1	BLEU-2	BLEU-3	BLEU-4
Evenki	15.47	7.81	3.4	1.59
Chukchi	10.03	3.0	0.0	0.0
Ket	22.04	10.66	4.76	0.0
Selkup	16.92	8.05	3.43	0.0
Ludic	16.38	6.81	2.86	1.62
Veps	18.23	7.66	3.5	1.85
Karelian	20.14	8.22	4.05	0.0

Table 3: Seq2Seq model results on translation task from 7 low-resource languages to Russian

Language	BLEU-1	BLEU-2	BLEU-3	BLEU-4
Evenki	36.8	24.8	16.9	12.2
Chukchi	13.9	6.9	4.1	2.5
Ket	36.8	28.1	20.7	14.9
Selkup	23.0	13.0	7.8	5.3
Ludic	25.1	14.2	8.7	5.6
Veps	28.0	15.3	8.3	4.7
Karelian	50.2	36.9	27.1	20.1

Table 4: mBART model results on translation task from 7 low-resource languages to Russian

late Karelian sentences correctly because of their length which was up to 220 symbols.

5.5 mBART with ruGPT-3 augmentation

Table 6 represents the BLEU scores that we obtained with the mBART model after fine-tuning it with the augmented data.

The results show that Evenki and Selkup models have improved some of their BLEU scores compared to the mBART models trained with the original datasets. As for the other models, we have noticed that the change in quality of the model is proportional to the size of the dataset. This correlation is shown in the figure 1. The training corpus size of each language is presented on the x axis, the difference between two BLEU-1 scores is presented on the y axis. We can see that the quality of the ruGPT-3 generation depends severely on the size of the training corpus. This fact is proved by the results of the translation models trained on the generated data. One can see that the results are much worse for the models with less than 1000 examples and starting from 1000 examples the difference becomes less and less. It means that the GPT model is able to generate coherent examples which are helpful during the training of the translation model starting from 2000 examples.

5.6 Example analysis

In the table 7 we present the example of the translation of one sentence by each system. The source sentence for all systems was the following phrase in the Evenki language: *tar ahi albaran ilatčami togoi.*. The expected output is the first line of the table.

As we can see, the statistical model did not manage to find the translation for the word *togoi* and left it unchanged in the text. As for the Seq2Seq model,

Language	BLEU-1	BLEU-2	BLEU-3	BLEU-4
Evenki	34.8	23.7	16.7	12.2
Chukchi	14.4	8.1	4.9	3.1
Ket	37.9	30.6	24.0	19.5
Selkup	20.6	11.5	6.6	4.4
Ludic	17.2	8.4	5.4	3.7
Veps	36.0	22.6	15.2	10.3
Karelian	27.0	16.1	9.9	6.2

Table 5: ruGPT-3 model on translation task from 7 low-resource languages to Russian

Language	BLEU-1	BLEU-2	BLEU-3	BLEU-4
Evenki	37.4	25.6	17.8	13.1
Chukchi	8.2	3.7	1.9	0.0
Ket	22.1	16.2	11.7	8.5
Selkup	23.4	13.3	7.6	4.9
Ludic	24.0	12.3	7.5	4.4
Veps	23.3	12.5	6.9	4.0
Karelian	49.2	35.2	26.0	19.9

Table 6: mBART model results after augmentation of the datasets by 10% on translation task from 7 low-resource languages to Russian

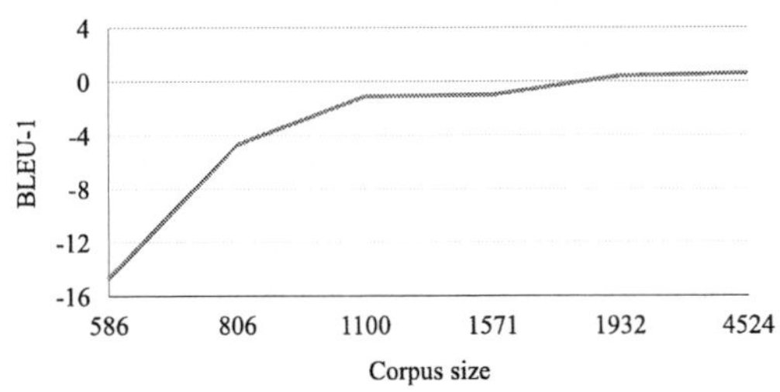

Figure 1: Correlation between the training corpus size and BLEU-1 difference between mBART and augmented mBART model. We did not include the Veps model results do to the problem explained in the Section 5.3

one can notice that it suffers from the lexical repetition problem and additionally it missed the main verb of a sentence. Both mBART models translated the sentence almost correctly, the only missing point is the possessive pronoun *svoj* which is expressed by the last letter *i* in the source word *togoi*. The ruGPT model translated the words correctly, but made 2 grammatical errors: in the subject by declining it to the instrumental case (*zenŝinoj* instead of *zenŝina*) and in the auxiliary verb by using the masculine ending instead of the feminine one (*smog* instead of *smogla*).

Overall, the translation quality is pretty high and it is possible to understand the source meaning of the sentence from all the generated translations.

6 Conclusion

In this study, we have presented our work on the machine translation for 7 low-resource languages of Eurasia. We have compared the phrase-based statistical model, the Seq2seq model, the mBART model and the ruGPT-3 model. We have shown that the statistical model achieves the highest quality for the majority of the languages and mBART model shows the best quality for the remaining ones.

We have also proposed the new way of augmenting the dataset with parallel sentences generated by the GPT-model fine-tuned for the translation task. The study has shown that this method allows to increase the quality of the model starting from a certain size of the training dataset, otherwise the quality decreases as the GPT model is not able to generate coherent examples.

Our future directions of research include training other Transformer-based architectures like M2M100 and using multi-task learning during the fine-tuning stage.

By this work, we would like to bring attention to the low-resource languages of Eurasia and encourage other researchers to continue our work. Every language is the part of the world's treasure and it is important to do our best trying to preserve them.

Model	Translation	English translation
Target	eta ženŝina ne smogla razžeč svoj ogon	this woman did not manage to start her fire
Moses	ta ženŝina ne smogla razžeč togoi	this woman did not manage to start *her fire*
Seq2Seq	eta ženŝina ne mogla i ogon ogon	this woman was not able and fire fire
mBART	ta ženŝina ne smogla razžeč ogon	that woman did not manage to start the fire
ruGPT-3	ženŝinoj i ne smog razžeč ogon	*woman* and *did not manage* to start the fire
mBART+	ta ženŝina ne smogla razžeč ogon	that woman did not manage to start the fire

Table 7: An example of the generated translations. The first line is the target translation from the corpus, other lines represent different models. mBART+ refers to the mBART model trained with the augmented dataset. Words in italics represent errors that are not obvious from the English translation and are explained in the Section 5.6

Acknowledgements

Experiments presented in this paper were carried out using the Grid'5000 experimental testbed, being developed under the INRIA ALADDIN development action with support from CNRS, RENATER and several Universities as well as other funding bodies (see `https://www.grid5000.fr`).

References

Peter F. Brown, Stephen A. Della-Pietra, Vincent J. Della-Pietra, and Robert L. Mercer. 1993. The mathematics of statistical machine translation. *Computational Linguistics*, 19(2):263–313.

Maria Brykina, Svetlana Orlova, and Beáta Wagner-Nagy. 2018. Inel selkup corpus. version 0.1. *The INEL corpora of indigenous Northern Eurasian languages., Hamburg, December. Hamburger Zentrum für Sprachkorpora.*

Julian Eberius, Maik Thiele, Katrin Braunschweig, and Wolfgang Lehner. 2015. Top-k entity augmentation using consistent set covering. SSDBM '15.

Xavier Garcia, Aditya Siddhant, Orhan Firat, and Ankur Parikh. 2021. Harnessing multilinguality in unsupervised machine translation for rare languages. In *Proceedings of the 2021 Conference of the North American Chapter of the Association for Computational Linguistics: Human Language Technologies*, pages 1126–1137, Online. Association for Computational Linguistics.

Jonas Gehring, Michael Auli, David Grangier, Denis Yarats, and Yann N Dauphin. 2017. Convolutional sequence to sequence learning. In *International conference on machine learning*, pages 1243–1252. PMLR.

Pranav Goel, Suhan Prabhu, Alok Debnath, Priyank Modi, and Manish Shrivastava. 2020. Hindi Time-Bank: An ISO-TimeML annotated reference corpus. In *16th Joint ACL - ISO Workshop on Interoperable Semantic Annotation PROCEEDINGS*, pages 13–21, Marseille. European Language Resources Association.

Kenneth Heafield, Ivan Pouzyrevsky, Jonathan H. Clark, and Philipp Koehn. 2013. Scalable modified Kneser-Ney language model estimation. In *Proceedings of the 51st Annual Meeting of the Association for Computational Linguistics (Volume 2: Short Papers)*, pages 690–696, Sofia, Bulgaria. Association for Computational Linguistics.

Guillaume Klein, Yoon Kim, Yuntian Deng, Jean Senellart, and Alexander Rush. 2017. OpenNMT: Open-source toolkit for neural machine translation. In *Proceedings of ACL 2017, System Demonstrations*, pages 67–72, Vancouver, Canada. Association for Computational Linguistics.

Philipp Koehn, Hieu Hoang, Alexandra Birch, Chris Callison-Burch, Marcello Federico, Nicola Bertoldi, Brooke Cowan, Wade Shen, Christine Moran, Richard Zens, et al. 2007. Moses: Open source toolkit for statistical machine translation. In *Proceedings of the 45th annual meeting of the association for computational linguistics companion volume proceedings of the demo and poster sessions*, pages 177–180.

Philipp Koehn, Franz Josef Och, and Daniel Marcu. 2003. Statistical phrase based translation. In *Proceedings of the Joint Conference on Human Language Technologies and the Annual Meeting of the North American Chapter of the Association of Computational Linguistics (HLT-NAACL)*.

Yinhan Liu, Jiatao Gu, Naman Goyal, Xian Li, Sergey Edunov, Marjan Ghazvininejad, Mike Lewis, and Luke Zettlemoyer. 2020. Multilingual denoising pre-training for neural machine translation. *Transactions of the Association for Computational Linguistics*, 8:726–742.

Minh-Thang Luong, Hieu Pham, and Christopher D. Manning. 2015. Effective approaches to attention-based neural machine translation.

Karima Meftouh, Salima Harrat, Salma Jamoussi, Mourad Abbas, and Kamel Smaili. 2015. Machine translation experiments on padic: A parallel arabic dialect corpus. In *Proceedings of the 29th Pacific Asia conference on language, information and computation*, pages 26–34.

Youness Moukafih, Nada Sbihi, Mounir Ghogho, and Kamel Smaïli. 2021. Improving Machine Translation of Arabic Dialects through Multi-Task Learning. In *20th International Conference Italian Association for Artificial Intelligence:AIxIA 2021*, MILAN/Virtual, Italy.

Franz Josef Och and Hermann Ney. 2003. A systematic comparison of various statistical alignment models. *Computational Linguistics*, 29(1):19–51.

Colin Raffel, Noam Shazeer, Adam Roberts, Katherine Lee, Sharan Narang, Michael Matena, Yanqi Zhou, Wei Li, and Peter J. Liu. 2020. Exploring the limits of transfer learning with a unified text-to-text transformer. *Journal of Machine Learning Research*, 21(140):1–67.

Tatiana Shavrina and Olga Shapovalova. 2017. To the methodology of corpus construction for machine learning:«taiga» syntax tree corpus and parser. *Proceedings of the "Corpora*, pages 78–84.

Oleh Shliazhko, Alena Fenogenova, Maria Tikhonova, Vladislav Mikhailov, Anastasia Kozlova, and Tatiana Shavrina. 2022. mgpt: Few-shot learners go multilingual.

Ilya Sutskever, Oriol Vinyals, and Quoc V. Le. 2014. Sequence to sequence learning with neural networks.

Yuqing Tang, Chau Tran, Xian Li, Peng-Jen Chen, Naman Goyal, Vishrav Chaudhary, Jiatao Gu, and Angela Fan. 2020. Multilingual translation with extensible multilingual pretraining and finetuning. *arXiv preprint arXiv:2008.00401*.

Ashish Vaswani, Noam Shazeer, Niki Parmar, Jakob Uszkoreit, Llion Jones, Aidan N. Gomez, Lukasz Kaiser, and Illia Polosukhin. 2017. Attention is all you need.

Kryzhanovskaya A.A. Pellinen N.A. Rodionova A.P. Zaytseva N. G., Kryzhanovskii A.A. 2017. Otkryty korpus vepsskogo i karelskogo yazykov (vepkar): predvaritelny otbop materialov i slovarnaya chast sistemi. *Trudi mezhdunarodnoi konferrencii «Korpusnaya lingvistika – 2017»*., pages 172–177.

A The comparison of all models

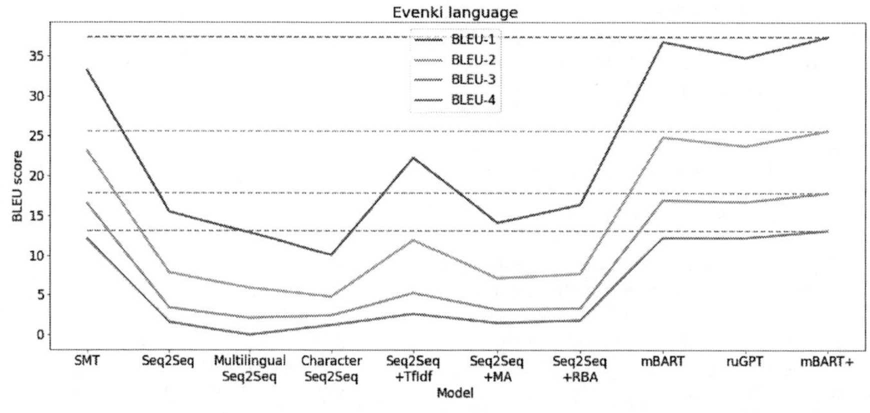

Figure 2: The comparison of the results of all the models trained from Evenki to Russian. Dashed lines represent the best result for the corresponding BLEU score. RBA = rule-based augmentation, MA = manual augmentation, mBART+ = mBART trained on the augmented with ruGPT dataset

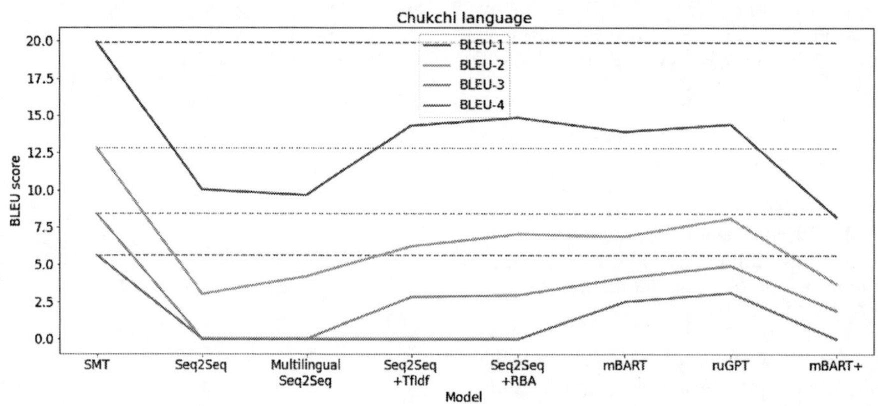

Figure 3: The comparison of the results of all the models trained from Chukchi to Russian. Dashed lines represent the best result for the corresponding BLEU score. RBA = rule-based augmentation, MA = manual augmentation, mBART+ = mBART trained on the augmented with ruGPT dataset

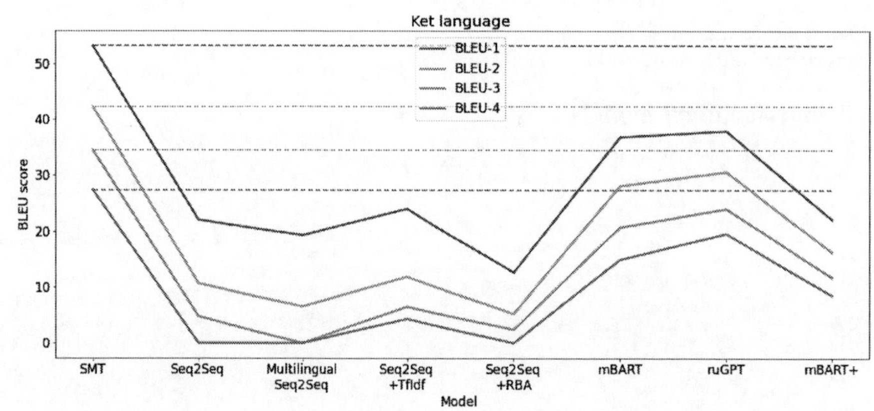

Figure 4: The comparison of the results of all the models trained from Ket to Russian. Dashed lines represent the best result for the corresponding BLEU score. RBA = rule-based augmentation, MA = manual augmentation, mBART+ = mBART trained on the augmented with ruGPT dataset

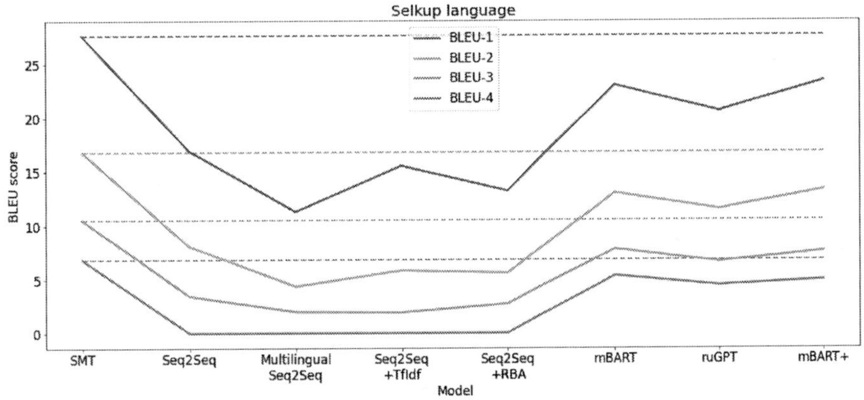

Figure 5: The comparison of the results of all the models trained from Selkup to Russian. Dashed lines represent the best result for the corresponding BLEU score. RBA = rule-based augmentation, MA = manual augmentation, mBART+ = mBART trained on the augmented with ruGPT dataset

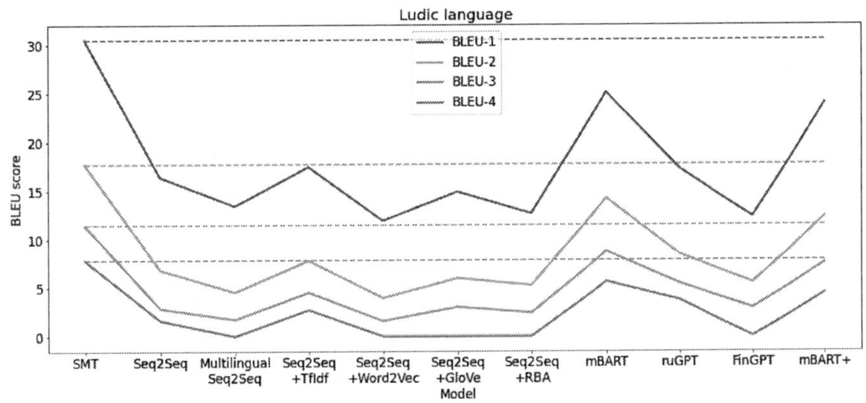

Figure 6: The comparison of the results of all the models trained from Ludic to Russian. Dashed lines represent the best result for the corresponding BLEU score. RBA = rule-based augmentation, MA = manual augmentation, mBART+ = mBART trained on the augmented with ruGPT dataset

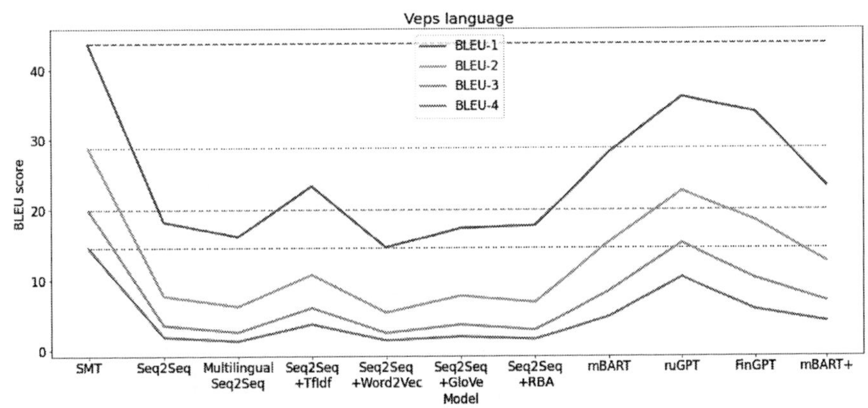

Figure 7: The comparison of the results of all the models trained from Veps to Russian. Dashed lines represent the best result for the corresponding BLEU score. RBA = rule-based augmentation, MA = manual augmentation, mBART+ = mBART trained on the augmented with ruGPT dataset

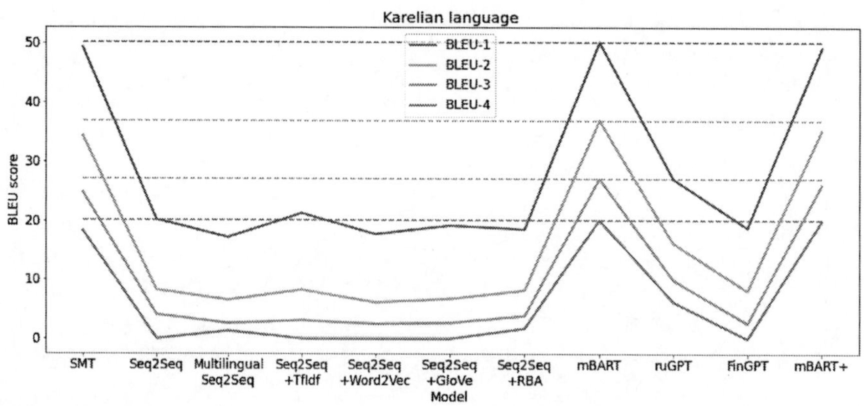

Figure 8: The comparison of the results of all the models trained from Karelian to Russian. Dashed lines represent the best result for the corresponding BLEU score. RBA = rule-based augmentation, MA = manual augmentation, mBART+ = mBART trained on the augmented with ruGPT dataset

Data-adaptive Transfer Learning for Translation: A Case Study in Haitian and Jamaican

Nathaniel R. Robinson
Language Technologies Institute
Carnegie Mellon University
Pittsburgh, PA, USA
nrrobins@cs.cmu.edu

Cameron J. Hogan
Department of Computer Science
Brigham Young University
Provo, UT, USA
camhogan@byu.net

Nancy Fulda
Department of Computer Science
Brigham Young University
Provo, UT, USA
nfulda@cs.byu.edu

David R. Mortensen
Language Technologies Institute
Carnegie Mellon University
Pittsburgh, PA, USA
dmortens@cs.cmu.edu

Abstract

Multilingual transfer techniques often improve low-resource machine translation (MT). Many of these techniques are applied without considering data characteristics. We show in the context of Haitian-to-English translation that transfer effectiveness is correlated with amount of training data and relationships between knowledge-sharing languages. Our experiments suggest that for some languages beyond a threshold of authentic data, back-translation augmentation methods are counterproductive, while cross-lingual transfer from a sufficiently related language is preferred. We complement this finding by contributing a rule-based French-Haitian orthographic and syntactic engine and a novel method for phonological embedding. When used with multilingual techniques, orthographic transformation makes statistically significant improvements over conventional methods. And in very low-resource Jamaican MT, code-switching with a transfer language for orthographic resemblance yields a 6.63 BLEU point advantage.

1 Introduction and Motivation

Machine translation (MT) for low resource languages (LRL) requires special attention due to data scarcity. Often LRL MT is aided by knowledge transfer from languages with more abundant resources (Tars et al., 2021; Neubig and Hu, 2018; Zoph et al., 2016). In this work we report a case study showing that transfer techniques based on back-translation can improve poor scores in very low-resource settings, but they can be counterproductive with more abundant authentic data. We demonstrate this in the case of a LRL for which augmentation data in the same genre as authentic data is not available.

We show that in some settings where authentic data amount renders back-translation less effective, multi-source MT methods (Zoph et al., 2016) are more reliable to make incremental improvements. In these settings, MT systems map from a small amount of data in a LRL and a larger amount of data in a related high resource language (HRL) to a target language (TGT), in order to improve LRL-to-TGT translation quality. (See §2.1.) In addition to applying these methods conventionally, we present novel techniques for harnessing syntactic, orthographic, and phonological similarities between source languages LRL and HRL. Prior to training, we employ multiple tools to transform HRL data to resemble LRL orthography and syntax by harnessing language relatedness. For phonologically similar languages, we present novel phonological word embeddings via PanPhon (Mortensen et al., 2016) and use these to initialize MT models to facilitate a model's learning the LRL from the HRL.

We conduct these experiments in a case study of Haitian-to-English MT. We also contribute a rule-based French-Haitian (FRA-HAT) orthographic and syntactic engine that transforms French to Haitian text with 59.5% character error rate (CER) and 1.60 BLEU (Papineni et al., 2002) on a single-reference set of 50 sentences.

To demonstrate how these techniques can be applied to other LRL, we adapt these strategies to Jamaican and show significant improvements over baseline performance, including improvements of up to 6.63 BLEU points.

Our findings suggest that despite back-

Proceedings of the 29th International Conference on Computational Linguistic, pages 35–42
October 12–17, 2022.

translation's reputation for usefulness in some settings, it cannot result in usable MT in others, in which case other transfer methods are needed for further, albeit marginal, improvement.

1.1 Case Study: Haitian

We consider Haitian as a low-resource language specimen. This language has critical importance for the global community, particularly in the context of recent immigration and disaster relief efforts (Heinzelman and Waters, 2010; Margesson and Taft-Morales, 2010; Rasmussen et al., 2015). Haitian is closely related to high-resource French, but the two have an unconventional relationship: high phonological and lexical similarity with low syntactic and orthographic similarity. This is comparable to a large number of language pairs such as Thai and Lao, Arabic and Maltese, Jamaican and English, etc.

The Haitian government did not formalize a Haitian writing system until the 20th century. (Valdman, 1988) Still today, Haitians often write in French rather than Haitian due to social pressures, which contributes to a lack of written and digitized materials. (Zimra, 1993) Despite this lack of resources, Haitian is a widely spoken language. Over 11 million people speak it natively (Bartens, 2021), including over 1 million immigrants in the USA, Brazil, the Bahamas, Canada, Chile, the Dominican Republic, France, Mexico, and elsewhere. (Audebert, 2017) Not many other residents of these countries learn Haitian. As a result, the lives of many Haitian speakers could be greatly improved by high-quality MT technology.

2 Related Work and Approach

We are not the first researchers to explore Haitian-to-English MT. Frederking et al. (1998) developed early statistical systems for Haitian MT and automatic speech recognition. In 2010 a devastating earthquake in Haiti's capital caused a global humanitarian disaster. This catastrophe renewed international interest in Haitian MT systems for disaster relief efforts, the deployment of which was a "widely heralded success story" (Neubig and Hu, 2018).

2.1 Back-translation Augmentation

Many researchers have employed back-translation to augment LRL data (Sennrich et al., 2016). This technique requires a small LRL-TGT bitext and a larger monolingual TGT corpus. Rather than mapping from LRL to TGT sentences by fitting on the small bitext, Sennrich et al. (2016) proposed a new method: (1) use the small bitext to train a TGT-to-LRL system, (2) translate the large TGT corpus to LRL, creating a large *synthetic* TGT-LRL bitext, then (3) train a system that maps from the LRL to the TGT on both the small authentic bitext and large synthetic bitext. In this paradigm, the quality of the synthetic translations may be low because they were produced by a system trained on a small bitext. The idea is that a small amount of high-quality data mixed with a large amount of low-quality data is preferable to a small amount of high-quality data alone. Back-translation has shown improvements in multiple MT settings (Popel et al., 2020). Xia et al. (2019) extended variations of this idea to a multilingual framework that we imitate. They investigated translating to English (ENG) from an LRL that has a closely related HRL. A large HRL-ENG bitext, and small bitexts between the LRL and the two other languages are assumed, as well as a large monolingual ENG corpus. They proposed producing synthetic LRL-ENG aligned data in three ways:

1. Train an ENG-to-LRL system on the small LRL-ENG bitext, and translate the large monolingual English corpus to LRL (i.e. back-translation)

2. Train an HRL-to-LRL system on the small LRL-HRL bitext, and translate the large ENG-aligned HRL data to LRL

3. Train an ENG-to-HRL system on the HRL-ENG bitext, and using the system from the previous step, translate the large ENG monolingual corpus to HRL and then to LRL

In the current work, we apply these augmentation methods for Haitian-to-English translation with HRL French. We refer to the synthetic bitext produced by step 1 as `synth_mono`, by step 2 as `synth_mix1`, and by step 3 as `synth_mix2`. Figure 1 displays a visual representation of the steps enumerated above.

2.2 Multi-source MT

Multi-source MT incorporating one or more HRL-TGT bitexts into training has been shown to improve LRL-TGT translation. (Freitag and Firat, 2020; Zoph et al., 2016; Peters and Martins, 2020).

Original French:	elle ne pensait pas descendre de sa maison pour lui rendre le livre, comme elle a fait ce matin
Orthography transform:	lwi panse pa dèsann son kay pou lwi rann la liv, konm lwi gen fè sa maten
Syntax transform:	il pas tape penser descendre maison il pour rendre li livre le comme il té faire matin ce
Both transforms:	li pa tap panse dèsann kay li pou rann li liv la konm li te fè maten sa
Actual Haitian translation:	li pa tap panse desann sòti kay li pou rann li liv la, jan li te fè maten sa
English:	she did not want to descend from her house to give him the book, like she did this morning

Table 1: Outputs of the Haitian-approximating orthographic and syntactic engines applied to transform French text.

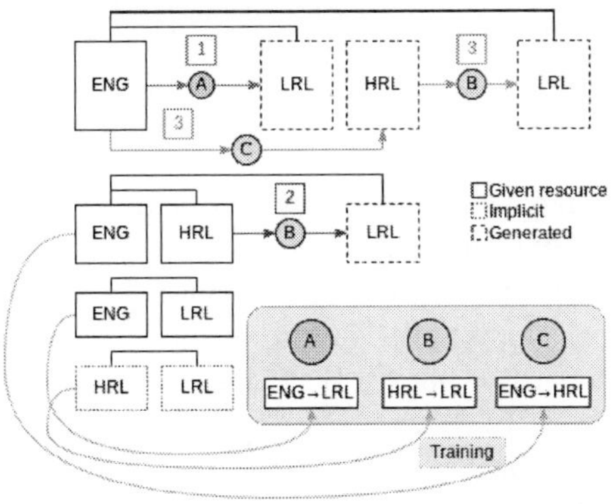

Figure 1: Visual representation of multilingual back-translation. Method adapted from Xia et al. (2019)

Neubig and Hu (2018) trained systems that map from an LRL and one related HRL to English. This improved LRL-ENG BLEU score significantly. In our work we show that this method can be more effective than back-translation when more authentic data is available, and we expand it through syntactic, orthographic, and phonological data representations to exploit relations between source languages.

3 Methodology and Experiments

Our experiments use a HAT-ENG bitext with 189,182 aligned sentence pairs (LRL-ENG) and a FRA-ENG bitext with 315,577 (HRL-TGT). These data come from broadcasts and literature produced by the Church of Jesus Christ of Latter-day Saints, with small additions from OPUS[1]. Because of overlap between the English portions of these two bitexts, we have an implicit FRA-HAT bitext of length 77,121. We have a large monolingual ENG corpus of text from Wikipedia, the Toronto book corpus (Zhu et al., 2015), and text scraped from Reddit. This monolingual augmentation data is not the same genre as the authentic aligned text. This setting is not ideal for back-translation, but it is meant to represent the realistic circumstance that no augmentation data in the authentic text genre is available, which may be the case for many low-resource languages.

All our models are attention-based (Vaswani et al., 2017), adapted from The Annotated Transformer (Klein et al., 2017), and trained using the Adam optimizer (Kingma and Ba, 2017). Hyperparameters are detailed in Appendix A.1 Because we are comparing data sets produced with different transfer methods, rather than model architecture or configuration, we used these same settings for all experiments.

We outline our methodology for the established methods of back-translation and multi-source training (§3.1 and §3.2) and then for our novel methods of linguistic transfer (§3.3).

3.1 Haitian Back-translation

We employed the same back-translation data augmentation strategies outlined in the numbered items of §2.1 and Figure 1. To observe effects of this augmentation on varying amounts of authentic data, we augmented gradually. We used three authentic data amounts as starting points: extremely low-resource (5K), low-resource (25K), and mid-resource (189K). To these starting amounts of authentic aligned data, we added 5K, then, 25K, then 200K lines of `synth_mono` data. Then to the 200K of `synth_mono` we added 5K, 25K, then 200K of `synth_mix1` data, and we followed suit with `synth_mix2` data. (Since `synth_mono` represents the simplest augmentation method and `synth_mix2` represents the most complicated, we reason that most practitioners would apply the former first of the three and the latter last.) Results from training on these 30 different sets are discussed in §4.

3.2 Multi-source Training

We also trained multi-source MT models with HAT and LRL, FRA as HRL, and ENG as TGT. We conducted the same experiment with Spanish (SPA) as the HRL and with all three source languages together. We selected French and Spanish because of their proximity to Haitian. However, the nature of this proximity introduces interesting challenges.

[1]https://opus.nlpl.eu

Roughly 90% of Haitian lexemes are of French origin, and the two languages are phonologically close. (Hall, 1953) However they have few shared word forms because of their distinct orthography systems. And they are syntactically different. Because traditional MT transformers do not access phonological information, this similarity does not provide any benefit in using French as co-source with Haitian.

3.3 Orthographic, Syntactic, and Phonological Transfer

Rule-based Orthographic and Syntactic Transformation To experiment with different methods of multi-source training, we developed a pipeline that orthographically transforms French to Haitian. The first engine changes word orthography via transformation rules based on French and Haitian grammar. The process resembles other automatic orthography transliterators like Epitran (Mortensen et al., 2018). The second engine uses the Berkeley Neural constituency parser (Kitaev et al., 2019) to change word order in French sentences, approximating Haitian syntax. This 922-line script tuned on zero data produces HAT reference translations from a single set with BLEU 1.60 and CER 59.5%[2].

In this manner we transform our French-English bitext into a pseudo-Haitian-English bitext and train jointly with that and our authentic Haitian-English data. To observe the different effects of transfer from orthographic similarity and from syntactic similarity in MT training, we also transform French to pseudo-Haitian using the two engines in isolation. See Table 1 for output examples.

Note how this method is distinct from the established method of code-switching for augmentation (Song et al., 2019; Yang et al., 2020). Our method here relies on deep linguistic knowledge and a collection of hand-crafted rules. Code-switching data, or replacing some source words with their translations in another language, may have a comparable effect but does not require linguistic knowledge; it is a less careful approach but more applicable to a wide variety of languages. We employ such a method for Jamaican MT in §5 and discuss it more there. Because hand-crafted rules do not provide complete coverage of a language, our orthographic transliterator does not always result in exact matches of Haitian words. This is one reason for the low BLEU score of its outputs and suggests the utility of using the phonological embeddings described below in tandem with orthographic and syntactic transformation.

Syntactic Transfer in Isolation Some languages are not orthographically or phonologically close but share syntactic features, such as Jamaican and Haitian or Spanish and French. We explore this more generalizable case of exploiting specifically syntactic relations between languages in §5.

Phonological Embedding We employ a separate method to exploit phonological similarity between source languages. We convert Haitian and French words to IPA feature vectors using Epitran (Mortensen et al., 2018) and PanPhon (Mortensen et al., 2016). We represent each word as the sum of its phone vectors and use these to initialize transformer embeddings. In this way, the model can know that French *unité* (IPA: `ynite`) and its Haitian translation *inite* (IPA: `inite`) are closely related. This method does not involve transforming or altering either language and can be applied readily to other language pairs. It is comparable to the way Chaudhary et al. (2018) produce phonological embeddings for low-resource named entity recognition.

In the case that we apply orthographic and syntactic transformation on French data in addition to phonological embeddings, we generate phonological embeddings for the psudo-Haitian text using Haitian pronunciation conventions. In this case the phonological embeddings theoretically serve as a way to fuzzy match during training: words with slight misspellings will be embedded close to their phonologically approximate correct spellings.

4 Results

Figure 2 shows translation performance scores across a progression of back-translation-based augmentation as discussed in §3.1. These techniques improve performance when the amount of authentic data is very small. But once it crosses a threshold, they become counter-productive. We do not identify the exact threshold, since we performed these experiments as a case study, and such a threshold would certainly vary, depending on the source language and training data genre. Our objective here is to illustrate a conceivable setting in which back-translation augmentation can hurt MT performance. In such circumstances, we note that there exist es-

[2]BLEU is a poor metric for this engine since a majority of its errors are word choice differences and misspellings.

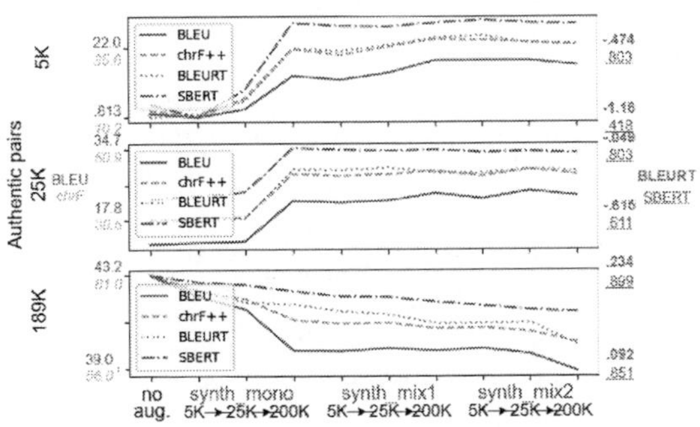

Figure 2: Scores in four performance metrics across models employing back-translation techniques. Back-translation augmentation increases to the right.

Source	BLEU	BLEURT
HAT	43.94*	.6810*
HAT+FRA	46.05*	.7026*
HAT+SPA	**46.51***	.7065
HAT+FRA+SPA	46.41*	**.7131***
HAT+JPN	30.41	-.1554

Table 2: HAT-ENG translation scores from multi-source training, best results **bolded**
*Significant improvement over next-best score, p=1e-6, details in Appendix B.1

tablished techniques for making back-translation more effective. (Burchell et al., 2022; Lakew et al., 2021) We, however, turn our attention to methods based on multi-source training.

Results for multilingual source training experiments are in Table 2. This illustrates that bi- and trilingual source training can improve MT even when we use all 189K authentic HAT-ENG pairs. As mentioned in §3.2, our MT models traditionally cannot take full advantage of Haitian's similarity to French. As the table shows, French does not help Haitian MT any better than Spanish does, despite the closer historical relationship. Note, however, that augmenting with a related language like French or Spanish is still more helpful than with an unrelated language, Japanese, which degrades performance. The best configurations we evaluated used Haitian and Spanish, per BLEU and BLEURT scores (Sellam et al., 2020).

Table 3 displays the results from different transfer methods from French source data to augment for HAT-ENG training. *Synt* and *Orth* refer to data transliteration from our syntactic and orthographic FRA-to-HAT engines, respectively. *Phon* indicates use of phonological encoded similarity via PanPhon. *All* indicates all of these transfers employed at once. Overall, our best HAT-to-ENG model uses orthographically transformed FRA data, and the second-best uses both *Synt* and *Orth*.

Transform.	BLEU	BLEURT
No HRL	43.94	.6810
No transf. on FRA	46.05*	.7026
Synt	46.08*	.7015
Orth	**46.88***	**.7061**
Synt+Orth	46.43*	.7057
Phon	44.52*	.6925*
Synt+Orth+Phon	45.55*	.6995*

Table 3: French co-source data transformed in three different ways to resemble Haitian, best results **bolded**
*Significant improvement over next-best score, p=1e-6

Although these methods all score significantly higher than zero augmentation (and significantly higher than the untransformed FRA baseline in BLEU), their margin of improvement is smaller than expected. We hypothesize this could be improved by learning phonological embeddings that preserve phone order in the case of *Phon* and by tuning our FRA-HAT pipeline to a small amount of real data in the case of *Synt* and *Orth*.

5 Rapid Adaptation to New Languages

We seek to apply these principles of orthographic, syntactic, and phonological transfer rapidly to new languages by exploring another case study: Jamaican. Jamaican (JAM) is an even lower-resource language than Haitian, with only 3.2 million native speakers[3].

We experiment with syntactic transfer in JAM-to-ENG translation. In these experiments we used Haitian in the HRL role because it is close to Jamaican syntactically but distant from it in terms of lexicon and orthography. Results in the top of Table 4 show that this transfer is helpful for JAM-to-ENG MT.

As mentioned in §3.3, our method for phonological embedding is readily applicable to other languages. To apply it to Jamaican, we created a new Jamaican setting in Epitran via 37 mapping rules. This step would be unnecessary, however, for adaption to any of the 77 languages supported by Epitran. We applied phonological transfer in JAM-to-FRA translation, where we used English as the HRL because it is phonologically close to Jamaican. Results from phonological embedding in the bottom of Table 4 are denoted "phon."

In the absense of a rule-based orthographic automatic transliterator from English to Jamaican, we sought to imitate the effects of orthographic transfer via code-switching. This is a method employed in multiple past works (Song et al., 2019; Yang

[3]According to Ethnologue

JAM→ENG Translation		
	BLEU	BLEURT
No aug.	4.868	.3873
HAT aug.	**10.32***	**.4483***

JAM→FRA Translation		
	BLEU	BLEURT
No aug.	1.176	.0452
ENG aug.	2.824*	.0773*
ENG aug. + CS	**7.807***	**.1698**
ENG aug. + phon	6.8312*	.1523*

Table 4: Experiments for harnessing syntactic, orthographic, and phonological relatedness to higher-resourced languages for Jamaican translation. Our formulations of syntactic and orthographic transfer are the most effective. "CS" refers to code-switching, which is used to imitate orthographic transfer.
*Significant improvement over next-best score, p=1e-6

et al., 2020; Xu and Yvon, 2021), however all of them employ code-switching by replacing source language (LRL) words with target langauge (TGT) words. In our experiments, we replace English (HRL) words with Jamaican (LRL) words using a dictionary of 200 Jamaican words with English translations. This causes the English augmentation text to resemble Jamaican orthography more closely. Of the methods we attempted to improve JAM-to-FRA translation, this was the most successful. As shown in the bottom of Table 4, it provides an advantage of 6.63 BLEU points over the baseline and of 4.98 BLEU points over conventional multisource training.

6 Conclusion

Although back-translation transfer methods are effective in some MT settings, in others they are unable to improve MT performance beyond a threshold or result in usable translation. Per our explorations, methods involving multilingual transfer from a HRL during training are able to make further improvements, even when more abundant authentic data yields higher baseline performance. In our experiments, employing strategies to transfer orthographic and syntactic information from the HRL outperform methods to transfer phonological information or no specific information. Our experiments on Haitian MT indicate the potential for future improvements and broad social impact. And our exploration of Jamaican demonstrates the capacity of these techniques for rapid adaptation to new settings and improvements in low-resource domains more generally.

References

Cedric Audebert. 2017. The recent geodynamics of haitian migration in the americas: refugees or economic migrants? *Revista Brasileira de Estudos de População*, 34:55–71.

Angela Bartens. 2021. The making of languages and new literacies: San andrés-providence creole with a view on jamaican and haitian. *Lingüística y Literatura*, 42(79):237–256.

Laurie Burchell, Alexandra Birch, and Kenneth Heafield. 2022. Exploring diversity in back translation for low-resource machine translation. In *Proceedings of the Third Workshop on Deep Learning for Low-Resource Natural Language Processing*, pages 67–79, Hybrid. Association for Computational Linguistics.

Aditi Chaudhary, Chunting Zhou, Lori Levin, Graham Neubig, David R. Mortensen, and Jaime G. Carbonell. 2018. Adapting word embeddings to new languages with morphological and phonological subword representations.

Robert E Frederking, Ralf D Brown, and Christopher Hogan. 1998. The diplomat rapiddeployment speech mt system. *MT Summit (1997)*, pages 261–262.

Markus Freitag and Orhan Firat. 2020. Complete multilingual neural machine translation. In *Proceedings of the Fifth Conference on Machine Translation*, pages 550–560, Online. Association for Computational Linguistics.

Robert Anderson Hall. 1953. *Haitian Creole: grammar, texts, vocabulary*, volume 43. American Anthropological Association.

Jessica Heinzelman and Carol Waters. 2010. *Crowdsourcing crisis information in disaster-affected Haiti.* JSTOR.

Diederik P. Kingma and Jimmy Ba. 2017. Adam: A method for stochastic optimization.

Nikita Kitaev, Steven Cao, and Dan Klein. 2019. Multilingual constituency parsing with self-attention and pre-training.

Guillaume Klein, Yoon Kim, Yuntian Deng, Jean Senellart, and Alexander M. Rush. 2017. Opennmt: Open-source toolkit for neural machine translation. In *Proc. ACL*.

Philipp Koehn. 2004. Statistical significance tests for machine translation evaluation. In *Proceedings of the 2004 conference on empirical methods in natural language processing*, pages 388–395.

Surafel M Lakew, Matteo Negri, and Marco Turchi. 2021. Self-learning for zero shot neural machine translation. *arXiv preprint arXiv:2103.05951*.

Rhoda Margesson and Maureen Taft-Morales. 2010. Haiti earthquake: Crisis and response. Library of Congress Washington DC Congressional Research Service.

David R. Mortensen, Siddharth Dalmia, and Patrick Littell. 2018. Epitran: Precision G2P for many languages. In *Proceedings of the Eleventh International Conference on Language Resources and Evaluation (LREC 2018)*, Paris, France. European Language Resources Association (ELRA).

David R. Mortensen, Patrick Littell, Akash Bharadwaj, Kartik Goyal, Chris Dyer, and Lori Levin. 2016. Pan-Phon: A resource for mapping IPA segments to articulatory feature vectors. In *Proceedings of COLING 2016, the 26th International Conference on Computational Linguistics: Technical Papers*, pages 3475–3484, Osaka, Japan. The COLING 2016 Organizing Committee.

Graham Neubig and Junjie Hu. 2018. Rapid adaptation of neural machine translation to new languages. In *Proceedings of the 2018 Conference on Empirical Methods in Natural Language Processing*, pages 875–880, Brussels, Belgium. Association for Computational Linguistics.

Kishore Papineni, Salim Roukos, Todd Ward, and Wei-Jing Zhu. 2002. Bleu: a method for automatic evaluation of machine translation. In *Proceedings of the 40th annual meeting of the Association for Computational Linguistics*, pages 311–318.

Ben Peters and André F. T. Martins. 2020. One-size-fits-all multilingual models. In *Proceedings of the 17th SIGMORPHON Workshop on Computational Research in Phonetics, Phonology, and Morphology*, pages 63–69, Online. Association for Computational Linguistics.

Martin Popel, Marketa Tomkova, Jakub Tomek, Łukasz Kaiser, Jakob Uszkoreit, Ondřej Bojar, and Zdeněk Žabokrtský. 2020. Transforming machine translation: a deep learning system reaches news translation quality comparable to human professionals. *Nature communications*, 11(1):1–15.

Maja Popović. 2017. chrf++: words helping character n-grams. In *Proceedings of the second conference on machine translation*, pages 612–618.

Andrew Rasmussen, Eddy Eustache, Giuseppe Raviola, Bonnie Kaiser, David J Grelotti, and Gary S Belkin. 2015. Development and validation of a haitian creole screening instrument for depression. *Transcultural psychiatry*, 52(1):33–57.

Nils Reimers and Iryna Gurevych. 2019. Sentence-bert: Sentence embeddings using siamese bert-networks. *arXiv preprint arXiv:1908.10084*.

Thibault Sellam, Dipanjan Das, and Ankur P Parikh. 2020. Bleurt: Learning robust metrics for text generation. *arXiv preprint arXiv:2004.04696*.

Rico Sennrich, Barry Haddow, and Alexandra Birch. 2016. Improving neural machine translation models with monolingual data. In *Proceedings of the 54th Annual Meeting of the Association for Computational Linguistics (Volume 1: Long Papers)*, pages 86–96, Berlin, Germany. Association for Computational Linguistics.

Kai Song, Yue Zhang, Heng Yu, Weihua Luo, Kun Wang, and Min Zhang. 2019. Code-switching for enhancing NMT with pre-specified translation. In *Proceedings of the 2019 Conference of the North American Chapter of the Association for Computational Linguistics: Human Language Technologies, Volume 1 (Long and Short Papers)*, pages 449–459, Minneapolis, Minnesota. Association for Computational Linguistics.

Maali Tars, Andre Tättar, and Mark Fišel. 2021. Extremely low-resource machine translation for closely related languages. In *Proceedings of the 23rd Nordic Conference on Computational Linguistics (NoDaLiDa)*, pages 41–52, Reykjavik, Iceland (Online). Linköping University Electronic Press, Sweden.

Albert Valdman. 1988. Ann pale kreyol: An introductory course in haitian creole.

Ashish Vaswani, Noam Shazeer, Niki Parmar, Jakob Uszkoreit, Llion Jones, Aidan N Gomez, Łukasz Kaiser, and Illia Polosukhin. 2017. Attention is all you need. In *Advances in neural information processing systems*, pages 5998–6008.

Mengzhou Xia, Xiang Kong, Antonios Anastasopoulos, and Graham Neubig. 2019. Generalized data augmentation for low-resource translation. In *Proceedings of the 57th Annual Meeting of the Association for Computational Linguistics*, pages 5786–5796, Florence, Italy. Association for Computational Linguistics.

Jitao Xu and François Yvon. 2021. Can you traducir this? machine translation for code-switched input. In *Proceedings of the Fifth Workshop on Computational Approaches to Linguistic Code-Switching*, pages 84–94, Online. Association for Computational Linguistics.

Zhen Yang, Bojie Hu, Ambyera Han, Shen Huang, and Qi Ju. 2020. CSP:code-switching pre-training for neural machine translation. In *Proceedings of the 2020 Conference on Empirical Methods in Natural Language Processing (EMNLP)*, pages 2624–2636, Online. Association for Computational Linguistics.

Yukun Zhu, Ryan Kiros, Rich Zemel, Ruslan Salakhutdinov, Raquel Urtasun, Antonio Torralba, and Sanja Fidler. 2015. Aligning books and movies: Towards story-like visual explanations by watching movies and reading books. In *Proceedings of the IEEE international conference on computer vision*, pages 19–27.

Clarisse Zimra. 1993. Haitian literature after duvalier: an interview with yanick lahens. *Callaloo*, 16(1):77–93.

Barret Zoph, Deniz Yuret, Jonathan May, and Kevin Knight. 2016. Transfer learning for low-resource neural machine translation. In *Proceedings of the 2016 Conference on Empirical Methods in Natural Language Processing*, pages 1568–1575, Austin, Texas. Association for Computational Linguistics.

A Hyperparameters, Infrastructure, and Efficiency

We will release our software publicly upon acceptance.

A.1 All Experiments

The following settings are true for all experiments reported in this paper:

architecture: Transformer (Vaswani et al., 2017)
layers: 2 encoder layers, 2 decoder layers
attention heads: 6
learning rate: 0.0005
dropout rate: 0.1
optimizer: Adam (Kingma and Ba, 2017)

Following subsections provide the settings for individual experiments.

A.2 Experiment 1: Hatian Back-Translation

parameters: 43283546
training set (sentences): 4375 (low-res.) - 690535 (high-res.)
evaluation set (sentences): 625 (low-res.) - 98647 (high-res.)
computing infrastructure: NVIDIA GeForce GTX 1080 Ti
average runtime: $<$ 1 hour

A.3 Experiment 2: Multi-Source Training

parameters: 43283546
training set (sentences): 165535 (no aug.) - 777440 (FRA+SPA aug.)
evaluation set (sentences): 23647 (no aug.) - 111062 (FRA+SPA aug.)
computing infrastructure: NVIDIA GeForce GTX 1080 Ti
average runtime: 2-3 hours

A.4 Experiment 3: Orthographic, Syntactic, and Phonological Transfer

parameters: 43283546
training set (sentences): 441665
evaluation set (sentences): 63094
computing infrastructure: NVIDIA GeForce RTX 2080 Ti
average runtime: 2 hours

A.5 Experiment 4: Jamaican MT

parameters: 43283546
training set (sentences): 6939 (no aug.) - 283069 (aug.)
evaluation set (sentences): 991 (no aug.) - 40438 (aug.)
computing infrastructure: NVIDIA GeForce RTX 2080 Ti
average runtime: 1 hour

B Evaluation Metrics

We employed four translation evaluation metrics: BLEU (Papineni et al., 2002), BLEURT (Sellam et al., 2020), chrF++ (Popović, 2017), and Sentence-BERT (SBERT) (Reimers and Gurevych, 2019)

B.1 Computing Statistical Significance

We computed statistical significance via a difference of means test over our evaluation set. We used the `stats.wilcoxon` from SciPy. For BLEURT we considered a simple difference of means, and for BLEU we bootstrapped 1000 document-level scores from our evaluation set (Koehn, 2004).

Augmented Bio-SBERT: Improving Performance For Pairwise Sentence Tasks in Bio-medical Domain

Sonam Pankaj
Rasa
s.pankaj@rasa.com

Amit Gautam
Saama Technologies
amit.gautam@saama.com

Abstract

One of the modern challenges in AI is the access to high-quality and annotated data, especially in NLP; that's why augmentation is gaining importance. In computer vision, where image data augmentation is standard, text data augmentation in NLP is complex due to the high complexity of language. And we have seen advantages of augmentation where there are fewer data available, and it can play a massive role in improving the model's accuracy and performance. We have implemented Augmentation in Pairwise sentence scoring in the biomedical domain.

By experimenting with our approach to downstream tasks on biomedical data, we have looked into the solution to improve Bi-encoders' sentence transformer performance using augmented data-set generated by cross-encoders fine-tuned on Biosses and MedNLI on pretrained Bio-BERT model. It has significantly improved the results with respect to the only the model only trained on Gold data for the respective tasks.

1 Introduction

Language models are data hungry; they consume massive amounts of data to identify patterns. For many niches, low-resource domains like that of Bio domain NLP, manually finding or annotating a substantial dataset is complicated. Bio-domain language models comparison (Peng et al., 2019). Fortunately, we don't need to label this new data; we can automatically generate or label data using one or more data augmentation techniques. Pairwise sentence scoring tasks are used widely in NLP Applications. (Thakur et al., 2020) like information retrieval, question answering, duplicate question detection, or clustering. Pre-trained transformers have led to remarkable progress in several tasks, especially BERT (Devlin et al., 2019) is an approach that sets new state-of-the-art performance for many tasks, including pairwise sentence scoring. For tasks that make pairwise comparisons between sequences, matching a given input with a corresponding label, two approaches are common: Cross-encoders and Bi-encoders. We pre-trained Cross-encoders on the gold dataset, then outputs of different pairs from random sampling and semantic sampling were fed to the cross-encoder. The silver dataset produced was then provided to Bi-encoder. There is a new approach like Poly-encoder, which mostly fits tasks around conversational AI. We have used BioBERT, a biomedical language representation model designed for biomedical text mining tasks such as biomedical named entity recognition, relation extraction, question answering, etc. cross- and bi- encoders, details on pretrained model architecture have been discussed in section 4.2 and 4.3. We worked on two tasks for pairwise sentences—semantic similarity and Language Inferences based on medical data such as Biosses and MedNLI. We have evaluated the results on the test set of each data set. In the end, we have compared our model results with results of textual similarity and inference tasks on a blue benchmark and have included the Table 1.

2 Related Work

There have been many NLP-augmentation methods based on paraphrasing models and non- paraphrasing models. A Survey of Data Augmentation Approaches for NLP highlights techniques used for popular NLP applications and tasks, (Feng et al., 2021) like mitigating biases and fixing class imbalance. Augmented SBERT: Data Augmentation Method for Improving Bi-Encoders for Pairwise Sentence Scoring Tasks have worked on sentence pair scor- ing through cross-encoder and Bi-encoder on general language(English). But available language evaluation doesn't fit bio-medical uses, given it can't relate to the biomedical domain.

Proceedings of the 29th International Conference on Computational Linguistic, pages 43–47
October 12–17, 2022.

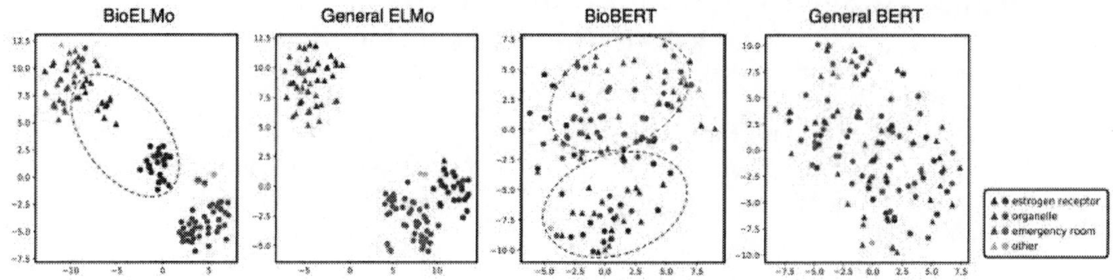

Figure 1: Comparison of BioELMO, General Elmo, BioBERT and General BERT

Probing Biomedical Embeddings from Language Models , (jin, 2019) this paper deals with the contrast in general, English and biomedical on any down- streaming tasks, and the results show that even pre-trained by in-domain corpus as a fixed feature extractor, BioBERT still cannot effectively encode biomedical relations compared to BERT. BioELMo is significantly better than ELMo in representing same relations closer to each other. Augmentation with general language BERT will perform poorly, as it has been compared in Figure 1.

3 Downstreaming Tasks

We have used two tasks for pairwise sentences: natural language inference and semantic textual similarity. The dataset for training and testing have been described in section 5.1.

Natural language inference (NLI): is the task (Romanov and Shivade, 2018) of determining whether a given hypothesis can be inferred from a given premise. We are using, MedNLI - a publicly available, expertly annotated dataset for NLI in the clinical domain.

Semantic textual similarity: Semantic textual similarity deals with determining how similar two pieces of texts are. Related tasks are paraphrase or duplicate identification. We have used the Biosses (Gizem Soganciogl̆u, 2017) dataset for the same.

4 Methods

In this section, we will describe the pre-trained model used, the fine-tuning, cross- and bi- encoders, and the step-by-step method of getting the predictions from the bi-encoder sentence transformer after fine-tuning it on a silver dataset. We will also discuss the sampling techniques used for creating a silver dataset.

1. Cross-Encoders are trained on gold label dataset of Biosses and MedNLI
2. Sample pairs of sentences by using methods of Random Sampling and Semantic Search Sampling
3. Predicting similarity on trained cross-encoder that we trained on a gold dataset. This makes the silver dataset
4. Training the Bi-Encoder SBERT based on the silver Dataset
5. Predicting the results and comparing the mix of (Gold and Silver dataset) to Gold Dataset

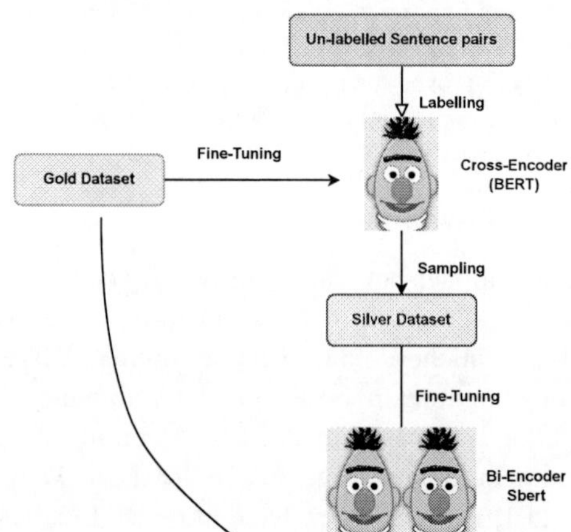

Figure 2: Architecture of training bi-encoders on silver dataset

4.1 Model

Pretrained Model: BioBERT largely outperforms BERT and previous state-of-the-art models

BLUE sentence-pair tasks dataset			
Corpus	gold	gold and silver	test-datset
Biosses	80	880	20
MedNLI	11232	67377	1422

Table 1: dataset for training and testing

in a variety of biomedical text mining tasks when pre-trained on biomedical corpora. Due to this, we have decided to use this sentence transformer based on this model.

SBERT: Given a pre-trained, well-performing cross-encoder, we sample sentence pairs according to a specific sampling strategy (discussed later) and label these using the cross-encoder. We call these weakly labeled examples the silver dataset, and will merge both with the gold training dataset. We then train the bi-encoder on this extended training dataset. We refer to this model as Augmented SBERT (AugSBERT). In Figure 2. we have illustrated the process of Augmented SBERT

Fine-tuning Model: Fine-tuning sentence transformer models requires pairs of labeled data, cross-encoder model fine-tuned on gold dataset, and the bi-encoder fine-tuned on gold and silver data [1].

4.2 Cross-encoder

In a cross-encoder, both sentences are passed to the network, and attention is applied across all tokens of the inputs. This approach is in Figure 3, where both sentences are simultaneously passed to the network. (Gizem Soganciogl u, 2017). It is a single Bio-BERT inference step that takes both sentences as a single input and outputs a similarity score.

Pretrained Model: We have used pretrained Bi-encoder dmis-lab/biobert-v1.1 from DMIS-Labs via hugging face, and finetuned it on gold data.

4.3 Bi-encoder

For a given sentence, bi-encoder produce a sentence embedding. We independently pass to a Bio-BERT the sentences A and B, which result in the sentence embedding u and v. These sentence embeddings can then be compared using cosine similarity, and thus we get similarity score as shown in Figure 4.

[1]codes available in supplementary

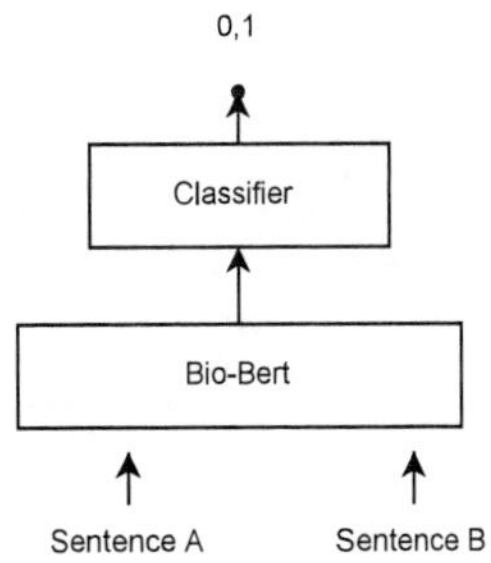

Figure 3: Scoring of Cross-encoder Architecture

Pretrained Model: We have used pretrained Bi-encoder dmis-lab/biobert-v1.1 from DMIS-Labs via hugging face, and finetuned it on gold+silver data.

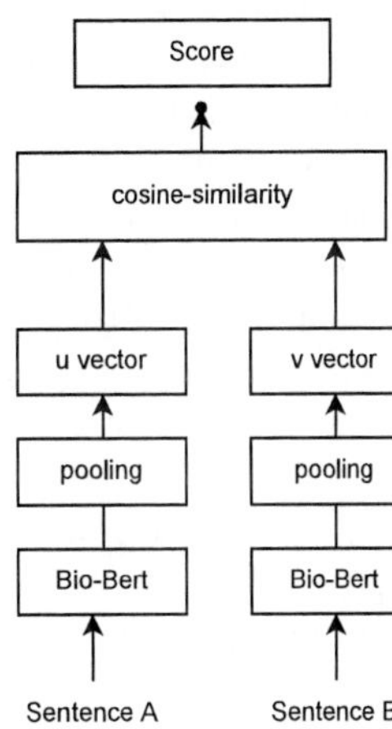

Figure 4: Bi-encoder Architecture

4.4 Sampling Techniques

We used random and semantic search sampling to make new pairwise data.

Random Sampling (RS) : We randomly sample a sentence pair and weakly label it with the cross-encoder. Randomly selecting two sentences usually leads to a dissimilar (negative) pair; positive pairs are extremely rare. This skews the label distribution of the silver dataset heavily towards negative pairs.

Semantic Search Sampling (SS) : We train a bi-encoder (SBERT) on the gold training set (Reimers and Gurevych) and use it to sample further similar sentence pairs. We use cosine-similarity and

Dataset Sampling	Biosses	MedNLI
Gold (baseline)	71.4	12.7
Gold and Silver (Random Sampling)	74.5	57.9
Gold and Silver (Semantic Sampling)	88.5	74

Table 2: Comparison with our model comparison of Gold with respect to Gold + Silver on Biosses and MedNLI

retrieve the top five most similar sentences in our collection on every sentence. We used pretrained-model which is BioBERT fine-tuned on the SNLI and the MultiNLI datasets using the sentence-transformers library to produce universal sentence embeddings.

5 Experiment-Setup

We conducted the experiments using PyTorch Hugging Face's transformers (Wolf et al., 2019), and we used google-colab to import the transformers, cross-encoders, and sentence transformers. The latter showed that BERT outperforms other transformer-like networks when used as a bi-encoder. Baselines are just Bio-Bert output on a gold dataset. Baseline with gold has been measured only with bi-encoder

5.1 Datasets

Sentence pair scoring can be differentiated in regression and classification tasks. Regression tasks assign a score to indicate the similarity between the inputs.

BIOSSES: Several approaches have been proposed for semantic sentence similarity estimation for generic English. Biosses is a benchmark data set consisting of 100 sentence pairs from the biomedical literature that is manually annotated by five human experts and used for evaluating the proposed methods.

MedNLI: MedNLI is a dataset annotated by doctors, performing a natural language inference task (NLI) grounded in patients' medical history. The MedNLI dataset consists of the sentence pairs developed by Physicians from the Past Medical History section of MIMIC-III clinical notes annotated for Definitely True, Maybe True, and False.

5.1.1 Benchmarks

Both the datasets are present in BLUE Benchmark, for pairwise sentences for similarity and inference.

Models	Biosses	MedNLI
ELMO	60.2	71.4
BioBERT	82.7	80.5

Table 3: Accuracy of different language models for corpus

Table 3 [2] gives us the comparison of different models on different tasks of BLUE benchmark.

6 Results

The results section includes experimentation on the only gold dataset and the gold and silver dataset, using both methods, random sampling, and semantic similarity sampling, given in the Table 3.

Depicting the silver dataset helps improve the model, produced by using SBERT augmentation and mixed with gold labels. We have also compared it with the results of ELMO and BIOBERT results given in Table 3.

7 Conclusion

As language models get bigger, so do datasets. And although we have seen an explosion of data in the past decade, it is often not accessible, especially in niche domains like Bio-domain. And there are datasets, like Biosses, which has only 100 pairs of sentences. Thus finding a substantial annotated dataset becomes difficult.

Sentence-BERT augmentation can be used to improve pairwise sentence models and sentence similarity datasets. Like in our case, it has improved results by up to 23.9 percent in the case of the Biosses and 482 percent in case of MedNLI, as discussed in Table 2.

[2]data has been taken from https://arxiv.org/pdf/1906.05474v2.pdf

References

Jacob Devlin, Ming-Wei Chang, Kenton Lee, and Kristina Toutanova. 2019. Bert: Pre-training of deep bidirectional transformers for language understanding.

Steven Y. Feng, Varun Gangal, Jason Wei, Sarath Chandar, Soroush Vosoughi, Teruko Mitamura, and Eduard Hovy. 2021. A survey of data augmentation approaches for nlp.

Özgür Gizem Sogancioglu, Öztürk H. 2017. Biosses: A semantic sentence similarity estimation system for the biomedical domain.

dhingra jin. 2019. probing biomedical embeddings from language models.

Yifan Peng, Shankai Yan, and Zhiyong Lu. 2019. Transfer learning in biomedical natural language processing: An evaluation of bert and elmo on ten benchmarking datasets.

Nils Reimers and Iryna Gurevych. Sentence-bert: Sentence embeddings using siamese bert-networks.

Alexey Romanov and Chaitanya Shivade. 2018. Lessons from natural language inference in the clinical domain.

Nandan Thakur, Nils Reimers, Johannes Daxenberger, and Iryna Gurevych. 2020. Augmented SBERT: data augmentation method for improving bi-encoders for pairwise sentence scoring tasks. *CoRR*, abs/2010.08240.

Machine Translation for a very Low-Resource Language - Layer Freezing approach on Transfer Learning

Amartya Roy Chowdhury and **S. R. Mahadeva Prasanna**
Indian Institute of Technology, Dharwad

Deepak K.T
Indian Institute of Information Technology, Dharwad

Samudra Vijaya K
Koneru Lakshmaiah Education Foundation, Vijayawada

Abstract

This paper presents the implementation of Machine Translation (MT) between Lambani, a low-resource Indian tribal language, and English, a high-resource universal language. Lambani is spoken by nomadic tribes of the Indian state of Karnataka and there are similarities between Lambani and various other Indian languages. To implement the English-Lambani MT system, we followed the transfer learning approach with English-Kannada as the parent MT model. The implementation and performance of the English-Lambani MT system are discussed in this paper. Since Lambani has been influenced by various other languages, we explored the possibility of getting better MT performance by using parent models associated with related Indian languages. Specifically, we experimented with English-Gujarati and English-Marathi as additional parent models. We compare the performance of three different English-Lambani MT systems derived from three parent language models, and the observations are presented in the paper. Additionally, we will also explore the effect of freezing the encoder layer and decoder layer and the change in performance from both of them.

1 Introduction

Machine Translation started way back in the 1950s as a way to bridge the communication gap. The techniques are broadly classified in three types (a) Rule-Based Machine Translation(RBMT) (Charoenpornsawat et al., 2002) (b) Statistical Based Machine Translation(SMT) (Zens et al., 2002) and (c) Neural-based approaches (NMT). Warren Weaver created the first computer-generated Machine Translation (Hutchins, 1997) during the 1980s by using Statistical methods using 'Shannon's Information Theory' (Stone). In the last couple of years, neural-based Machine Translation has achieved state-of-the-art performance where large amounts of parallel data are available. With the introduction of the encoder-decoder-based architecture (Eriguchi et al., 2016; Vaswani et al., 2018), there was a surge of interest and a lot of research has been conducted. However, it was quickly realized that these initial systems require a huge amount of data to get a performance close to that of a SMT system. (Koehn, 2009). Transfer learning has proved successful for low resource settings (Yi et al., 2018; Tits et al., 2019; Maimaiti et al., 2019; Imankulova et al.,

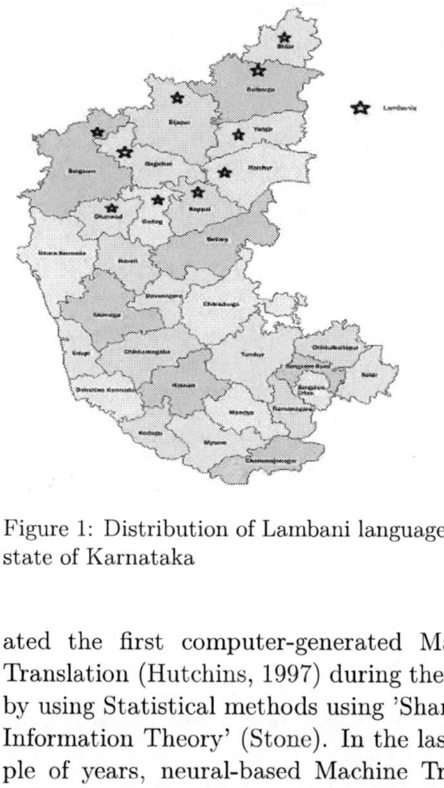

Figure 1: Distribution of Lambani language in the state of Karnataka

Proceedings of the 29th International Conference on Computational Linguistic, pages 48–55
October 12–17, 2022.

2019) and achieves higher translation performance. In this paper, we will specifically be focusing on NMT although transfer learning has been used for SMT in the past. Specifically for low-resourced languages SMT seem to give better performance in case of domain mismatch (Kumar et al., 2018)

In this paper, we focus on Lambani language (Chandramouli and General, 2011) which is generally spoken by the banjaras (Varady, 1979; Childers et al., 2003) and study how the language draws its influence from various other languages. We show how morphological similarity can improve the performance of a language. We focus on three different languages and how are they related to Lambani. However, it is a major challenge to collect a large amount of data for languages which are not spoken by a lot of people. Despite the recent emphasis on low resource languages, we are not aware of any research that has done any work in the Lambani language.

The paper is organized as follows. A summary of the background work is given in section 2. The proposed approach is explained in section 3. The details of the dataset used are given in section 4. The effect of layer freezing is presented in Section 5.

2 Background

In this section we give an overview of the transfer learning approach in the context of Machine Translation.

2.1 Transfer Learning

Transfer learning was first conceptualized in 2016 (Do and Ng, 2005; Zoph et al., 2016) and was mainly used for the text classification task. Transfer learning is the transfer of knowledge from one model to another. We apply the same concept in our work for MT between various languages.

2.2 Transfer learning in Machine Translation

(Zoph et al., 2016) used transfer learning for MT between four languages, viz. Uzbek, Hausa, Turkish, and Urdu. In the paper, the parent model was trained on a high-resource data set and the model parameters were transferred to the low-resource setting. By using this method Zoph et al. were able to improve the BLEU (Papineni et al., 2002) score by an additional 5 to 6, on average. In the case of Urdu, we see the largest change in BLEU score from 5.2 to 13.5 was seen in case of English to Urdu MT. An increase in BLEU score of 16 was observed in case of a Spanish to English MT when transfer learning approach was used with English to French as the parent model Based on the above results we can be sure that using transfer learning we get a performance improvement. Also the study showed that performance depends on the proximity of the languages.

(Kocmi and Bojar, 2018) in 2018 explored a very similar scenario where they have trained multiple parent models having no relations between them. By this method, the child model was performing significantly better as compared to baseline models. In the paper, the improvement was also noticed for unrelated languages that are languages that don't show any similarities like Czech and Estonia. There was an improvement of +3.38 BLEU for the EN-ET pair when EN-CS was taken as the parent model. This is in direct contradiction with what Zoph et. al (Zoph et al., 2016) reported that more related the models are better will be the translation. The paper also explored completely unrelated languages like Arabic and Russian, Although there were some improvements, the gains are very small (+0.49 to +0.78). Therefore, compared to the baseline models it is preferable to do the transfer learning from the related parent model to target model.

(Maimaiti et al., 2021) tried to improve the performance of transfer learning models by incorporating lexicon information as well as lexical embedding of low-resource child languages. In this work, the parent model was trained using a hybrid approach where the lexical information was shared between the parent and child model before fine-tuning. Using this method, there was an improvement in BLEU score of +0.25 on the Azerbijan-Chinese child pair and an improvement of +0.38 on the Farsi to Chinese language pair. But the method of incorporating the lexical information doesn't give better performance with morphologically poor language.

3 Proposed Approach

In this proposed work we will first train a parent pair containing a large number of sentences for a given number of iterations and then switch to the child language pair without changing any of the hyperparameters. Then subsequently the performance is improved by freezing some of the layers where weights of some layers are frozen.

Transfer learning in Machine translations was first proposed by (Zoph et al., 2016). We will be applying the same principle in this work . The Lambani language has no script of its own and it is generally written in Kannada script. Whereas, Marathi and Gujarati generally follow Devanagari script. To avoid script mismatch we will be transliterating both Marathi and Gujarati to Kannada script. To the best of our knowledge this work demonstrates the effectiveness of transfer learning for very low resource Indian tribal language. The novel part of this paper is that we will not be sharing any vocabulary instead we will use distinct vocabularies for the parent and child models. A shared vocabulary will not work in our case as some of the parent models don't share lexical features with the child model. We will also incorporate encoder and decoder layer freezing and how they impact the performance of our child model.

During our training, we train our NMT model on high resource data and this is called our parent model. Then we will be using the parent model to train the child model on low-resource data using the transfer learning approach.

3.1 Model Architecture

We will use the Transformer Sequence-to-Sequence model (Kalchbrenner and Blunsom, 2013) as proposed by (Vaswani et al., 2017) Initially we will train three different parent models namely English-Kannada, English-Marathi, and English-Gujarati. As there was no existing data available on Lambani, so

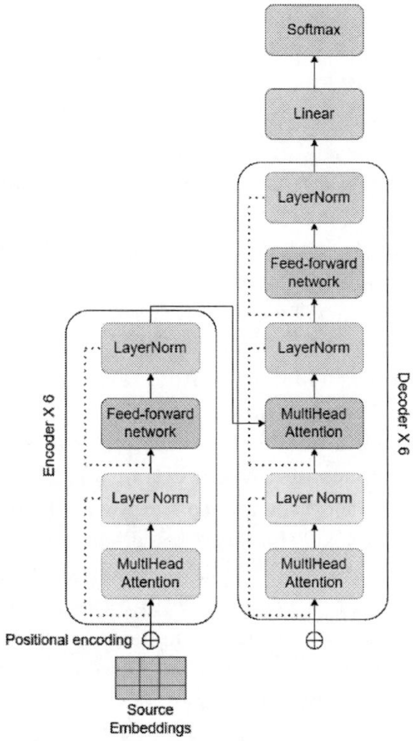

Figure 2: Transformer (Vaswani et al., 2017) architecture

it was mostly a manual process. The parent model will be used to fine-tune the child model. We will also use the parent model to try and understand the role of language relatedness in transfer learning.

For both the models we will be using Transformer model (Vaswani et al., 2017) containing six encoder and six decoder layers and eight attention heads. The tokenization method is SentencePiece (Kudo and Richardson, 2018) which produces a vocabulary of 32,000 for every parent model and 4000 for the child model. The parent languages pair are chosen based on similarity. As explained above we have two models. All our languages are summarized in the table below. Without modifying the architecture of the MT models, the architecture of the parent models is identical to the child model. As for hyper-parameters we have a beam search width of five. The batch size is set to 25. The parent models are trained for 500000 steps on Samanantar dataset (Ramesh et al., 2021). The average checkpoint with the lowest validation loss is then selected. For all our experiments we will be using OpenNMT-tf

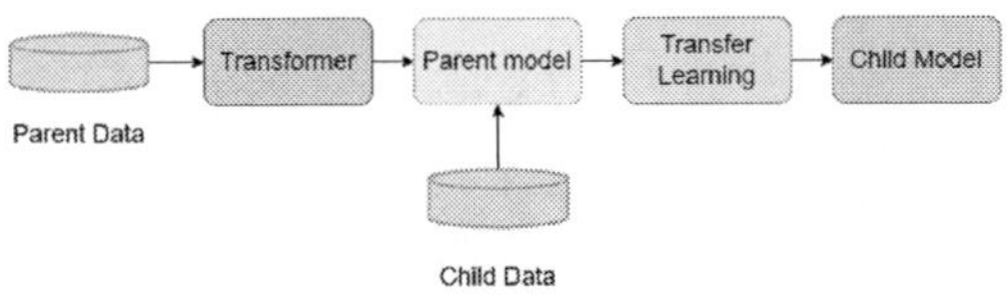

Figure 3: Block diagram of the entire process

Language		Sentence	Vocab	
Source	Target		Source	Target
English	Kannada	4M	32K	32K
English	Marathi	3.32M	32K	32K
English	Gujrati	3M	32K	32K
English	Lambani	6K	4K	6K

Table 1: Details of the dataset used for our experiment. Here, vocab means vocabulary of the Source and target language

by Google (Klein et al., 2017).

4 Dataset

In our experiment, we are be mainly working on a low-resource dataset. We consider Lambani as a very low-resource language reason being that no text-based resources are available to the best of our knowledge. While Kannada, Marathi, and Gujrati are considered to be medium resources languages. The size of the dataset is given in table 1. Preparing the Lambani dataset was mostly a manual process. (a) Firstly raw sentences were extracted from NCERT books (Upreti et al., 2014) and Wikipedia articles (Wikipedia contributors, 2022). (b) Then the sentences were pre-processed and longer sentences were removed. Most of the sentences in our dataset are within 6-10 words. We have also removed any semantically or syntactically incorrect sentences (c) Then the sentences were translated by a Lambani native speaker and was quality checked by other Lambani native speakers. Almost similar level of prepossessing was followed for the parent Pairs, sentences with less than three words and with more than 100 words are removed from the parent dataset, along with that any 'URLs' and unknown characters are also removed.

Language	Role	Train	Test	Valid
Kannada	Parent	3.5M	0.5M	0.5M
Marathi	Parent	3M	0.15M	0.15M
Gujrati	Parent	2.7M	0.15M	0.15M
Lambani	Child	5.4K	0.3K	0.3K

Table 2: Details of the number of sentences in the Train, Validation and Test

Language Pair		Transfer		Baseline
Parent-Pair	Child-Pair	Valid	Test	Parent-only
EN-KN	EN-LA	9.90	13.28	17.2
EN-MR	EN-LA	8.44	10.25	14.4
EN-GU	EN-LA	9.88	12.24	15.5

Table 3: Our transfer learning method applied to various parent models. Note that we are getting the best BLEU(Papineni et al., 2002) score when kannada is treated as the Parent model.

Language Pair		Transfer			
		Encoder		Decoder	
Parent-Pair	Child-Pair	Valid	Test	Valid	Test
EN-KN	EN-LA	12.42	14.25	7.64	11.78
EN-MR	EN-LA	11.44	14.43	7.56	10.23
EN-GU	EN-LA	9.93	14.83	7.37	9.93

Table 4: BLEU (Papineni et al., 2002) score obtained by freezing the first five layers of encoder and the decoder. If we compare it with our previous transfer result from Table 2. we can see that we are getting better performance while encoder is frozen.

4.1 Experiments

For our experiments, we are using Kannada, Marathi, and Gujrati models as our parent models. All three of these parent models has almost similar dataset size. While our child pair contains only 6000 sentence pairs. As mentioned above the parent model was trained for 500K steps while the child model is trained for 50K steps.We are representing the models with a pair of source and target codes. For example, the English-to-Kannada is denoted by EN-Kn and transfer learning models will be represented as EN-XX-LA (where XX represents the target code). The size of the vocabularies used for all these models are also given in Table 1.

For both the parent and child model we have used English as the common language (that

	English	Lambani
Test	7.0%	6.7%
Validation	6.3%	5.2%

Table 5: Details of vocabulary overlap of the Test and Validation set with the training set

means EN-XX). Table 3. summarizes the various results from both the high-resource and low-resource languages. From the table we can see that we get the best performance when EN-KN is used as the parent model. with a BLEU (Papineni et al., 2002) score of almost 9.9 on the validation set and 13.28 on the test set. This score is expected as the data used in this experiment was collected from Lambani speakers located in Karnataka. So, their language would be influenced by Kannada language. Further, the score is not restricted to related language when EN-GU pair we reach a score of 9.88 a -0.02 over the best performing pair. Now we interpret that these two BLEU scores are almost comparable. For the EN-MR we are seeing the worst performance which is almost -1.44 degradation over the best model indicating that EN-MR is the least related language as compared to Lambani.
Freezing analysis in Automatic Speech Recognition (ASR) shows an improvement in performance (Eberhard and Zesch, 2021). Motivated by the study we have applied it in the current Machine Translation study. Details of freezing and experimental setup is explained in section 5. Figs 4, 5 and 6 show the BLEU score curves on the validation set for all the three parent models. In all of the three plots we can see that we are getting better performance when we are freezing the first five layers of the encoder (represented in 'orange' color). Whereas freezing the layers in the decoder may not help in improving the performance as can be noticed from the plot (represented in 'green' color) over the baseline performance (represented by 'blue' color)
The baselines are models trained entirely on parent data. Table 3. also summarizes the results on the Test which are quite higher compared to the validation set, we think this may be due to higher vocabulary overlap between the Training and Test sets as given in table 5.

5 Freezing

5.1 Freezing encoder layers

We are interested to measure the overall change in performance upon freezing the encoder layers. We perform continued training while freezing the layers of the encoder(i.e. keeping the layers fixed to the values while training the child model while adapting the rest of the components). The results are shown in Table 4. For all of the language pairs, we are seeing a performance improvement. For the EN-MR-LA model, we are seeing the largest improvement in performance followed by EN-KN-LA (+3 BLEU and +2.52 BLEU respectively) on the validation set. This increase in performance may be because the initial few layers of a model are generally well trained. This shows that by freezing the encoder during training, the model can find a local minimum that is better than the one when the models are transfer learned.

Sr.No.	Sentence	
1	Source	I do nothing on Sundays.
	Ground Truth	ಮ ರವಿವಾರೆರ್ ಕಾಂಯಿ ಕರುನಿ.
	Transliterated Sentence	ma ravivaarer kaanyi karuni.
	EN-KN-LA	ಕಾಂಯಿ ರವಿವಾರೇರ ಕಾಂಯಿ ಕರೆನಿ.
	EN-MR-LA	ರವಿವಾರೇರ ಖಾಲಿ ರೆಚಿ ಕ?
	EN-GU-LA	ಮ ರವಿವಾರೇರ ಕಾಂಯಿ ಕರು?
2	Source	I get up early in the morning
	Ground Truth	ಮ ಪರ್ಬಾತಿ ಜಲ್ದಿ ವುಟುಚು.
	Transliterated Sentence	ma parbaati jaldi vutuchu.
	EN-KN-LA	ಮ ಪರ್ಬಾತಿ ಜಲ್ದಿ ವುಟುಚು
	EN-MR-LA	ಮ ಪರ್ಬಾತಿ ಜಲ್ದಿ ವೂಟೇನಿ
	EN-GU-LA	ಮ ಪರ್ಬಾತಿ ಜಲ್ದಿ ವೂಟೇನಿ

Table 6: Some example sentences from all the three parent models along with transliterated sentences

5.2 Freezing the decoder layers

If we freeze the entire decoder layer it is noticed that the results are inferior. From Table 4. we can see that for all the models we are getting degradation in performance when the decoder is frozen. We can see the largest drop in performance occur in the case of EN-KN (-3.8) followed by EN-GU (-2.56) on the validation set. One interesting thing to note here and also can be seen from the curves Fig 4, 5, and 6 is that the BLEU score on the validation set for all the models are very close to one another (an experiment we keep for future study). This reduction in the performance may be because the layers in the decoder need more training as compared to the Encoder as the final layers of the model are more task-specific.

6 Future work

Although there may have been a couple of research on transfer language of related and unrelated languages there is very little research

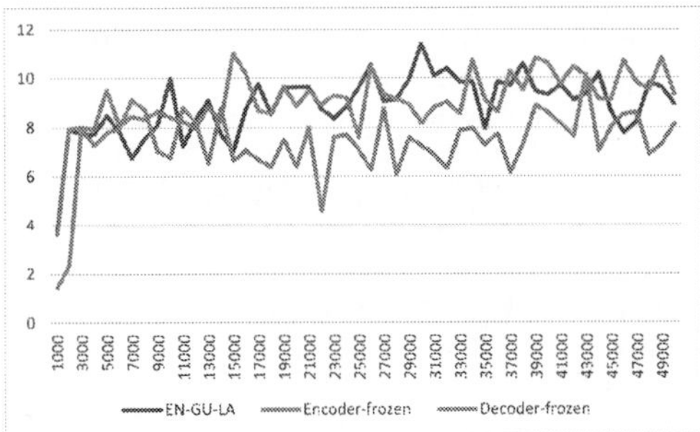

Figure 4: BLEU score curves on the val set for EN-GU as parent

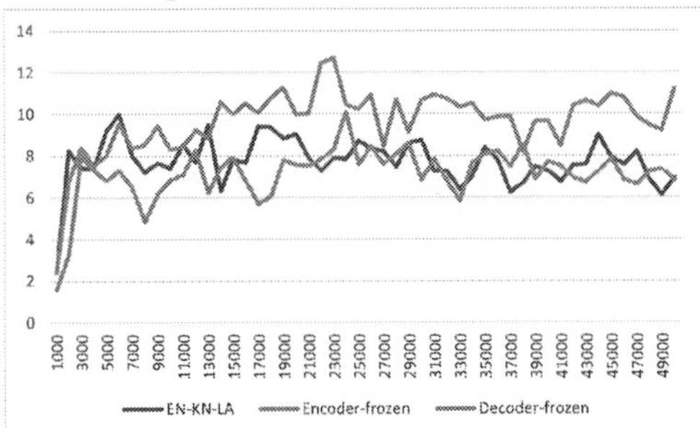

Figure 5: BLEU score curves on the val set for EN-KN as parent

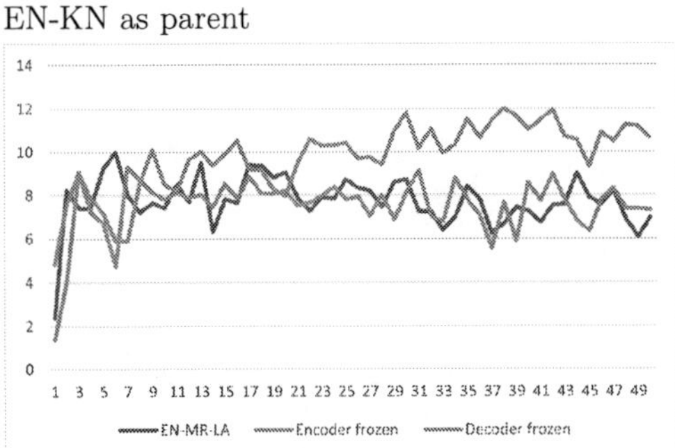

Figure 6: BLEU score curves on the val set for EN-MR as parent

as to why transfer learning is giving better results for related languages from a linguistic perspective. As in our case Lambanis a nomadic tribe before they settled in the modern state of Karnataka. As a result, the language is morphologically rich and may share some linguistic similarities with other language.

According to (Edunov et al., 2018) adding noise to the training data has improved Neural Machine Translation. The same idea can be applied to our model. We can randomly drop words from the training data and replace them with filler words in order for the model to learn better. Noisy sentence help in learning as it makes it harder to predict translation.

7 Conclusion

Our experiment is limited to a transfer learning method between closely related languages. From our experiments, we are seeing much better performance when similar languages are taken for transfer learning while for unrelated languages we are not seeing a drastic change in BLEU (Papineni et al., 2002) score which may be because of our dataset size of all the parent models is almost similar. We have further improved our model performance by incorporating encoder freezing and reached a performance improvement of +3 over the EN-MR-LA model. From our experiments we also notice that freezing the decoder is reducing the performance. This may be because the decoder needs more data than an encoder.

8 Acknowledgement

The authors like to thank "Anatganak", high-performance computation (HPC) facility, IIT Dharwad, for enabling us to perform our experiments. And Ministry of Electronics and Information Technology (MeitY), Govt. of India, for supporting us through the "Speech to Speech translation for tribal languages" project. We would also like to thank Tonmoy Rajkhowa for his valuable help in setting up the paper

References

C Chandramouli and Registrar General. 2011. Census of india. *Rural urban distribution of population, provisional population total. New Delhi: Office of the Registrar General and Census Commissioner, India.*

Paisarn Charoenpornsawat, Virach Sornlertlamvanich, and Thatsanee Charoenporn. 2002. Improving translation quality of rule-based machine translation. In *COLING-02: machine translation in Asia.*

CH Childers et al. 2003. *Banjaras.* Oxford University Press.

Chuong B Do and Andrew Y Ng. 2005. Transfer learning for text classification. *Advances in neural information processing systems*, 18.

Onno Eberhard and Torsten Zesch. 2021. Effects of layer freezing when transferring deepspeech to new languages.

Sergey Edunov, Myle Ott, Michael Auli, and David Grangier. 2018. Understanding back-translation at scale. In *Proceedings of the 2018 Conference on Empirical Methods in Natural Language Processing*, pages 489–500, Brussels, Belgium. Association for Computational Linguistics.

Akiko Eriguchi, Kazuma Hashimoto, and Yoshimasa Tsuruoka. 2016. Character-based decoding in tree-to-sequence attention-based neural machine translation. In *Proceedings of the 3rd Workshop on Asian Translation (WAT2016)*, pages 175–183, Osaka, Japan. The COLING 2016 Organizing Committee.

John Hutchins. 1997. From first conception to first demonstration: the nascent years of machine translation, 1947-1954. a chronology. *Machine Translation*, 12(3):195–252.

Aizhan Imankulova, Raj Dabre, Atsushi Fujita, and Kenji Imamura. 2019. Exploiting out-of-domain parallel data through multilingual transfer learning for low-resource neural machine translation. *arXiv preprint arXiv:1907.03060.*

Nal Kalchbrenner and Phil Blunsom. 2013. Recurrent continuous translation models. In *Proceedings of the 2013 Conference on Empirical Methods in Natural Language Processing*, pages 1700–1709, Seattle, Washington, USA. Association for Computational Linguistics.

Guillaume Klein, Yoon Kim, Yuntian Deng, Jean Senellart, and Alexander Rush. 2017. OpenNMT: Open-source toolkit for neural machine translation. In *Proceedings of ACL 2017, System Demonstrations*, pages 67–72, Vancouver, Canada. Association for Computational Linguistics.

Tom Kocmi and Ondřej Bojar. 2018. Trivial transfer learning for low-resource neural machine translation. *arXiv preprint arXiv:1809.00357.*

Philipp Koehn. 2009. *Statistical machine translation.* Cambridge University Press.

Taku Kudo and John Richardson. 2018. SentencePiece: A simple and language independent subword tokenizer and detokenizer for neural text processing. In *Proceedings of the 2018 Conference on Empirical Methods in Natural Language Processing: System Demonstrations*, pages 66–71, Brussels, Belgium. Association for Computational Linguistics.

Nirmal Kumar, K. Mrinalini, and P. Vijayalakshmi. 2018. Improving the performance of low-resource smt using neural-inspired sentence generator. In *2018 International Conference on Computer, Communication, and Signal Processing (ICCCSP)*, pages 1–4.

Mieradilijiang Maimaiti, Yang Liu, Huanbo Luan, and Maosong Sun. 2019. Multi-round transfer learning for low-resource nmt using multiple high-resource languages. *ACM Transactions on Asian and Low-Resource Language Information Processing (TALLIP)*, 18(4):1–26.

Mieradilijiang Maimaiti, Yang Liu, Huanbo Luan, and Maosong Sun. 2021. Enriching the transfer learning with pre-trained lexicon embedding for low-resource neural machine translation. *Tsinghua Science and Technology*, 27(1):150–163.

Kishore Papineni, Salim Roukos, Todd Ward, and Wei Jing Zhu. 2002. Bleu: a method for automatic evaluation of machine translation.

Gowtham Ramesh, Sumanth Doddapaneni, Aravinth Bheemaraj, Mayank Jobanputra, Raghavan AK, Ajitesh Sharma, Sujit Sahoo, Harshita Diddee, Mahalakshmi J, Divyanshu Kakwani, Navneet Kumar, Aswin Pradeep, Srihari Nagaraj, Kumar Deepak, Vivek Raghavan, Anoop Kunchukuttan, Pratyush Kumar, and Mitesh Shantadevi Khapra. 2021. Samanantar: The largest publicly available parallel corpora collection for 11 indic languages.

James V Stone. Information theory: A tutorial introduction.

Noé Tits, Kevin El Haddad, and Thierry Dutoit. 2019. Exploring transfer learning for low resource emotional tts. In *Proceedings of SAI Intelligent Systems Conference*, pages 52–60. Springer.

K. Upreti, G. Khanna, and SK Singh. 2014. *NCERT Solutions - Science for Class X.* Arihant Publication India Limited.

Robert Gabriel Varady. 1979. North indian banjaras: Their evolution as transporters. *South Asia: Journal of South Asian Studies*, 2(1-2):1–18.

Ashish Vaswani, Samy Bengio, Eugene Brevdo, Francois Chollet, Aidan N. Gomez, Stephan Gouws, Llion Jones, Łukasz Kaiser, Nal Kalchbrenner, Niki Parmar, Ryan Sepassi, Noam Shazeer, and Jakob Uszkoreit. 2018. Tensor2tensor for neural machine translation.

Ashish Vaswani, Noam Shazeer, Niki Parmar, Jakob Uszkoreit, Llion Jones, Aidan N. Gomez, Lukasz Kaiser, and Illia Polosukhin. 2017. Attention is all you need.

Wikipedia contributors. 2022. India — Wikipedia, the free encyclopedia. `https://en.wikipedia.org/w/index.php?title=India&oldid=1100411060`. [Online; accessed 30-July-2022].

Jiangyan Yi, Jianhua Tao, Zhengqi Wen, and Ye Bai. 2018. Language-adversarial transfer learning for low-resource speech recognition. *IEEE/ACM Transactions on Audio, Speech, and Language Processing*, 27(3):621–630.

Richard Zens, Franz Josef Och, and Hermann Ney. 2002. Phrase-based statistical machine translation. In *KI 2002: Advances in Artificial Intelligence*, pages 18–32, Berlin, Heidelberg. Springer Berlin Heidelberg.

Barret Zoph, Deniz Yuret, Jonathan May, and Kevin Knight. 2016. Transfer learning for low-resource neural machine translation. *arXiv preprint arXiv:1604.02201*.

HFT: High Frequency Tokens for Low-Resource NMT

Edoardo Signoroni and **Pavel Rychlý**
Faculty of Informatics
Masaryk University
Brno, CZ, 602 00
e.signoroni@mail.muni.cz, pary@fi.muni.cz

Abstract

Tokenization has been shown to impact the quality of downstream tasks, such as Neural Machine Translation (NMT), which is susceptible to out-of-vocabulary words and low frequency training data. Current state-of-the-art algorithms have been helpful in addressing the issues of out-of-vocabulary words, bigger vocabulary sizes and token frequency by implementing subword segmentation. We argue, however, that there is still room for improvement, in particular regarding low-frequency tokens in the training data. In this paper, we present "High Frequency Tokenizer", or HFT, a new language-independent subword segmentation algorithm that addresses this issue. We also propose a new metric to measure the frequency coverage of a tokenizer's vocabulary, based on a frequency rank weighted average of the frequency values of its items. We experiment with a diverse set of language corpora, vocabulary sizes, and writing systems and report improvements on both frequency statistics and on the average length of the output. We also observe a positive impact on downstream NMT.

Introduction

Tokenization is a fundamental preprocessing step for NMT and it was shown to impact the quality of the final output (Domingo et al., 2018; Gowda and May, 2020; Sennrich et al., 2016) . It involves splitting a longer text in smaller parts called tokens, separating punctuation from words, with current algorithms also implementing subword segmentation. These methods enable NMT models capable of open-vocabulary translation by encoding rare and unknown words as sequences of subword units. This is even more relevant for languages that produce words by agglutination or compounding. Subword segmentation, while usually not adhering to morphological constraints, mimics these processes by learning the most optimal segmentation from training data, thus generating vocabularies of subword tokens capable of generating new words not seen at training time.

For training of an NMT system, the frequency of tokens in the training data is vital. The more frequent the token, the better its representation. While still performing better than Statistical MT, NMT still shows weakness in translating low-frequency words (Koehn and Knowles, 2017). Therefore it is desired that a vocabulary contains a series of well represented, and so, high-frequency tokens. In this regard, some metrics have been proposed in to determine the best settings for training a NMT system (Gowda and May, 2020): i. Frequency at the 95th percentile $F_{95\%}$; ii. Mean Average Sequence length μ. These metrics can be used as an index of the performance of a tokenization algorithm. In our evaluation, we compare different tokenization algorithms against these metrics. Nonetheless, we argue that $F_{95\%}$ is not optimal to measure the frequency coverage of the vocabulary: due to its punctual nature it does not represent the whole vocabulary. Thus, we propose to use a weighted average of the frequencies. All these metrics will be discussed in Section 2.

Usually the tokenization process involves some normalization, often in the form of lower casing or true casing, to handle the difference in spelling in real data and reduce the low-frequency problem. This is even more relevant for small datasets, in which the tokens are inherently less well represented. We argue that this solution is not optimal, as in some cases retaining explicit information regarding uppercase, lowercase, white spaces, and caps lock text can be useful for downstream tasks.

To address these issues, we present "High Frequency Tokenizer", or HFT, a new language-independent subword tokenization algorithm aimed at improving the frequency of the tokens in the vocabulary.

Thus our contributions are the following:

- **High Frequency Tokenizer**, or **HFT**, a new

Proceedings of the 29th International Conference on Computational Linguistic, pages 56–63
October 12–17, 2022.

language-independent subword segmentation algorithm to improve the frequency coverage of tokens;

- a **new metric** to evaluate the performance of tokenizers in this regard, which improves on the Frequency at the 95th percentile proposed by (Gowda and May, 2020)

This paper is structured as follows: Section 1 details the HFT segmentation algorithm; Section 2 relates our evaluation, its experimental setup and results, Section 3 relates to some limitations to be addressed in the future; Section 4 gives an overview of some related work; Section 5 outlines our conclusions.

1 High Frequency Tokenizer

HFT uses the advantage of pretokenization, where sentences are split into tokens on the borders of alphanumeric and non-alphanumeric characters. The current prototype uses the regular expression `\b` of the Unix `sed`[1] command . Both the beginning and the end of each token is explicitly annotated.

HFT subwords are learnt from these tokens, they never cross the token boundaries, each token from the pretokenization is handled independently from other tokens. It speeds up both vocabulary learning and actual subword tokenization.

We also use case normalization for characters with both uppercase and lowercase. A single uppercase letter is changed to a special <uppercase-next> character and lowercase version of the given letter. A sequence of uppercase letters is changed to lowercase with a special <all-uppercase> and <end-of-uppercase> characters attached to the beginning and the end of the sequence. Figure 2 gives the special characters `hft` uses in pretokenization and tokenization.

The learning algorithm starts from a vocabulary containing all characters from the training text as possible subwords. The vocabulary contains the number of occurrences of the given subword (character). Then it gradually increase the vocabulary in the following steps:

1. it processes all the words (tokens) from the pretokenized text to find the best subword segmentation using only subwords from the current vocabulary, counts the frequencies of each subword and of all possible subword candidates (pairs of succeeding subwords);
2. selects the top K candidates with the highest frequency and adds them as new subwords to the vocabulary (K is 5% of the target vocabulary size as default);
3. removes from the vocabulary all non-single-character subwords with frequency lower than the last added candidate;
4. repeat from 1. until the requested vocabulary size is reached

The best subword tokenization (in step 1) searches in all possible subword segmentation sequences the one with the lowest number of tokens and (for same number of tokens) the highest minimum frequency.

2 Evaluation

We train and compare `hft` with the `sentence piece` (Kudo and Richardson, 2018) implementation of `bpe` (Sennrich et al., 2016) and `unigram` (Kudo, 2018) on two of the metrics presented by Gowda and May (2020). We use portions of different bilingual and monolingual datasets: The English section of the English-Marathi and the Irish part of the English-Irish from the LoResMT 2021 shared task[2]; a sample of the Hindi half of the English-Hindi IITB parallel corpus (Kunchukuttan et al., 2018) and of the Lithuanian portion of the Lithuanian-English of Europarl (Koehn, 2005) used in the WMT19 News Translation Shared Task[3]. As for monolingual corpora, we used different translations of the Bible[4] (Christodoulopoulos and Steedman, 2014) in a diverse range of languages and writing systems retrieved from OPUS (Tiedemann and Nygaard, 2004). Figure 3 gives an overview of the size of the datasets.

2.1 Experimental Setup

Following Gowda and May (2020), we evaluate our tokenizer on two statistics: **Frequency at 95% Class Rank**($F_{95\%}$), defined as the least frequency in the 95th percentile of most frequent tokens, and **Mean Sequence Length**(μ), which is computed as the arithmetic mean of the lengths of the tokenized sequences. We also propose and test a new metric, **Frequency Rank Weighted Average** ν, to improve on the intuition of $F_{95\%}$.

[1] https://www.gnu.org/software/sed/manual/sed.html

[2] https://github.com/loresmt/loresmt-2021

[3] https://www.statmt.org/wmt19/translation-task.html

[4] We are aware of the shortcomings of the Bible as a NLP dataset

```
↑¦state¦ ↑¦health¦ ↑¦minister¦ ↑¦rajesh¦ ↑¦tope¦ ¦also¦ ¦acknowledged¦ ¦the¦ ¦situation¦ ,_ ¦saying¦ ,_" ↑¦efforts¦
↑¦currently¦ ,_ ¦there¦ ¦are¦ ¦2,56,278¦ ¦isolation¦ ¦beds¦ _( ¦excluding¦ Δ¦icu¦∇ )_ ¦available¦ ¦in¦ ¦the¦ ¦state¦
```

Figure 1: A sample of pretokenized text from the English dataset.

¦	<token-delimiter>
↑	<single-uppercase>
_	<explicit-whitespace>
∇	<all-uppercase>
Δ	<end-of-uppercase>

Figure 2: Special characters in the pretokenization and tokenization.

$F_{P\%}$ is a way to quantify the minimum number of training examples for at least the *P*th percentile of tokens, while the bottom (1-*P*) is discarded to account for noise inherent in real-world data. An higher value of $F_{95\%}$ reflects the presence of many training examples per token, and thus is the desired setting for ML methods.

We argue that this metric is not optimal to capture the frequency coverage of a tokenizer's vocabulary, since it considers just one value, and not the whole structure of the vocabulary. Instead, we propose a **Frequency Rank Weighted Average** ν. Assuming a vocabulary ranked according to descending frequencies, we compute ν as:

$$\nu = \frac{\sum_{i=1}^{n}(i \cdot f_{x_i})}{\sum_{i=1}^{n} i} \quad (1)$$

where f_{x_i} is the frequency of the token x at the vocabulary index i, and n is the length of the vocabulary. We improved on the intuition of $F_{95\%}$, which purpose is to assure good token coverage even at lower frequency ranks. Following this objective, our metric gives more weight to lower frequency tokens in the vocabulary, all the while considering all of its length.

Gowda and May (2020) cast NMT as a classification task in an autoregressive setting, where the total error accumulated grows proportionally with the length of the sequence, altering the prediction of subsequent tokens in the sentence. Thus, a smaller sequence length is preferred.

We compare `hft` with `bpe` and `unigram`, the latter two being trained with the `sentence piece` module. We train models separately for each language and for different vocabulary sizes. Following previous work (Gowda and May, 2020; Sennrich et al., 2016; Sennrich and Zhang, 2019), we limit our investigation between vocabulary sizes of 500 and 8k tokens, since it was shown that bigger vocabulary sizes for small datasets harm the quality of the translation. Other parameters for the `sentence piece` trainer are left in the default setting.

We compute $F_{95\%}$, μ, and ν on the same train portion of the data, since these metrics do not involve any downstream task or validation on external data.

Figure 4 gives a sample of the results of our experiments regarding the metrics mentioned above.

We also report on some preliminary evaluation of the impact of HFT against BPE on downstream NMT. We train BPE and HFT tokenizers for both source and target language separately and then we tokenize the data with BPE (Sennrich et al., 2016), as implemented in `subword-nmt`[5], and HFT, with our implementation. We used a vocabulary size of 2000 for *en-ga* and 3000 for *en-mr*. The size of the vocabulary is set at the same value for both tokenization methods for the same dataset. For this evaluation, we do not optimize any other hyperparameter nor we employ techniques such as backtranslation.

2.2 Results

The following sections detail our results: Section 2.3 relates to the metrics explained in Section 2.1, while Sections 2.4 and 2.5 report some preliminary results on downstream NMT.

2.3 Metrics

`hft`'s performance on both $F_{95\%}$ and the Average Length μ seems promising, improving on both `bpe` and `unigram` in most of the cases. Recall that according to Gowda and May (2020) a higher value of $F_{95\%}$ and a lower value of μ is the desired outcome. For each vocabulary size, a higher value of ν means a better frequency coverage.

In the case of $F_{95\%}$, it starts at lower values, and then picks up the pace after some vocabulary size threshold. From our qualitative evaluation of the models, we deduce that this is due to the choice of storing every character occurring in the data at least

[5]https://github.com/rsennrich/subword-nmt

Language		Dataset		Sent.	Script	Sample
Amharic	Afro-Asiatic	am	Bible	30.580	Ge'ez	በመጀመሪያ እግዚአብሔር ሰማያትንና
Arabic	Afro-Asiatic	ar	Bible	31.102	Arabic	في البدء خلق الله السموات والارض
Cherokee	Iroquian	chr	Bible-NT	7.957	Cherokee	ᎯᎠ ᎠᏇᏑ ᎣᏃᏢᎰ ᏧᏂᏢᏔᏅᏒ ᏥᏌ ᎦᎶᏁᏛ,
Czech	Indo-Eur.	cs	Bible	38.116	Latin(Czech)	Na počátku stvořil Bůh
English	Indo-Eur.	en	LoResMT	20.933	Latin	It is also doubtful whether
Finnish	Ugro-Finnic	fi	Bible	38.613	Latin	Alussa loi Jumala taivaan
Irish	Indo-Eur.	ga	LoResMT	8.112	Latin	Cén chaoi a n-oibríonn
Hindi	Indo-Eur.	hi	IITB	20.000	Devanagari	यह कार्य दोनों प्रकार के हैं - ऑनलाइन और बाहरी।
Italian	Indo-Eur.	it	Bible	38.536	Latin	In principio Dio creò il
Japanese	Japonic	ja	Bible	31.087	Kana/Kanji	はじめに神は天と地とを創造された。
Jakaltek	Mayan	jak	Bible-NT	12.509	Latin(Jak.)	Ha' icham Abraham yeb naj
Lithuanian	Indo-Eur.	lt	Europarl	20.000	Latin(Lith.)	Tačiau balsavau prieš prane
Marathi	Indo-Eur.	mr	LoResMT	20.933	Devanagari	राज्यात हळूहळू अनलॉक होण्यास सुरुवात झाली
Burmese	Sino-Tibetan	my	Bible	30.928	Burmese	အစအဦး၌ ဘုရားသခင်သည် ကောင်းကင်နှင့်
Ojibwe	Algic	ojb	Bible-NT	7.945	Ojibwe	ᒦᑕᐦ ᐅᐅᐌ ᐁᔑᐲᐃᑳᑌᓂᑲ ᐋᓃᑎ ᒥᓭ x ᑳᐱᐅᒥ ᓂᑖᐎᑭᓐ
Swedish	Indo-Eur.	sv	Bible	38.879	Latin	I begynnelsen skapade Gud
Syriac	Afro-Asiatic	syr	Bible-NT	7.954	Syriac	ܕܝܫܘܥ ܡܫܝܚܐ ܒܪܗ ܕܕܘܝܕ ܒܪܗ ܕܐܒܪܗܡ
isiZulu	Niger-Congo	zu	Bible-NT	9.095	Latin(Zulu)	Incwadi yokuzalwa kukaJesu

Figure 3: Overview of the datasets. From left to right, the table gives: the name of the language and its family, the name of the dataset, its size, the name of the writing system used, and a sample of the text.

once. This is done to prevent out-of-vocabulary tokens, similarly to both `bpe` and `unigram`, but leads to a bigger portion of smaller vocabularies being made up of characters. This is particularly evident in the Japanese dataset, which contains a larger amount of ideograms. This issue will be addressed in future research.

Regarding the Average Length μ of the segmented output, we find bigger improvements on some of the datasets, such as Jakaltek, isiZulu, and Lithuanian. In other cases, the performance increase is smaller, depending on the dataset. Conversely, we observe a significant increase of μ for other languages, such as Burmese and Japanese. The reason of this behavior is worthy of further investigation.

When looking at the Frequency Rank Weighted Average ν, `hft` outperforms `bpe` slightly and `unigram` by a bigger margin on each vocabulary size. However, a more in-depth analysis is need for specific datasets, such as Japanese, which are more problematic than others.

Taking a look at the frequency distribution of a vocabulary's elements, plotted in Figure 5, it is noticeable that our algorithm trades off frequency values between the most frequent elements, which are better represented in `bpe` and `unigram`, and the tokens with lower frequency, which frequency counts in `hft` are higher. In fact, we can see that `hft` consistently has higher values for the bottom part of the vocabulary. We argue that this is in fact a very good trade: while the higher ranking tokens are still very well represented, we also achieve better frequencies and representations on the lower occurring tokens.

`hft` often achieves better performance than other methods with regards to $F_{95\%}$ and μ. Nevertheless, our segmentation algorithm is not free from issues. We will discuss these in section 3.

2.4 Downstream NMT

We also report on a preliminary evaluation of the impact of `hft` against `bpe` on downstream NMT. We train `bpe` and `hft` tokenizers for both source and target language separately and then we tokenize the data with `bpe` (Sennrich et al., 2016), as implemented in `subword-nmt`[6], and `hft`, with our implementation. We used a vocabulary size of 2000 for *en-ga* and 3000 for *en-mr*. The size of the vocabulary is set at the same value for both tokenization methods for the same dataset. For this evaluation, we do not optimize any other hyperparameter nor we employ techniques such as backtranslation.

[6]https://github.com/rsennrich/subword-nmt

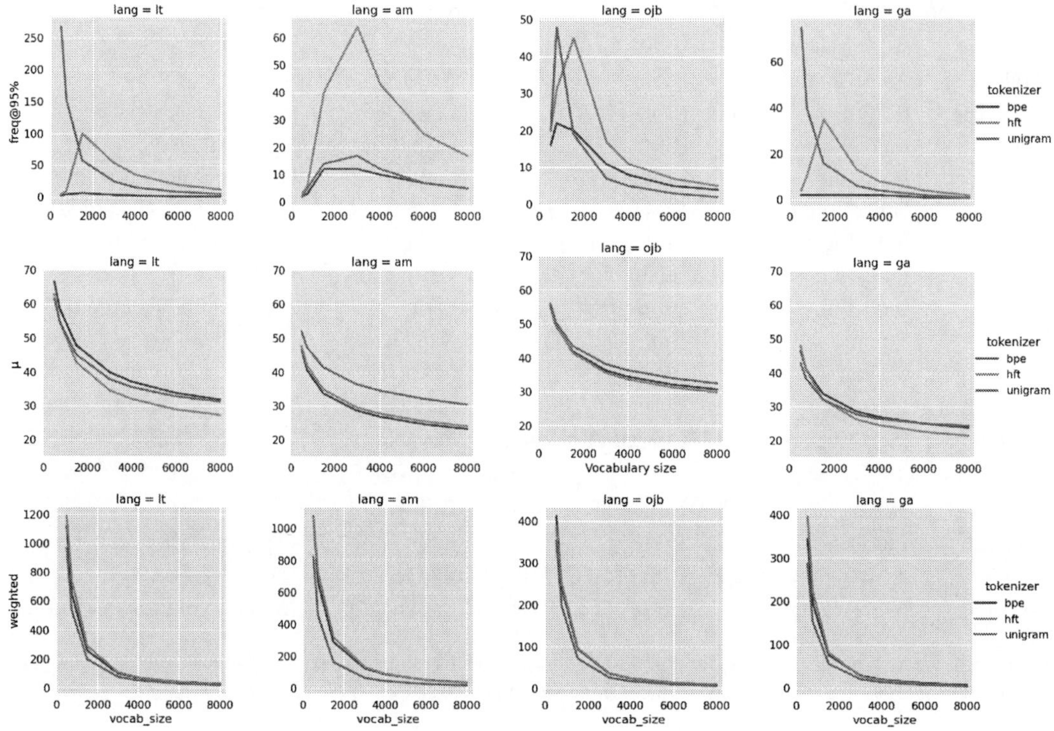

Figure 4: $F_{95\%}$ (higher is better), μ (lower is better), and ν weighted average (higher is better) plotted against vocabulary size on the Lithuanian, Amharic, Ojibwe, and Irish datasets.

We use Fairseq (Ott et al., 2019) to train 5 default Transformers (Vaswani et al., 2017) for both directions and tokenizer type for 30 epochs with dropout of 0.1, label smoothing of 0.1, and 4096 maximum tokens for each training batch. We use *adam* as optimizer, a learning rate of 0.0005 and the inverted square root scheduler.

We optimize for BLEU during training on the validation set at each epoch, with detokenized text for `bpe` (obtained with the Fairseq `-remove-bpe` argument) and tokenized text for `hft`, since we currently do not have a custom Fairseq plugin to allow detokenized training on `hft`. These preliminary results are summarized in Table 1.

Training the Transformer on data tokenized with `hft` leads to a better average NMT performance on both datasets we experimented on, with an increment in BLEU from +0.82 to +2.15. The overall low BLEU scores can be explained by the fact that we did not optimized neither the architecture nor the parameters of the Transformer to the specific low-resource dataset.

2.5 Qualitative Evaluation

We conduct some preliminary analysis of the translation systems' output. To obtain our candidates for manual evaluation, we compute sentence-level sacreBLEU score on the output of both `bpe`- and `hft`-based systems, against a reference translation. We then compute the difference in BLEU score between the two different outputs, and list them by decreasing size of the gap, that is the most changed first. This is done to observe where `hft` has the biggest impact. We consider the first 50 candidates for both *en-ga* and *en-mr* parallel corpora. Due to linguistic constraints, however, we are able to manually analyze only the *ga-en* and the *mr-en*.

While more in-depth examination is warranted in this regard, we can already see that `hft` provides some benefits, such as the one shown in Figure 6. In this case, the named entity *Naxals*[7] was correctly generated by the `hft`-based model, while the bpe-based one gives an almost nonsensical translation.

[7]A group of Maoist communists currently leading an insurgency against the Indian Government in the so-called "Red corridor" area of east and central India.

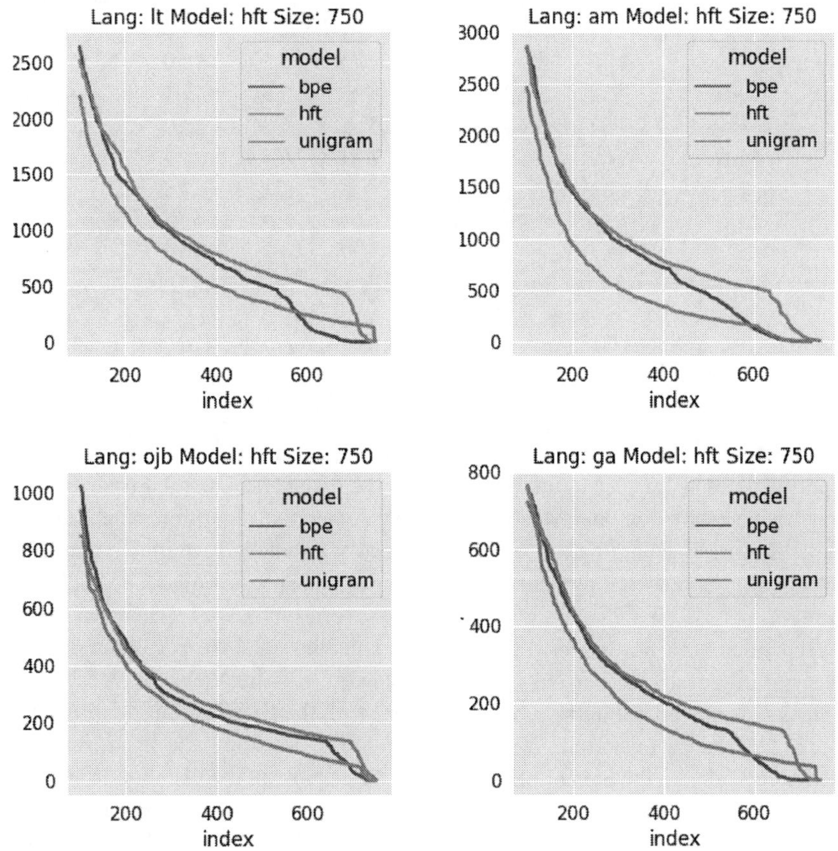

Figure 5: Frequency distribution of tokens in a sample of the 0.75k vocabularies. We do not plot the first 100 most frequent tokens to obtain cleaner plots and to focus on the bottom of the vocabulary.

3 Limitations and Future Work

As we mentioned in section 2.2, we opted to include in the final vocabulary each character seen in the training data at least once to avoid out-of-vocabulary tokens. This, however, has the side-effect of saturating and inflating the vocabulary with low-frequency tokens. At lower vocabulary sizes, these entries make up a bigger percentage of the overall vocabulary, becoming less and less relevant as the size increases. This explains why our method becomes effective over a threshold in the size of the vocabulary, which varies depending on the size and, more importantly, on the amount of unique characters in the dataset.

The presence of these character may be due to the inherent complexity of the writing system. This is the case of Japanese, which uses two sets of syllabic characters, *hiragana* and *katakana* (collectively referred to as *kana*), and a huge amount of Chinese-derived ideograms, called *kanji*.

The other source for unique characters in the data is noise, in the form of non-standard orthography, special characters, non-linguistic text, and so on. If present in the dataset, these sections can quickly saturate our vocabulary. This issue makes the method somewhat susceptible to noise, and must be addressed in future work.

Another aspect to investigate further is the relationship between μ and different writing systems. From our evaluation, we have seen that `hft` improves the performance on this metric for most of the data and writing systems we included in our evaluation. However, for Japanese and Burmese, μ is higher than other methods. It is worthwhile to investigate this matter in the future.

While the preliminary evaluation of `hft`'s impact on downstream NMT seems to show promising results, we acknowledge that the testing sample is not vast. Moreover, using an unoptimized Transformer does not completely reflect real-world appli-

DATASET	MODEL	BLEU						INCREMENT
		1	2	3	4	5	avg	
en-ga	t-bpe	4.46	4.54	4.06	4.69	4.73	4.50	
	t-hft	**5.34**	**5.49**	**5.95**	**5.69**	**5.59**	**5.61**	**+1.11**
ga-en	t-bpe	5.57	5.48	5.12	5.80	5.51	5.50	
	t-hft	**6.09**	**6.49**	**6.57**	**6.10**	**6.33**	**6.32**	**+0.82**
en-mr	t-bpe	7.49	7.21	6.88	6.57	6.12	6.85	
	t-hft	**7.33**	**7.99**	**8.80**	**8.31**	**8.31**	**8.14**	**+1.29**
mr-en	t-bpe	9.58	8.56	10.15	8.58	9.56	9.29	
	t-hft	**11.05**	**12.09**	**12.19**	**11.06**	**10.82**	**11.44**	**+2.15**

Table 1: Results of the evaluation on NMT given in sacreBLEU scores, for each dataset and trained model. The last column reports the increment of hft models over the bpe baseline.

cations, where the NMT system would be carefully tuned to the specific dataset. We plan to undertake a more comprehensive evaluation on downstream translation in the future, by enlarging the testing sample and employing hft in settings closer to real applications.

Lastly, we report that hft has longer training time than other algorithms in the current implementation, which are however still in the range of minutes for the bigger datasets we used. We plan to work on this shortcoming in the next implementation of the tokenizer.

4 Related Work

Before Sennrich et al. (2016), MT coped with the problem of out-of-vocabulary words by backing off to a dictionary with sub-optimal assumptions regarding morphological identities and transliterations. bpe addressed this issue by adapting a compression algorithm to the task of word segmentation. The methods initializes the symbol vocabulary with the character vocabulary, plus a special end-of-word symbol. Then it iteratively counts all symbols pairs and replaces every occurrence of the most frequent pair ('A', 'B') with the new symbol 'AB'. These character *n*-grams are then merged together in a similar fashion. They do not consider pairs that cross word boundaries. Following these steps, bpe allows for open-vocabulary NMT, which better handles out-of-vocabulary and rare words, by representing them as a sequence of subword units.

The unigram method by Kudo (2018) is based on a unigram language model. This makes the assumption that each subword occurs independently, thus formulating the probability of a subword sequence $X = (x_1, ..., x_M)$ as the product of the subword occurrence probabilities $p(x_i)$. To find the vocabulary set and their probabilities, they employ an iterative algorithm which starts by creating a seed vocabulary of unique characters and most frequent substrings, without considering those that cross word boundaries. Then the following steps are repeated until the vocabulary reaches the desired size: i. fixing the set of vocabulary, optimize $p(x)$ with the Expectation Maximization (EM) algorithm; ii. compute the $loss_i$, for each subword x_i, as the amount the likelihood L is reduced when removing x_i from the vocabulary; iii. sort the symbols by loss, and keeping the top $n\%$ of subwords, while always keeping single characters to avoid out-of-vocabulary. Thus unigram can output multiple segmentations and their probabilities, making it more flexible than bpe.

In sentence piece (Kudo and Richardson, 2018) both these segmentation algorithms are implemented in a way that removes the need for preprocessing steps, such as pretokenization, and trains subword models directly from the raw sentences. This allows for the creation for a purely end-to-end and language-independent system.

5 Conclusions

In this paper we present **High Frequency Tokenizer**, or HFT, a new language-independent subword tokenization algorithm to improve on the frequency coverage of tokens in the vocabulary of NMT systems. We demonstrate its performance on a diverse dataset of languages and writing systems, and show that our approach can be beneficial to downstream NMT.

However, some issues still remain to be investigated, such as the frequency coverage for smaller vocabularies and the mean output length for some

```
ref: Hundreds of Naxals have been infected with corona throughout the penance.

bpe: Help teachers to have died the corona infection.

hft: Hundreds of Naxals have been infected with corona.
```

Figure 6: Example from the *mr-en* translation systems. The first line gives the reference translation, the second gives the translation from a `bpe`-based system, while the last gives the translation from an `hft`-based system. The named entity *Naxals* is preserved by `hft`.

languages. This will be the matter for future research. We also plan to further evaluate `hft`'s impact on downstream NMT.

The `hft` scripts are available on GitHub,[8] together with the evaluation's data and results.[9]

Acknowledgements

We thank the reviewer for their useful inputs. This work was partly supported by the Internal Grant Agency of Masaryk University, Lexical Computing, and the Ministry of Education of the Czech Republic within the LINDAT-CLARIAH-CZ project LM2018101.

References

Christos Christodoulopoulos and Mark Steedman. 2014. A massively parallel corpus: the bible in 100 languages. *Language Resources and Evaluation*, 49:1–21.

Miguel Domingo, Mercedes Garcıa-Martınez, Alexandre Helle, Francisco Casacuberta, and Manuel Herranz. 2018. How much does tokenization affect neural machine translation?

Thamme Gowda and Jonathan May. 2020. Finding the optimal vocabulary size for neural machine translation. In *Findings of the Association for Computational Linguistics: EMNLP 2020*, pages 3955–3964, Online. Association for Computational Linguistics.

Philipp Koehn. 2005. Europarl: A parallel corpus for statistical machine translation. In *Proceedings of Machine Translation Summit X: Papers*, pages 79–86, Phuket, Thailand.

Philipp Koehn and Rebecca Knowles. 2017. Six challenges for neural machine translation. In *Proceedings of the First Workshop on Neural Machine Translation*, pages 28–39, Vancouver. Association for Computational Linguistics.

Taku Kudo. 2018. Subword regularization: Improving neural network translation models with multiple subword candidates. In *Proceedings of the 56th Annual Meeting of the Association for Computational Linguistics (Volume 1: Long Papers)*, pages 66–75, Melbourne, Australia. Association for Computational Linguistics.

Taku Kudo and John Richardson. 2018. SentencePiece: A simple and language independent subword tokenizer and detokenizer for neural text processing. In *Proceedings of the 2018 Conference on Empirical Methods in Natural Language Processing: System Demonstrations*, pages 66–71, Brussels, Belgium. Association for Computational Linguistics.

Anoop Kunchukuttan, Pratik Mehta, and Pushpak Bhattacharyya. 2018. The IIT Bombay English-Hindi parallel corpus. In *Proceedings of the Eleventh International Conference on Language Resources and Evaluation (LREC 2018)*, Miyazaki, Japan. European Language Resources Association (ELRA).

Myle Ott, Sergey Edunov, Alexei Baevski, Angela Fan, Sam Gross, Nathan Ng, David Grangier, and Michael Auli. 2019. fairseq: A fast, extensible toolkit for sequence modeling. In *Proceedings of the 2019 Conference of the North American Chapter of the Association for Computational Linguistics (Demonstrations)*, pages 48–53, Minneapolis, Minnesota. Association for Computational Linguistics.

Rico Sennrich, Barry Haddow, and Alexandra Birch. 2016. Neural machine translation of rare words with subword units. In *Proceedings of the 54th Annual Meeting of the Association for Computational Linguistics (Volume 1: Long Papers)*, pages 1715–1725, Berlin, Germany. Association for Computational Linguistics.

Rico Sennrich and Biao Zhang. 2019. Revisiting low-resource neural machine translation: A case study. In *Proceedings of the 57th Annual Meeting of the Association for Computational Linguistics*, pages 211–221, Florence, Italy. Association for Computational Linguistics.

Jörg Tiedemann and Lars Nygaard. 2004. The OPUS corpus - parallel and free: `http://logos.uio.no/opus`. In *Proceedings of the Fourth International Conference on Language Resources and Evaluation (LREC'04)*, Lisbon, Portugal. European Language Resources Association (ELRA).

Ashish Vaswani, Noam Shazeer, Niki Parmar, Jakob Uszkoreit, Llion Jones, Aidan N. Gomez, Lukasz Kaiser, and Illia Polosukhin. 2017. Attention is all you need.

[8] https://github.com/pary42/hftoks

[9] https://github.com/edoardosignoroni/hftoks-eval

Romanian language translation in the RELATE platform

Vasile Păiș and **Maria Mitrofan** and **Andrei-Marius Avram**
Research Institute for Artificial Intelligence "Mihai Drăgănescu", Romanian Academy
vasile,maria,andrei.avram@racai.ro

Abstract

This paper presents the usage of the RELATE platform[1] for translation tasks involving the Romanian language. Using this platform, it is possible to perform text and speech data translations, either for single documents or for entire corpora. Furthermore, the platform was successfully used in international projects to create new resources useful for Romanian language translation.

1 Introduction

Translation platforms represent a subset of Language Technology (LT) platforms, providing services and resources for written or spoken language translation. Artificial intelligence (AI) methods are used to implement the platform functionalities. These can be used either online, following a request-response model, or offline for processing large corpora, following an initial upload in the platform.

Rehm et al. (2020a) notes that instead of competing with one another, platforms should be constructed to be interoperable and interact with each other to create synergies toward a productive LT ecosystem. We agree with this observation and consider that one way to achieve interoperability is through standardized formats for both input and output, allowing data to be exchanged between platforms. Furthermore, web services can expose internal functionality, allowing for integration into other systems.

This paper provides a detailed presentation of the translation functionalities of the RELATE platform . RELATE was developed as a modular, state-of-the-art platform for processing the Romanian language. Available functions are provided by modules developed in multiple national and international projects, both in-house and by partner institutions. Since its inception, one of its main goals was using standardized and easy-to-use file formats, combined with web APIs, thus allowing integration with other systems (Păiș, 2020) , as needed. Component integration is performed directly by consuming the provided APIs from a partner's servers or utilizing Docker containers hosted on one or multiple servers associated with the platform. Thus, it follows the philosophy behind the European Language Grid[2].

RELATE contains multiple translation functions for both text and speech. Furthermore, it allows for development of translation related corpora. The paper is organized as follows: Section 2 presents related work, Section 3 describes the current architecture of the platform and its evolution. Text translation functions are presented in Section 4. Speech to speech translation is covered in Section 5. Examples of large corpora, useful for translation, created within the platform in the context of international projects are given in Section 6. Finally we conclude in Section 7.

2 Related work

Coleman et al. (2020) presents an architecture developed for a Machine Translation (MT) platform that uses specific components and pre-existing services of Amazon Web Services to assure the security, robustness and scalability of the platform. Its main functionality is to provide translation services for news using a single integration point. With the needed translation technology integrated into one place, this platform facilitates news publication in multiple languages and through different virtual environments.

Franceschini et al. (2020) presents ELITR (European Live Translator) project, that aims to combine different NLP technologies such as automatic speech recognition, machine translation, and spo-

[1] https://relate.racai.ro

[2] https://www.european-language-grid.eu/

Proceedings of the 29th International Conference on Computational Linguistic, pages 64–74
October 12–17, 2022.

ken language translation to create end-to-end systems mainly for face-to-face conferences (interpreting official speeches and workshop-style discussions) and for remote conferences (live video streaming for which the platform automatically transcribes and translate subtitles). For now, ELITR's ASR technology is available for 6 EU languages. Since ELITR services work in real-time, the translation of the conversations starts immediately as the ASR service has an output available. ELITR technology is based upon PerVoice Service Architecture, a proprietary software solution that enables the concatenation of different services.

Khanna et al. (2021) presents Apertium, a free open-source platform for rule-based machine translation (RBMT) for under-resourced languages. Apertium is a complex pipeline consisting of multiple modules such as deformatter, source language morphological analyzer, source language morphological disambiguator, source language retokenization, lexical transfer, lexical selection, source language anaphora resolution, shallow structural transfer, recursive structural transfer, target language retokenization, target language morphological generator, target language post-generator, reformatter. One of the platform's main advantages is that users can add or remove modules according to their needs. Currently, the platform offers translation for eleven of the forty-four languages considered vulnerable or endangered.

Juremy[3] is an intelligent concordance search tool available for all combinations of the 24 EU official languages. It can be used to search legal and technical terminology in documents. In order to display the results, Juremy uses EUR-Lex and IATE databases and to reference the source document, Juremy provides the user with a series of metadata such as document title, topic, IATE evaluation, or work date. A plus of this online service is that it allows the user a customized search, but the services of Juremy are only available after registration on the website.

Rehm et al. (2020b) emphasize that numerous AI domains are underdeveloped at the national and international levels. Even though AI technologies such as deep neural networks offer significant opportunities for many societal and economic challenges, there is still work to do until LT technologies can be considered viable solutions for all 24 EU official languages. Another essential aspect underlined by the authors is the enormous fragmentation of the European AI and LT landscape and consider that efforts should be made to ensure that all these platforms can exchange information, data and services to identify synergies in market capitalization. Furthermore, the authors propose implementing standardized ways of exchanging repository entries that enable multiplatform and multi-vendor service workflows. Ai4EU[4] and ELG[5] platforms are presented as large European ecosystems that can assure interoperability between language technologies in Europe.

3 Architecture of the RELATE platform

The RELATE platform was implemented primarily for processing large text corpora (Păiș et al., 2019). In addition, it also offers access to state-of-the-art (SOTA) tools for the Romanian language on a "per request" use case. Recent developments allow speech processing of the Romanian language by integrating tools for automatic speech recognition (ASR), text-to-speech (TTS) and speech-to-speech translation.

Modules available in the platform include: TEPROLIN (Ion, 2018), NLP-Cube (Boroș et al., 2018) , UDPipe (Straka et al., 2016), TTL (Ion, 2007), MLPLA (Boroș et al., 2018), RomanianTTS (Stan et al., 2011), Legal-domain NER (Păiş et al., 2021), Biomedical NER (Mitrofan and Păiș, 2022). Also, some of the older, existing tools were exposed as web services and integrated in the platform. These modules account for the following operations: text segmentation (paragraph, sentence, token), phonetic transcription, lemmatization, syllabification, dependency parsing, text classification, term extraction, named entity recognition, diacritic restoration, abbreviation and numeral expansion, speech recording, ASR, TTS, text translation, and speech translation. Additionally, web interfaces are available for querying the Representative Corpus of Contemporary Romanian Language (CoRoLa) (Tufiș et al., 2019) and the Romanian WordNet (Tufiș and Barbu Mititelu, 2015).

From a user perspective, the platform provides two interfaces: document-based and corpus-based. In the document-based interface, the user can work with a single file (text document or speech recording) and obtains the processing results in near real-

[3] https://juremy.com/)

[4] https://www.ai4europe.eu/

[5] https://www.european-language-grid.eu/

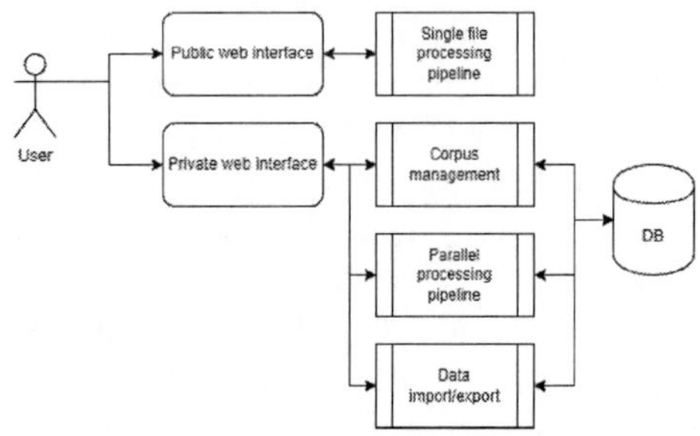

Figure 1: User perspective on the RELATE platform functionality

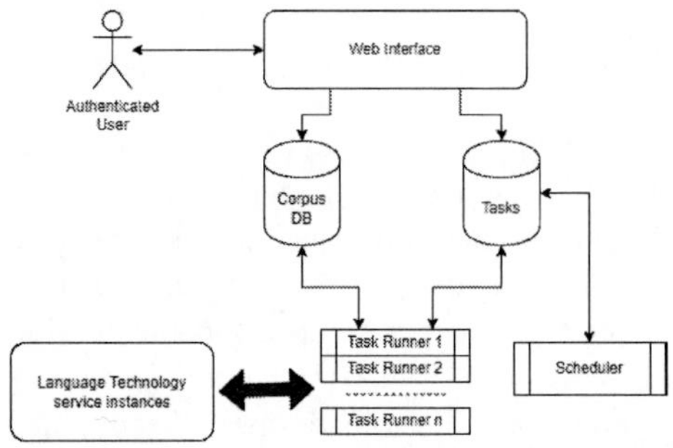

Figure 2: Task-based architecture in the RELATE platform

time. In the corpus-based interface, the user must first upload a corpus, then schedule processing tasks and finally obtain the results once all the tasks have been completed. Both interfaces are free for users, but the corpus-based interface requires the user to be registered (registration is provided free of charge for research purposes). This separation is presented in Figure 1.

From a technical point of view, the platform uses the same underlying LT services to operate in a single document and task-based modes. For performance purposes, different services can be instantiated multiple times on the same hardware nodes or servers. This methodology allows scaling the platform annotation capabilities with the size of the corpora to be processed. A scheduling component distributes the tasks across the available services. The number of instances associated with each LT service differs based on the service's speed. Faster services require fewer instances, while slower services benefit from more instances, thus allowing for increased parallelization of the processing queue. Figure 2 depicts the scheduling component with associated task runner processes.

The corpus management component provides basic functions such as file uploading (either a file-by-file process or an entire archive with multiple files), processing using the task-based system (task scheduling, task monitoring), visualization of both raw files and resulting annotations, and data export. Processed files can be exported in the internal format or converted to project-specific formats available within the platform. The internal platform format is based on the CoNLL-U Plus[6] specification, which in turn is derived from the basic CoNLL-U format[7], employed in the Universal Dependencies[8] project. This is a tabular format with an additional document or segment-specific metadata. The file starts with a metadata field ("global.columns") which describes the content associated with each column. For the RELATE platform, we keep the first ten columns corresponding to the basic CoNLL-U file and add additional columns, as needed, based on the tasks executed on each corpus. Therefore, the final annotated format may differ between corpora if different annotation tasks were executed. This can be further changed using format converters. Currently, converters are available for exporting in other CoNLL-U Plus structures or XML documents. Furthermore, due to our interest in Linguistic Linked Data, various Romanian language resources (Barbu Mititelu et al., 2020; Păiș and Barbu-Mititelu, 2022; Barbu Mititelu et al., 2022), some of which were created within the RELATE platform, were converted into RDF format. Examples of such resources are represented by the LegalNERo (Păiș et al., 2021) named entity corpus and the ROBIN Technical Acquisition Speech Corpus (RTASC) (Păiş et al., 2021).

Figure 3 presents the different components available in the RELATE platform. The web front-end is the graphical user interface employed to interact with the components. It handles unauthenticated interactions, user authentication and authenticated requests. The back-end exposes platform functionality as web APIs that can be consumed from the front end. This layer also allows for potential integration into other applications or platforms. At this level, corpus management functions are implemented, together with the task scheduling component. The other components, implementing specific processing functions, are called directly from the web back-end or task execution processes. Ro-

[6]https://universaldependencies.org/ext-format.html
[7]https://universaldependencies.org/format.html
[8]https://universaldependencies.org/

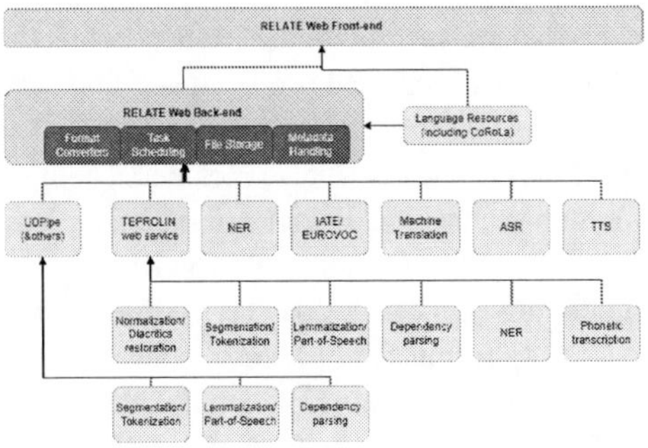

Figure 3: RELATE platform architecture

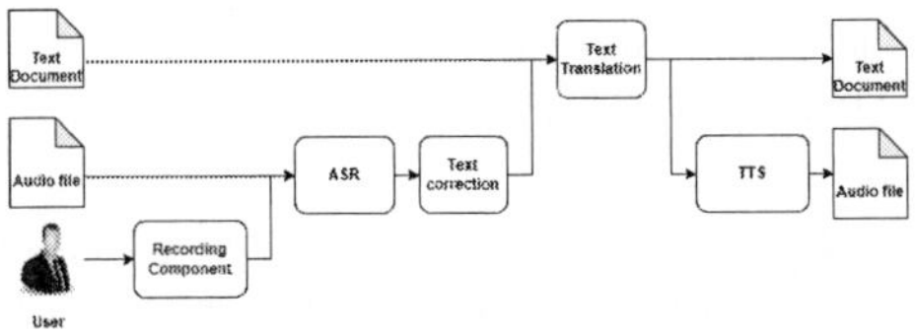

Figure 4: Translation flows in the RELATE platform

manian language resources can be downloaded or queried from the RELATE platform, such as pre-trained language models (for both word representations and annotation tasks) and gold annotated corpora. Considering the CoRoLa corpus, the user can directly access the main query interface of the text component, using the KorAP corpus analysis platform (Bański et al., 2012), and the speech component, allowing searching in audio files (Boroş et al., 2018) and listening to words being pronounced by Romanian speakers.

Translation in the RELATE platform is performed around a text translation component. However, due to the integration of both ASR and TTS components (for Romanian and English), it is possible to translate also speech (by using pre-recorded audio files or by using the integrated speech recording functionality), resulting in new audio files (available for download or direct playback). Different translation scenarios are depicted in Figure 4. As described above, depending on the use case, the translation pipeline can be invoked on a request basis or for entire corpora. Details on the text translation component are given in Section 4 and the speech-to-speech translation component is further described in Section 5.

4 Text translation

The "CEF Automated Translation toolkit for the Rotating Presidency of the Council of the EU" Action aimed to make the European Commission's

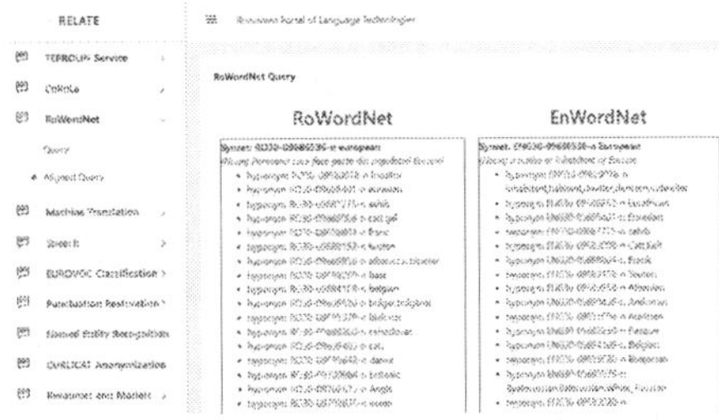

Figure 5: Aligned WordNet query using Romanian and English WordNets in the RELATE platform

eTranslation platform available to users from EU member states by extending the eTranslation platform with a set of custom MTs tailored for the EU Presidency domain. The Romanian-English and English-Romanian translation systems were improved by developing high-quality custom MT systems for the EU Presidency and DSI domains. For the Romanian language, the Research Institute for Artificial Intelligence "Mihai Drăgănescu" contributed to developing the translation system (Ro-En and En-Ro), a component of a wider system for the Presidency of the Council of the EU. The current MT platform[9] allows users to translate entire documents and local websites, including secure automated translation systems for all EU official languages.

Using the TILDE Machine Translation API[10], the textual translation component for Ro-En and En-Ro was integrated into the RELATE platform so that users can translate documents directly in the platform and also analyse the resulting document using the platform's functionalities.

In addition to the full-text translation, a version of the Romanian WordNet (Tufiş and Barbu Mititelu, 2015) aligned with the English WordNet (Miller, 1995) is available for querying. In this case, the user can look up a Romanian word and see the equivalent synset from the English WordNet. Figure 5 shows an example query for the word "european" (in English is written similarly, except with a capital letter "European").

5 Speech to speech translation

Automatic S2ST plays a core role in allowing people to communicate more naturally using spoken utterances when they do not share a common language, and nowadays, two methods are usually em-

[9] `https://ro.presidencymt.eu`

[10] `https://www.tilde.com/developers/machine-translation-api`

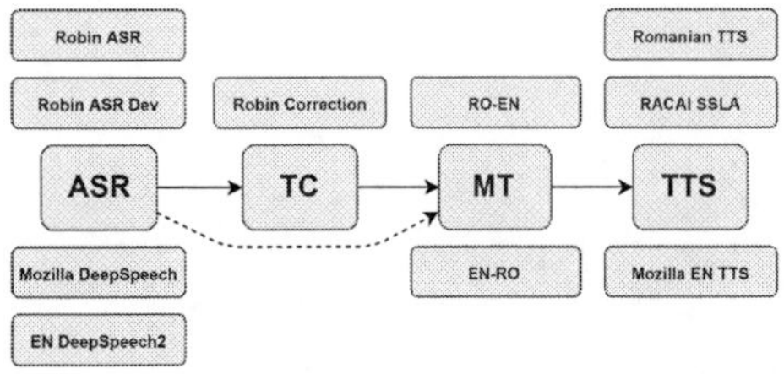

Figure 6: The proposed S2ST architecture with the four components: (1) automatic speech recognition (ASR), (2) textual correction (TC), (3) machine translation (MT) and (4) text-to-speech (TTS). The available models of each component are depicted in the upper part for Romanian and in the lower part for English (Avram et al., 2021b).

ployed for solving this problem: cascaded systems and end-to-end (E2E) models. Cascaded systems usually obtain better results compared to E2E models (Federico et al., 2020), but they have the drawback of propagating the error from one component to the next, making the overall system brittle. On the other hand, E2E models do not have this issue, and recent research has tried to minimize the gap between these two architectures (Jia et al., 2019).

Due to the limited amount of Romanian resources that are available for directly training an E2E model on this task, it was created a cascaded S2ST service for both Romanian to English[11] and English to Romanian[12] speech translation that contains four components in their respective pipeline (Avram et al., 2021b), as depicted in Figure 6. Each component incorporates at least one configurable model for the Romanian and English languages, enabling simple integration of new models into the system and improved flexibility in choosing a specific configuration given a potential requirement.

The first component of the cascaded S2ST system is the ASR to transcribe the audio input. The Romanian version has two models: Robin ASR and Robin ASR Dev. The former used the DeepSpeech2 architecture (Amodei et al., 2016) and was trained on approximately 230 hours of public speech data, obtaining a 9.91% word-error-rate (WER) on a customized dataset that was created by randomly extracting 5,000 samples from the training set (Avram et al., 2020). The Robin ASR Dev model is a specialized speech recognition system developed to better recognize utterances from the technical domain, specific to the ROBIN project[13]. ROBIN was a user-centred project designing software systems and services to use robots in an interconnected digital society. It also included a component for human-machine dialogue in specific microworld scenarios (Ion et al., 2020). The Robin ASR Dev model (Avram et al., 2022) was trained only on the RTASC corpus and, in order to leverage the benefits of transfer learning on small datasets, we started from a Wav2Vec2 (Baevski et al., 2020) model that was pre-trained on the whole unlabeled audio data from VoxPopuli[14] (Wang et al., 2021) that is publicly available on HuggingFace[15]. Robin ASR Dev achieved 13.93% WER on the RTASC test set.

The English version of the ASR component also contains two models: Mozilla DeepSpeech, which is based on the DeepSpeech (Hannun et al., 2014) architecture and that contains the latest speech-to-text system offered by Mozilla [16], and EN DeepSpeech2 which, as Robin ASR, is based on the DeepSpeech2 model and was trained only on LibriSpeech (Panayotov et al., 2015). Both models were evaluated on the clean test set of LibriSpeech and obtained 7.06% WER and 9.19% WER, respectively. This difference in performance comes from the training set used for each model, Mozilla DeepSpeech being trained on more data than EN DeepSpeech2 which is not available for public usage.

The RELATE platform offers, at the time of writing this paper, a single model for textual correction on Romanian - Robin Correction that applies two postprocessing algorithms to the incoming transcriptions. Firstly, the component capitalizes the first character of the words that are found in a list of known named entities and then, in the second part, it replaces the unknown words from the transcription with known words from a vocabulary. This component is optional and can be removed from the cascaded system if needed (e.g. when working with uncased text or with an open vocabulary). A new neural punctuation restoration component for the Romanian language is still under active development and will become available in the future(Păiş and Tufiş, 2022; Păiș, 2022). A prototype is avail-

[11]https://relate.racai.ro/index.php?path=translate/speech_ro_en

[12]https://relate.racai.ro/index.php?path=translate/speech_en_ro

[13]https://aimas.cs.pub.ro/robin/en/

[14]https://huggingface.co/facebook/wav2vec2-large-100k-voxpopuli

[15]https://huggingface.co/facebook/wav2vec2-base-100k-voxpopuli

[16]https://github.com/mozilla/DeepSpeech

able for testing[17], but is not yet fully integrated and is not available in the speech translation pipeline. The Romanian to English and English to Romanian machine translation components use the API introduced in Section 4.

The English language comes with one model for the TTS component in our cascaded system - Mozilla EN TTS, a pretrained Tacotron2 with Dynamic Convolution Attention (Battenberg et al., 2020), that was developed by Mozilla[18] using the LJSpeech dataset[19]. The model obtained a median opinion score (MOC) of 4.31±0.06 using a 95% confidence interval. For the Romanian language, we offer two models that are not based on deep neural networks but use the classical Hidden Markov Models (HMM) to generate the audio output for a given sentence: Romanian TTS (Stan et al., 2011) and RACAI SSLA (Boroș et al., 2018). The difference between these two versions is that the former model outputs a synthesis of higher quality than the former model but at a slower rate, thus allowing a user to trade off computational speed for a better synthesis, or vice-versa, depending on the requirements.

6 Creating corpora relevant for machine translation

6.1 The MARCELL legislative corpus

The CEF Telecom project Multilingual Resources for CEF.AT in the legal domain (MARCELL) [20] had as the primary goal the enhancement of the eTranslation system developed by the European Commission. Within this project, seven legislative corpora have been created that contain the total body of national legislative documents in effect for seven countries included in the consortium: Bulgaria, Croatia, Hungary, Poland, Romania, Slovakia and Slovenia. All the corpora were tokenized, lemmatized and morphologically annotated, dependency parsed, named entities were also added, nominal phrases were identified together with IATE [21] terms and EuroVoc [22] descriptors. Interactive Terminology for Europe (IATE) has been the EU's terminology database since 2004. The primary purpose of this resource is to help translators working for the European Commission; that is why it is used in EU institutions and agencies for the collection, dissemination and management of terminology. It contains over 8 million terms in 24 official languages of the EU.

EuroVoc is a multilingual thesaurus developed and maintained by the Publications Office of the European Union. The main purpose for which it was built is to help process the information contained in documents issued by the EU institutions. The current version, EuroVoc 4.4, was released in 2012 and includes 6,883 unique IDs for thesaurus concepts, organized in 21 top-level domains, which are further refined in 127 micro-tesauri. It serves as the basis for the main domains of the IATE database. All the corpora are in CoNLL-U Plus format with fourteen columns in each file, the first ten columns keep the standard CONLL-U values (ID, FORM, LEMMA, UDPOS, XPOS, FEASTS, HEAD, DEPREL, DEPS and MISC), while the following four columns (NER, NP, IATE and EUROVOC) are specific to the MARCELL project.

Since texts from each corpus came from different sources, metadata harmonization was necessary to create a homogeneous resource in file format. Therefore, many fields were established, some mandatory for each language and others optional. The obligatory keys that assure the harmonization of the data are: id - unique identifier of the document, date - date of the document in ISO 8601 format, title - the title of the document in the original language, type - the legal type of the document in the original language, entype - the legal type of the document in English. The optional keys are: url - the address of each document, keywords - several keywords in the original language, and topic - the human-readable topic of the document in the original language. In (Váradi et al., 2020) are presented all the available metadata keys and attributes in source archives for each language.

The MARCELL Romanian language corpus contains approximately 144k processed legislative documents that can be classified into five main categories: governmental decisions (25%), ministerial orders (18%), decisions (16%), decrees (16%) and laws (6%). In terms of document length, most of them contain more than 1,000 words per document, and only 6,000 can be considered short documents because they contain less than 100 words per docu-

[17] https://relate.racai.ro/index.php?path=punctuation_restoration/demo

[18] https://github.com/mozilla/TTS

[19] https://keithito.com/LJ-Speech-Dataset/

[20] https://marcell-project.eu/

[21] https://iate.europa.eu/home

[22] https://eur-lex.europa.eu/browse/eurovoc.html?locale=ro

ment. A general overview of the Romanian legislative corpus can be seen in Table 1.

No. of raw documents	144,131
No. of sentences	4,300,131
No. of tokens	66,918,022
No. of unique lemmas	200,888
No. of unique tokens	281,532

Table 1: General statistics of the Romanian legal corpus

The Romanian legal corpus (Tufiş et al., 2020) was processed in the RELATE platform, using the integrated TEPROLIN web service (Ion, 2018). In terms of dependency parsing annotation, NLP-Cube (Boroș et al., 2018) was used, which according to the evaluation made by Păiș et al. (2021a), has a labelled attachment score (LAS) of 85.87 for Romanian. One of the objectives of the MARCELL project was the classification into EuroVoc topics and enrichment with EuroVoc and IATE terms identified in each of the seven monolingual corpora. The algorithm we employed for EuroVoc classification was based on static word embeddings representations (Păiș and Tufiș, 2018), trained on the CoRoLa corpus (Tufiș et al., 2019). These were used to train a classifier utilizing the FastText tool (Joulin et al., 2017). Currently, the RELATE platform also offers a transformer-based classification with EuroVoc descriptors that were developed later, using the PyEuroVoc toolkit (Avram et al., 2021a). After this step, all the corpora were compiled into a comparable corpus of seven languages aligned at the topic level domains identified by EuroVoc descriptors. This project activity has positively impacted both MT systems in the seven languages concerned and the improvement of both the e-justice and the Online Dispute Resolution Digital Service infrastructures. Regarding the identification of IATE and EuroVoc terms, the Romanian team used a custom algorithm similar to the Aho-Corasick algorithm (Aho and Corasick, 1975), that uses a language-specific compression function (Coman et al., 2019) and which has a term matching rate of approximately 98%. All these services were integrated into the RELATE platform (Păiș et al., 2019) so that its output is as visually descriptive as possible and can configure each processing step according to different algorithms integrated into the platform. As a result, the user only needs to specify the type of annotation desired to build the processing chain.

6.2 The CURLICAT corpus

Curated Multilingual Resources for CEF.AT (CURLICAT) [23] is an ongoing project that, similar to the MARCELL project, aims to deliver language resources, in particular monolingual corpora, in the EU/CEF languages: Bulgarian, Croatian, Hungarian, Polish, Romanian, Slovak and Slovenian. Unlike the MARCELL project, in which legislative documents belonging to each country in the consortium were collected, the CURLICAT project's main aim is to create seven monolingual corpora containing texts from the following fields: culture, education, economy, health, nature, politics, science. Creating these resources for the under-resourced languages will contribute to breaking down linguistic barriers to the creation of the Digital Single Market in Europe and implicitly will lead to improvements in automatic translations between EU's languages.

In order to assure a harmonized structure of the resulting resources, all the corpora use the CONLL-U Plus format; each language-specific sub-corpus has the same format. The first ten columns have the standard CONLL-U values, and the last three are specific to the CURLICAT project. Regarding the metadata for each document, the principles used in the MARCELL project have been adopted. After the harmonization of the metadata phase ends, all the metadata information will be classified as: obligatory - information that all partners have to provide, optional - information that can be missing or that contains an empty value in some language corpora, and local - information specific to a given language corpus. At the end of the project, each consortium partner will provide a corpus of at least 2 million sentences containing at least 20 million words. Each corpus will consist of at least 500k sentences (5 million words) for the five main domains: culture, economy, finances, health and science.

Regarding the Romanian component of the CURLICAT corpus, most texts were extracted from The Reference Corpus of the Contemporary Romanian Language (CoRoLa) (Tufiș et al., 2019). The documents were selected based on different metadata attributes present in CoRoLa metadata scheme. After selecting the texts according to the established criteria, they went through an automatic cleaning phase. Next, the texts were processed with the RELATE platform, so each corpus was tokenized, lemmatized, annotated with part of speech

[23] `https://curlicat-project.eu/`

tags, and dependency parsed. In Table 2 are given relevant statistics for each domain of the current version of the Romanian sub-corpus created for the CURLICAT project.

Domain	No. of sentences
culture	577,307
education	320,484
economy	311,721
health	417,681
nature	338,953
politics	379,188
science	2,113,454
TOTAL	4,458,788

Table 2: Current statistics of the CURLICAT-RO corpus

Since "the protection of natural persons in relation to the processing of personal data is a fundamental right" (Spiekermann, 2012), text anonymization is one of the natural processing phases that all the corpora need to go through. Therefore, for the Romanian language, an anonymization solution was implemented (Păiș et al., 2021b) and the "local" pseudonymization approach was considered. Since most anonymization requirements appear in relation to news and other blog posts, to allow NLP algorithms to use this resource better, it was decided to keep suffixes specific to Romanian named entities as part of the pseudonym being used. Experiments [24] have shown that this is a viable solution for anonymizing texts for the Romanian language. It was integrated into the RELATE platform to automatically allow the entire corpus to be anonymized. Upon completion, this project will make a significant contribution to different kinds of linguistic research, such as neural machine translation training, cross-lingual legal terminology extraction, or cross-lingual entity mapping.

7 Conclusion

In this paper, we described the usability of the RELATE platform in the context of machine translation of the Romanian language. It provides options for text and speech translation using a modular architecture. Additionally, the platform successfully created considerable language resources relevant for machine translation. Sections 6.1 and 6.2 described the creation of two large comparable corpora in 7 official EU languages, including the Romanian language.

The platform is designed to be highly customizable and easily extensible, while the standardized file formats ensure interoperability with other systems. Furthermore, the service-oriented architecture (SOA), based on REST APIs, allows for additional integration options with external applications or other language platforms. The RELATE platform is available open source on GitHub[25]. Its current form resulted from integration of components developed in many research projects. We aim to continue the development, both in terms of translation capabilities and more generally with regard to language technology for Romanian language.

Acknowledgements

Part of this research was conducted in the context of the "Curated Multilingual Language Resources for CEF.AT" (CURLICAT) project, CEF-TC-2019-1 – Automated Translation grant agreement number INEA/CEF/ICT/A2019/1926831. Part of this research was conducted in the context of the European Language Equality (ELE) project, action ELE/101018166, work programme PPPA-LANGEQ2020.

References

Alfred V Aho and Margaret J Corasick. 1975. Efficient string matching: an aid to bibliographic search. *Communications of the ACM*, 18(6):333–340.

Dario Amodei, Sundaram Ananthanarayanan, Rishita Anubhai, Jingliang Bai, Eric Battenberg, Carl Case, Jared Casper, Bryan Catanzaro, Qiang Cheng, Guoliang Chen, et al. 2016. Deepspeech 2: End-to-end speech recognition in English and Mandarin. In *International conference on machine learning*, pages 173–182. PMLR.

Andrei-Marius Avram, Vasile Păiș, and Dan Tufiș. 2021a. PyEuroVoc: A tool for multilingual legal document classification with EuroVoc descriptors. In *Proceedings of the International Conference on Recent Advances in Natural Language Processing (RANLP 2021)*, pages 92–101.

Andrei-Marius Avram, Vasile Păiș, and Dan Tufiș. 2020. Towards a Romanian end-to-end automatic speech recognition based on Deepspeech2. *Proceedings of the Romanian Academy Series A*, 21:395–402.

[24] `https://github.com/racai-ai/ROAnonymization_CURLICAT`

[25] `https://github.com/racai-ai/RELATE`

Andrei-Marius Avram, Vasile Păiş, and Dan Tufiş. 2021b. A modular approach for Romanian-English speech translation. In *International Conference on Applications of Natural Language to Information Systems*, pages 57–63. Springer.

Andrei-Marius Avram, Vasile Păiș, and Dan Tufiș. 2022. Self-supervised pre-training in speech recognition systems. In Vasile Păiș, editor, *Speech Recognition Technology and Applications*, pages 27–56. Nova Science Publishers.

Alexei Baevski, Yuhao Zhou, Abdelrahman Mohamed, and Michael Auli. 2020. Wav2Vec 2.0: A framework for self-supervised learning of speech representations. *Advances in Neural Information Processing Systems*, 33:12449–12460.

Piotr Bański, Peter M. Fischer, Elena Frick, Erik Ketzan, Marc Kupietz, Carsten Schnober, Oliver Schonefeld, and Andreas Witt. 2012. The new IDS corpus analysis platform: Challenges and prospects. In *Proceedings of the Eighth International Conference on Language Resources and Evaluation (LREC'12)*, pages 2905–2911, Istanbul, Turkey. European Language Resources Association (ELRA).

Verginica Barbu Mititelu, Elena Irimia, Vasile Păiș, Andrei-Marius Avram, Maria Mitrofan, and Eric Curea. 2020. Romanian resources in LLOD format. In *Proceedings of the 15th International Conference Linguistic Resources and Tools for Natural Language Processing*, pages 29–40, online.

Verginica Barbu Mititelu, Elena Irimia, Vasile Păiș, Andrei-Marius Avram, and Maria Mitrofan. 2022. Use case: Romanian language resources in the lod paradigm. In *Proceedings of the Linked Data in Linguistics Workshop @ LREC2022*, pages 35–44. European Language Resources Association (ELRA).

Eric Battenberg, RJ Skerry-Ryan, Soroosh Mariooryad, Daisy Stanton, David Kao, Matt Shannon, and Tom Bagby. 2020. Location-relative attention mechanisms for robust long-form speech synthesis. In *ICASSP 2020-2020 IEEE International Conference on Acoustics, Speech and Signal Processing (ICASSP)*, pages 6194–6198. IEEE.

Tiberiu Boroș, Stefan Daniel Dumitrescu, and Ruxandra Burtica. 2018. NLP-cube: End-to-end raw text processing with neural networks. In *Proceedings of the CoNLL 2018 Shared Task: Multilingual Parsing from Raw Text to Universal Dependencies*, pages 171–179, Brussels, Belgium. Association for Computational Linguistics.

Tiberiu Boroș, Ștefan Dumitrescu, and Vasile Păiș. 2018. Tools and resources for Romanian text-to-speech and speech-to-text applications. In *Proceedings of the International Conference on Human-Computer Interaction (RoCHI)*, pages 46–53.

Susie Coleman, Andrew Secker, Rachel Bawden, Barry Haddow, and Alexandra Birch. 2020. Architecture of a scalable, secure and resilient translation platform for multilingual news media. In *Proceedings of the 1st International Workshop on Language Technology Platforms*, pages 16–21, Marseille, France. European Language Resources Association.

Andrei Coman, Maria Mitrofan, and Dan Tufiș. 2019. Automatic identification and classification of legal terms in Romanian law texts. In *The 14th International Conference on Linguistic Resources and Tools for Natural Language Processing*, pages 39–49.

Marcello Federico, Alex Waibel, Kevin Knight, Satoshi Nakamura, Hermann Ney, Jan Niehues, Sebastian Stüker, Dekai Wu, Joseph Mariani, and Francois Yvon, editors. 2020. *Proceedings of the 17th International Conference on Spoken Language Translation*. Association for Computational Linguistics, Online.

Dario Franceschini, Chiara Canton, Ivan Simonini, Armin Schweinfurth, Adelheid Glott, Sebastian Stüker, Thai-Son Nguyen, Felix Schneider, Thanh-Le Ha, Alex Waibel, et al. 2020. Removing european language barriers with innovative machine translation technology. In *Proceedings of the 1st International Workshop on Language Technology Platforms*, pages 44–49.

Awni Hannun, Carl Case, Jared Casper, Bryan Catanzaro, Greg Diamos, Erich Elsen, Ryan Prenger, Sanjeev Satheesh, Shubho Sengupta, Adam Coates, et al. 2014. Deep speech: Scaling up end-to-end speech recognition. *arXiv preprint arXiv:1412.5567*.

Radu Ion. 2007. *Word sense disambiguation methods applied to English and Romanian*. Ph.D. thesis, Romanian Academy. In Romanian.

Radu Ion. 2018. TEPROLIN: An extensible, online text preprocessing platform for Romanian. In *The 13th International Conference on Linguistic Resources and Tools for Natural Language Processing*, pages 69–76.

Radu Ion, Valentin Gabriel Badea, George Cioroiu, Verginica Barbu Mititelu, Elena Irimia, Maria Mitrofan, and Dan Tufiș. 2020. A dialog manager for micro-worlds. *Studies in Informatics and Control*, 29(4):411–420.

Ye Jia, Ron J Weiss, Fadi Biadsy, Wolfgang Macherey, Melvin Johnson, Zhifeng Chen, and Yonghui Wu. 2019. Direct speech-to-speech translation with a sequence-to-sequence model. *Proc. Interspeech 2019*, pages 1123–1127.

Armand Joulin, Edouard Grave, Piotr Bojanowski, and Tomas Mikolov. 2017. Bag of tricks for efficient text classification. In *Proceedings of the 15th Conference of the European Chapter of the Association for Computational Linguistics: Volume 2, Short Papers*, pages 427–431, Valencia, Spain. Association for Computational Linguistics.

Tanmai Khanna, Jonathan N Washington, Francis M Tyers, Sevilay Bayatlı, Daniel G Swanson, Tommi A Pirinen, Irene Tang, and Hèctor Alòs i Font. 2021. Recent advances in apertium, a free/open-source rule-based machine translation platform for low-resource languages. *Machine Translation*, pages 1–28.

George A. Miller. 1995. WordNet: A lexical database for English. *Commun. ACM*, 38(11):39–41.

Maria Mitrofan and Vasile Păiș. 2022. Improving Romanian BioNER using a biologically inspired system. In *Proceedings of the 21st Workshop on Biomedical Language Processing*, pages 316–322, Dublin, Ireland. Association for Computational Linguistics.

Vasile Păiş, Maria Mitrofan, Carol Luca Gasan, Vlad Coneschi, and Alexandru Ianov. 2021. Named entity recognition in the Romanian legal domain. In *Proceedings of the Natural Legal Language Processing Workshop 2021*, pages 9–18.

Vasile Păiș. 2020. Multiple annotation pipelines inside the RELATE platform. In *The 15th International Conference on Linguistic Resources and Tools for Natural Language Processing*, pages 65–75.

Vasile Păiş, Radu Ion, Andrei-Marius Avram, Elena Irimia, Verginica Barbu Mititelu, and Maria Mitrofan. 2021. Human-machine interaction speech corpus from the ROBIN project. In *2021 International Conference on Speech Technology and Human-Computer Dialogue (SpeD)*, pages 91–96. IEEE.

Vasile Păiş, Dan Tufiș, and Radu Ion. 2019. Integration of Romanian NLP tools into the RELATE platform. In *The 14th International Conference on Linguistic Resources and Tools for Natural Language Processing*, pages 181–192.

Vassil Panayotov, Guoguo Chen, Daniel Povey, and Sanjeev Khudanpur. 2015. Librispeech: an ASR corpus based on public domain audio books. In *2015 IEEE international conference on acoustics, speech and signal processing (ICASSP)*, pages 5206–5210. IEEE.

Vasile Păiș, Radu Ion, Andrei-Marius Avram, Maria Mitrofan, and Dan Tufiș. 2021a. In-depth evaluation of Romanian natural language processing pipelines. *Romanian Journal of Information Science and Technology (ROMJIST)*, 24(4):384–401.

Vasile Păiș, Elena Irimia, Radu Ion, Dan Tufiș, Maria Mitrofan, Verginica Barbu Mititelu, Andrei-Marius Avram, and Eric Curea. 2021b. Romanian text anonymization experiments from the CURLICAT project. In *The 17th Edition of the International Conference on Linguistic Resources and Tools for Natural Language Processing - CONSILR*.

Vasile Păiş and Dan Tufiş. 2018. Computing distributed representations of words using the CoRoLa corpus. *Proceedings of the Romanian Academy Series A - Mathematics Physics Technical Sciences Information Science*, 19(2):185–191.

Vasile Păiş, Maria Mitrofan, Carol Luca Gasan, Vlad Coneschi, and Alexandru Ianov. 2021. Named entity recognition in the Romanian legal domain. In *Proceedings of the Natural Legal Language Processing Workshop 2021*, pages 9–18, Punta Cana, Dominican Republic. Association for Computational Linguistics.

Vasile Păiş and Dan Tufiş. 2022. Capitalization and punctuation restoration: a survey. *Artificial Intelligence Review*, 55(3):1681–1722.

Vasile Păiș. 2022. Punctuation recovery for romanian transcribed documents. In Vasile Păiș, editor, *Speech Recognition Technology and Applications*, pages 119–154. Nova Science Publishers.

Vasile Păiș and Verginica Barbu-Mititelu. 2022. Linguistic linked open data for speech processing. In Vasile Păiș, editor, *Speech Recognition Technology and Applications*, pages 155–188. Nova Science Publishers.

Georg Rehm, Kalina Bontcheva, Khalid Choukri, Jan Hajič, Stelios Piperidis, and Andrejs Vasiļjevs, editors. 2020a. *Proceedings of the 1st International Workshop on Language Technology Platforms*. European Language Resources Association, Marseille, France.

Georg Rehm, Dimitris Galanis, Penny Labropoulou, Stelios Piperidis, Martin Welß, Ricardo Usbeck, Joachim Köhler, Miltos Deligiannis, Katerina Gkirtzou, Johannes Fischer, Christian Chiarcos, Nils Feldhus, Julian Moreno-Schneider, Florian Kintzel, Elena Montiel, Víctor Rodríguez Doncel, John Philip McCrae, David Laqua, Irina Patricia Theile, Christian Dittmar, Kalina Bontcheva, Ian Roberts, Andrejs Vasiļjevs, and Andis Lagzdiņš. 2020b. Towards an interoperable ecosystem of AI and LT platforms: A roadmap for the implementation of different levels of interoperability. In *Proceedings of the 1st International Workshop on Language Technology Platforms*, pages 96–107, Marseille, France. European Language Resources Association.

Sarah Spiekermann. 2012. The challenges of privacy by design. *Communications of the ACM*, 55(7):38–40.

Adriana Stan, Junichi Yamagishi, Simon King, and Matthew Aylett. 2011. The Romanian speech synthesis (RSS) corpus: Building a high quality HMM-based speech synthesis system using a high sampling rate. *Speech Communication*, 53(3):442–450.

Milan Straka, Jan Hajič, and Jana Straková. 2016. UDPipe: trainable pipeline for processing CoNLL-U files performing tokenization, morphological analysis, POS tagging and parsing. In *Proceedings of the 10th International Conference on Language Resources and Evaluation (LREC 2016)*, Portorož, Slovenia. European Language Resources Association.

Dan Tufiș and Verginica Barbu Mititelu. 2015. *The Lexical Ontology for Romanian*, pages 491–504. Springer International Publishing, Cham.

Dan Tufiș, Verginica Barbu Mititelu, Elena Irimia, Vasile Păiș, Radu Ion, Nils Diewald, Maria Mitrofan, and Mihaela Onofrei. 2019. Little strokes fell great oaks. creating CoRoLa, the reference corpus of contemporary Romanian. *Revue Roumaine de Linguistique*, 64(3):227 – 240.

Dan Tufiş, Maria Mitrofan, Vasile Păiș, Radu Ion, and Andrei Coman. 2020. Collection and annotation of the Romanian legal corpus. In *Proceedings of the 12th Language Resources and Evaluation Conference*, pages 2773–2777.

Tamás Váradi, Svetla Koeva, Martin Yamalov, Marko Tadić, Bálint Sass, Bartłomiej Nitoń, Maciej Ogrodniczuk, Piotr Pęzik, Verginica Barbu Mititelu, Radu Ion, Elena Irimia, Maria Mitrofan, Vasile Păiș, Dan Tufiș, Radovan Garabík, Simon Krek, Andraz Repar, Matjaž Rihtar, and Janez Brank. 2020. The MARCELL legislative corpus. In *Proceedings of the 12th Language Resources and Evaluation Conference*, pages 3761–3768, Marseille, France. European Language Resources Association.

Changhan Wang, Morgane Riviere, Ann Lee, Anne Wu, Chaitanya Talnikar, Daniel Haziza, Mary Williamson, Juan Pino, and Emmanuel Dupoux. 2021. VoxPopuli: A large-scale multilingual speech corpus for representation learning, semi-supervised learning and interpretation. In *Proceedings of the 59th Annual Meeting of the Association for Computational Linguistics and the 11th International Joint Conference on Natural Language Processing (Volume 1: Long Papers)*, pages 993–1003.

Translating Spanish into Spanish Sign Language: Combining Rules and Data-driven Approaches

Luis Chiruzzo
Universidad de la República
Montevideo, Uruguay
luischir@fing.edu.uy

Euan McGill **Santiago Egea-Gómez** **Horacio Saggion**
Universitat Pompeu Fabra, Barcelona, Spain
{euan.mcgill,santiago.egea,
horacio.saggion}@upf.edu

Abstract

This paper presents a series of experiments on translating between spoken Spanish and Spanish Sign Language glosses (LSE), including enriching Neural Machine Translation (NMT) systems with linguistic features, and creating synthetic data to pretrain and later on finetune a neural translation model. We found evidence that pretraining over a large corpus of LSE synthetic data aligned to Spanish sentences could markedly improve the performance of the translation models.

1 Introduction

The widening of access to technology is crucial in today's highly interconnected online world, and it is important that technologies are made available across languages and for people with different needs. The World Federation of the Deaf[1] states that 70 million people communicate in one of the 400 sign languages (SLs) around the world. Jointly with the United Nations, they supported a resolution[2] in order to include the Deaf and Hard-of-Hearing (DHH) community in all matters concerning the provision of technology for them[3], respect the linguistic and cultural identity of signers, and improve access to education and services.

According to the Spanish National Confederation of Deaf People (CNSE)[4], approximately 2.3% of Spain's population experience hearing loss to some degree and a large number of them use *Lengua de Signos Española* (LSE) as their primary means of communication. Also, ethnologue estimates that there are between 45 to 75 thousand LSE signers. LSE was first described in the late 18th Century, while only recently a grammar (Rodríguez González, 2003) has been written to capture the features of the language. In 2011, LSE was recognized as an official language, and there has been a greater focus on providing resources for signers and learners.

As with other SLs, LSE is produced in the visual-spatial modality (Baker, 2015) rather than the oral-auditory modality of spoken languages. Manual and non-manual (facial expression, body position) features including the space around the signer can be articulated simultaneously to produce meaning. Whereas textual forms are well-established in spoken languages, those capturing the spatio-temporal nature of SLs including HamNoSys (Hanke, 2004) are long extant but not widely known or used by signers (Jantunen et al., 2021). The most frequently encountered representation of SLs are glosses – a lexeme-based representation using the ambient spoken language of the region where the SL is native. For example, glosses for LSE are written in Spanish. One criticism of glosses is that a great deal of semantic information is lost (Zhang and Duh, 2021). However, their linearity as text is a beneficial input format for machine learning (ML) models.

Machine translation (MT) has advanced significantly in recent years, specially thanks to the development of methods based on Deep Neural Networks, reaching quality levels comparable to humans (Hassan et al., 2018) for spoken languages. Despite these advances, MT is in its infancy when it comes to translation between spoken and sign languages or between different sign languages. In this paper we address a little researched topic in MT, that of translating between Spanish and LSE using a combination of rule-based and neural approaches. We present experiments on building MT systems between spoken Spanish and LSE using a small parallel corpus of sentences and gloss sequences. We first show a baseline system using

[1] https://wfdeaf.org/our-work/

[2] UN Resolution 72/161: "International Day of Sign Languages"

[3] This resolution emphasises the 'nothing about us without us' method of working with the DHH community.

[4] https://www.cnse.es/inmigracion/index.php?lang=en

Proceedings of the 29th International Conference on Computational Linguistic, pages 75–83
October 12–17, 2022.

only the parallel data, and then present two techniques for improving this baseline: enriching the representation of words and glosses with linguistic information; and using a large corpus of synthetic data for creating a pretrained model, and then fine-tuning using the original training data. As we will see, this last approach is the one with the most promising results.

The rest of this paper is structured as follows: Section 2 presents related work on LSE and SLs in general; section 3 introduces the dataset we base our research on, the ID/DL corpus; section 4 describes the different experiments we carried out with this dataset; section 5 shows the evaluation of the experiments over the test partition; and finally section 6 presents some conclusions and future work.

2 Related Work

The scarcity of linguistic resources constitutes a major barrier in the adaptation of latest technology to SLs (Yin et al., 2021). In fact, SLs are considered *extremely* low resource languages (Moryossef et al., 2021) for MT models. This section explores computational resources and systems existing for LSE, SL Translation (SLT) and processing.

2.1 LSE technologies and resources

There has been a wide range of work focusing on LSE, including resources such as image and video signbanks and lexica (Cabeza and García-Miguel, 2019; del Carmen Cabeza-Pereiro et al., 2016; Gutierrez-Sigut et al., 2016), language learning resources (Herrero-Blanco, 2009), and corpora containing full utterances for academic purposes (Porta et al., 2014). The largest barrier to create technologies on par with those available to spoken languages, one that is shared with all SLs (Bragg et al., 2019; Holmes et al., 2022), is the size and tendency towards domain-specificity in LSE parallel corpora.

Outside of static reference resources, there also exist rule-based translation systems from Spanish into LSE. Porta and colleagues (Porta et al., 2014) worked with a psycholinguistics-based corpus consisting of one SL interpreter reciting six passages translated from Spanish into LSE in varied domains. There are 229 parallel sentences in total, with 611 unique sign types. The LSE glosses are transcribed to an extent in a convention which incorporates prosodic, morphological and syntactic phenomena. This study leverages knowledge of LSE grammar, a language-agnostic dependency parser, the bilingual corpus, and the DILSE dictionary (Fundación CNSE, 2008) to form the rule-based MT system. The BLEU (Papineni et al., 2002) and Translation Error Rate (TER) (Snover et al., 2006) metrics are commonly used in MT studies. This system reported a reasonable BLEU of 30.0 and TER of 42%, especially coming from a domain-unspecific testbed.

In addition, Vegas-Cañas (Vegas Cañas et al., 2020) outlines their web-based Text2LSE system. This system is also rule-based, and translates between simple Spanish text and LSE text, or LSE videos from the ARASAAC resource[5]. Text2LSE was evaluated on 137 simple utterances, and was shown to be severely limited as 82.5% of output sentences were deemed 'errorful'. The lack of crossover between output glosses and existing signs in an LSE lexicon was the most salient factor. It is therefore important to check whether SLT outputs have a grounding in the real language.

In this work, we focus on the ID/DL corpus created by San-Segundo and colleagues (San-Segundo et al., 2008), based on utterances drawn from Spanish identity card and driving license application data. They also used it to design a statistical rule-based end-to-end (E2E) translation system from speech recognition through translation and outputting to a 3D avatar. They achieved a BLEU score of 49.4 when using them with a phrase-based statistical MT model. Using a rule-based system with 153 linguistically-motivated rules crafter by the authors and tuned specifically to the dataset, they achieved a BLEU score of 57.8. These findings are of importance for the present study, which is comparable as it is trained on the same ID/DL dataset.

2.2 Current methods in Sign Language Translation

SLT is inherently multimodal (Bragg et al., 2019), where it is necessary to incorporate audiovisual processing, speech recognition, and SL generation through technologies such as avatars. E2E systems between text and sign exist (Camgoz et al., 2020), but modular systems with intermediate representations such as Text2Gloss (Yin and Read, 2020) before transforming to a sign appear to currently yield higher accuracy (Zhang and Duh, 2021) in

[5] `https://arasaac.org/`

translation.

Transformer-based neural machine translation (NMT) (e.g. Klein et al. 2017; Xue et al. 2021) has been instrumental in forming the current state-of-the-art between a wide range of languages, including low-resource spoken languages. Due to the unique multimodal nature of the SLT task, as well as the status of most SLs as *extremely* low-resource languages, further strategies are necessary to perform adequate SLT. One example is data augmentation methods to boost the amount of training data available. These strategies include backtranslation (Zhou et al., 2021), and a rule-based strategies between parallel corpora (Moryossef et al., 2021). Another method is to supplement the encoder of a transformer model with linguistic information (Sennrich and Haddow, 2016). Our previous work on German-DGS[6] using linguistic feature embeddings (Egea Gómez et al., 2021) and transfer learning methods (Egea Gómez et al., 2022) result in an increase in performance of more than 5 BLEU over a baseline not incorporating linguistic information. In the present study, we propose using methods of data augmentation based on the linguistic features of LSE, as well as incorporating part-of-speech and syntactic dependency tags on input data for translation models.

3 Corpus

For our experiments, we use the ID/DL corpus (San-Segundo et al., 2008)[7], made up of 416 parallel Spanish-LSE utterances. Below, we show one example of the parallel text samples composing this corpus:

> **Spanish**: deberá tener preparadas las fotografías y documentos necesarios
> **LSE**: FUTURO TÚ OBLIGATORIO PREPARAR PLURAL FOTOGRAFíA Y PLURAL DOCUMENTO PLURAL NECESARIO

We randomly split the dataset into 266 training utterances, 75 dev utterances and 75 test utterances. Table 1 presents the data composition of the different partitions used in our experiments and the LSE Lexicon (Gutierrez-Sigut et al., 2016) for comparison.

As can be observed, the train partition contains 290 unique glosses, which cover 89.9% of dev glosses and 85.6% of test glosses. Consequently, there are a lot of glosses both in the dev and test sets that the MT models will never see at training time (out-of-vocabulary glosses). The models might overfit train patterns while some of the input sequences may not be properly learnt leading to inaccurate predictions. Also, we notice that the glosses in the LSE Lexicon seem not to be representative enough of the glosses found in the ID/DL corpus, as less than 50% of the glosses found on the train, dev and test sets are in the lexicon, which is in line with the problems mentioned in Section 2.1.

	Train	Dev	Test	Lexicon
Sentences	266	75	75	-
Total words	3153	859	917	-
Unique words	531	312	289	-
Total glosses	2952	803	885	2243
Unique glosses	290	188	181	2243
Glosses coverage between sets in %				
	Train	Dev	Test	Lexicon
Train coverage	100	58.3	53.4	37.9
Dev coverage	89.9	100	64.4	35.6
Test coverage	85.6	66.9	100	45.3
Lexicon coverage	4.9	3.0	3.7	100

Table 1: The top part shows the sizes of the training, development and test splits, and the lexicon set. The bottom part shows the coverage of glosses between each pair of sets.

4 Experiments

We have carried out a series of experiments on building MT models between (spoken) Spanish and LSE. Although ID/DL corpus is not a fully comprehensive representation of LSE, it is one of the few available LSE resources with a suitable format to experiment with ML algorithms.

In the present work, we first create a baseline for both translation directions *LSE↔Spanish* (section 4.1); then we incorporate linguistic features to boost our MT model (section 4.2); and finally we pretrain a transformer model on synthetic data generated using data augmentation rules, and fine-tune it with the ID/DL training data (section 4.3). All the results in this section are evaluated against the ID/DL development set, while section 5 shows results over the test set.

4.1 Baseline model

In the preliminary experiment a DL model is trained using only the parallel word and gloss sequences from ID/DL. We used the Open-

[6]Deutsche Gebärdensprache (German Sign Language)

[7]Enquiries about the corpus should be addressed to: `https://www.fundacioncnse.org/`

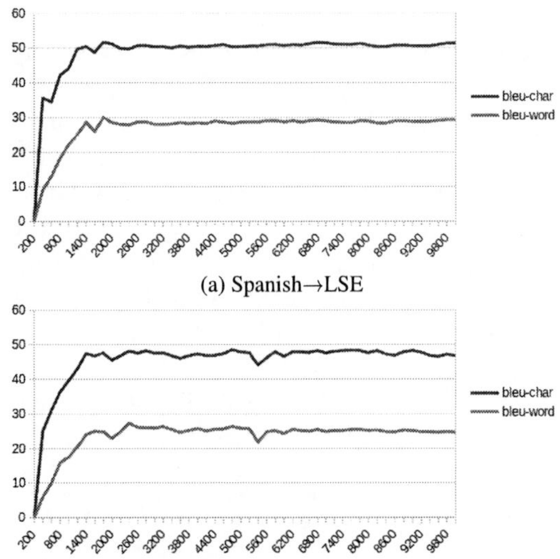

(a) Spanish→LSE

(b) LSE→Spanish

Figure 1: Performance of the baseline experiment during training, calculated over the development set.

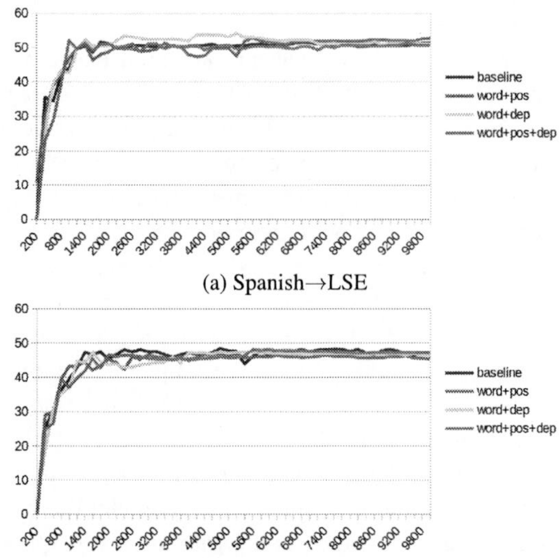

(a) Spanish→LSE

(b) LSE→Spanish

Figure 2: BLEU-char performance for the models with linguistic features during training, calculated over the development set. The baseline model (in blue) is also shown for comparison.

NMT (Klein et al., 2017) system in its default configuration, consisting in a stack of Long Short-term Memory (LSTMs) layers with a general attention mechanism. The model was trained for 10,000 steps taking a snapshot every 200 steps to evaluate it against the dev corpus; this training setting is used in all experiments reported here. Fig. 1 shows the performance of this experiment on the dev set for both directions, according to the BLEU (Papineni et al., 2002) metric calculated using SacreBLEU (Post, 2018) both at word and character level, which we refer to as BLEU-word and BLEU-char respectively. The BLEU-char metric is also used in other works related to SLT (Egea Gómez et al., 2021).

Regarding *Spanish→LSE*, convergence is achieved between 2000 and 2500 steps, while for the other direction convergence happens after 2600 but the performance fluctuates more than in the other case. Both metrics (at word and character level) seem to be very correlated, but the best performance is not necessarily achieved at the same time. For example, for the *LSE→Spanish* direction, peak BLEU-char performance is 48.43 at 4800 steps, while peak BLEU-word performance is achieved much earlier, 27.32 at 2400 steps. On the other hand, for the *Spanish→LSE* direction, the best BLEU-char and BLEU-word performances are obtained at 1800 steps, 51.60 and 29.94 respectively. Since both metrics are correlated, and for the sake of better chart visualisation, in the rest of this section we report only the BLEU-char metric for the dev partition, while both metrics will be examined on test data.

4.2 Enriching models with linguistic features

Following (Egea Gómez et al., 2021), linguistic information is incorporated into our model in order to boost translation performances. We used the Spanish spaCy model[8] to analyse the spoken Spanish utterances, obtaining their part-of-speech (POS) and dependency parsing information (DEP). Then we trained three different models where the source text uses these combinations of features: (1) words + POS, (2) words + DEP label, and (3) words + POS + DEP label. The OpenNMT models, in this case, use separate dictionaries for words, POS and DEP features, creating separate embedding models for each of the feature spaces. Then, the embedding vectors are concatenated and fed to the LSTM network.

The experimental setting described so far can only be employed in the *Spanish→LSE* direction; because the Spanish spaCy model manages only Spanish sentences, while sign glosses follow different linguistic rules and the annotation model is not applicable to them. Even the dependency grammars and treebanks for other sign languages are

[8]`https://spacy.io/models`

still under development or are too small to work with (Östling et al., 2017). Therefore, in order to try the same configuration in the *LSE→Spanish* direction, we transfer POS and DEP features generated for spoken Spanish to glosses using the statistical-based alignment model fast_align (Dyer et al., 2013). We use the following rules to create silver-standard POS and DEP data for glosses:

- (1) If gloss `j` is aligned to word `i`, assign the label for `i` to the gloss `j`.
- (2) If gloss `j` is not aligned to any word, assign the most common label for gloss `j` found in the gloss side of the corpus.
- (3) Otherwise, use the label `UNK` for the gloss.

This feature transfer schema is independently applied for each data partition. However, it is important to remark that in a real scenario this process will not be applicable, since DEP and POS features are annotated on gloss utterances based on their corresponding spoken ground truths, which are not available in a real scenario. Consequently, the results on *LSE→Spanish* must be seen as an unrealistic upper bound, and further research is needed to build actual POS and DEP models for LSE.

Fig. 2 shows the evolution of performance over the dev set for these experiments. We can see that all models behave in a similar way, but the word+DEP model overcomes the others in *Spanish→LSE* between steps 2600 and 5600 in up to 3 points, reaching a BLEU-char of 54.1. Conversely, this improvement is not clear for *LSE→Spanish*.

4.3 Augmenting the corpus with synthetic data

Previous work like (Moryossef et al., 2021) have shown that it is possible to use corpus augmentation strategies for improving performance of MT models in sign language scenarios. In our case, we follow a strategy with two steps: first we *pretrain* over a large set of synthetic data, and then we *finetune* using the ID/DL training set. Based on the LSE grammar (Rodríguez González, 2003) and our observations of the training data, we created a rule-based system that tries to mimic the most salient rules for getting the sequence of glosses from the corresponding sequence of words. We first obtain morphosyntactic and dependency information for a spoken sentence using spaCy, and then we use three sets of rules shown in table 2 to create a rough

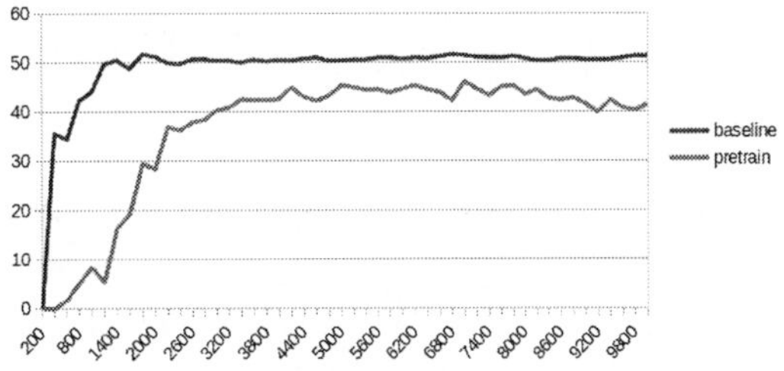

(a) *Spanish→LSE*

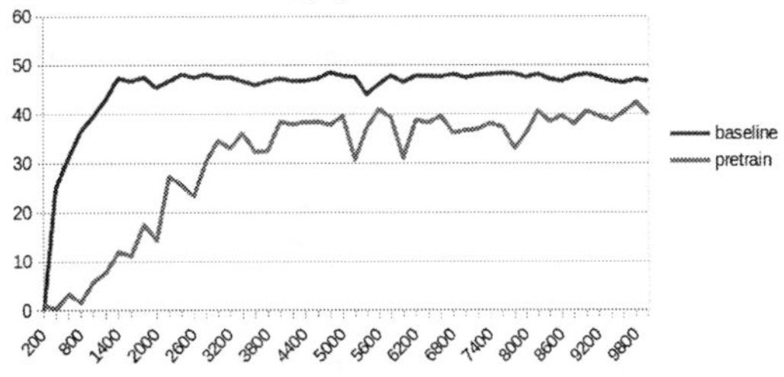

(b) *LSE→Spanish*

Figure 3: BLEU-char performance of the pretrained models (trained over the synthetic corpus), calculated over the development set. The baseline model (in blue) is also shown for comparison.

translation. Using these rules already yields somewhat good results on the development set: 63.42 BLEU-char and 29.73 BLEU-word, compared to 51.60 BLEU-char and 29.94 BLEU-word obtained in the baseline MT system described in section 4.1.

Using this rule-based system, we translated the whole Spanish set of the Ancora corpus (Taulé et al., 2008). This corpus contains 17k sentences of from newspaper text, around 500k words. After translating all the sentences, the resulting gloss sequences corpus has around 400k glosses. With this, we created a silver-standard synthetic corpus of glosses aligned to their corresponding sentences in spoken Spanish. Then we pretrained neural translation systems with this synthetic corpus for 10,000 steps in both directions. Of course, the results of these pretrained models over the ID/DL development corpus were much lower than for the rest experiments described so far, because even if the synthetic Ancora parallel set is much larger, its sentences are very different from the ones in ID/DL. However, as we will see, we can use this pretrained model as a starting point for finetuning with the ID/DL training data, which achieves much better results. Fig. 3 shows the BLEU-char performance of the pretrained models compared to the baseline model, where we can see that the performance of the pretrained model is always below the baseline model.

Inclusion of explicit morphological markers	Example
1) Add the "PLURAL" token before any plural word.	perros → PLURAL PERRO
2) Add the "FUTURO" token before any verb in future tense.	comerá → FUTURO COMER
3) Add the "TÚ" token before any verb in second person.	vienes → TÚ VENIR
4) Change a possessive determinant to "PROPIO" + the pronoun.	mi madre → PROPIO YO MADRE
Removal of words not used in LSE	**Example**
5) Remove determinants (except the possessive, which are changed by rule 4).	el perro → PERRO
6) Remove prepositions "de" and "en".	de tarde →TARDE
Particular lexical transformations	**Example**
7) Copula words are changed to the token "SE-LLAMA".	esto es importante → ESTO SE-LLAMA IMPORTANTE
8) Sequences whose lemmas correspond to the sequence "TENER QUE", are changed to "NECESITAR".	tiene que llevar → NECESITAR LLEVAR
9) Instances of "denei" are changed to "DNI".	llevar denei → LLEVAR DNI
10) All other words are represented as their uppercase lemmas.	perros → PERRO

Table 2: Rules used in the rule-based system for creating synthetic data.

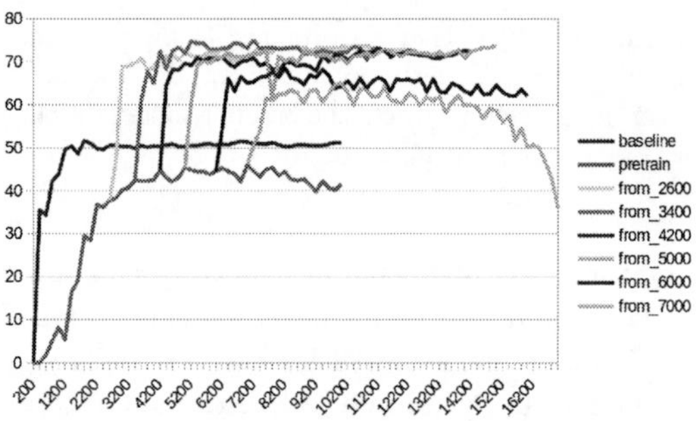

(a) Spanish→LSE

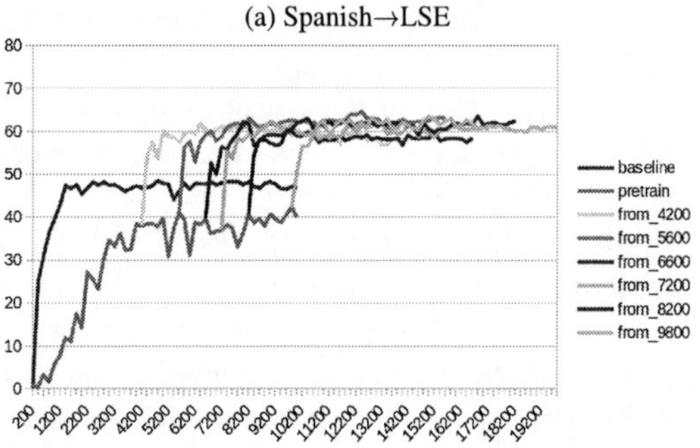

(b) LSE→Spanish

Figure 4: BLEU-char performance of the finetuned models (trained over the training set but starting from different steps of the pretrained model), calculated over the development set. The baseline model (in blue) and the pretrained model (in red) are also shown for comparison.

The pretrained model also seems to converge much more slowly than the baseline, and shows some spikes in performance at some points. We chose some of those points where performance seems to peak (six in each direction) as starting points for finetuning. We then finetuned the model using the original ID/DL training data for 10,000 more steps in each case. Fig. 4 shows the BLEU-char performance of these new models over the development set, the baseline model (blue) and the pretrained model (red) are shown for comparison. Note that there is a considerable leap in performance for all finetuned models, which start from the pretrained line and suddenly jump much higher than the baseline.

In the *LSE→Spanish* direction, the performance of all finetuned models plateau between 55 and 65 BLEU-char.

5 Results and Discussion

We chose the model that yielded the best results according to BLEU-char for each of the described experiments, and we evaluated them over the test set. Table 3 shows the results of this evaluation. The first thing to notice is that all the finetuned models behave much better than the baseline model and the models infused with linguistic features, having as much as 20 more points in BLEU-char or 15 points in BLEU-word in both directions. Besides BLUE-char and BLEU-word, we show other usual MT metrics: Meteor, TER and ROUGE-L. All these metrics also show a similar trend, having substantial improvements when using the finetuned models. Our best result for the finetuned models is a BLEU-word of 58.98, which is higher than any configuration in San Segundo's work (San-Segundo et al., 2008).

The models that incorporated linguistic features performed similarly for the dev split. However, this performance is not reflected on the test split,

Direction	Experiment	BLEU char	BLEU word	Meteor	ROUGE L F1	TER
	baseline	49.92	30.87	0.4382	0.4772	0.6785
	word+pos	52.23	31.99	0.4590	0.4914	0.6715
	word+dep	49.80	28.60	0.4296	0.4772	0.6746
	word+pos+dep	43.94	21.46	0.3689	0.4141	0.7387
	pretrain	42.34	9.63	0.2841	0.3748	0.7311
Spanish→LSE	from 2600	74.16	57.11	0.7139	0.7316	0.3691
	from 3400	70.93	52.12	0.6978	0.7270	**0.3424**
	from 4200	**75.42**	**58.98**	**0.7153**	**0.7351**	0.3438
	from 5000	72.16	53.82	0.6945	0.7250	0.3794
	from 6000	65.78	49.02	0.6360	0.6815	0.4007
	from 7000	67.33	47.20	0.6478	0.6718	0.4425
	baseline	46.08	24.97	0.4026	0.4206	0.7387
	word+pos	43.72	22.84	0.3746	0.4037	0.7438
	word+dep	45.03	24.35	0.3834	0.4061	0.7419
	word+pos+dep	45.16	23.66	0.3963	0.4121	0.7359
	pretrain	36.62	4.88	0.2646	0.2974	0.9568
LSE→Spanish	from 4200	**64.59**	41.02	**0.6037**	0.6047	0.4658
	from 5600	63.23	41.12	0.5946	0.6016	0.4829
	from 6600	62.71	40.15	0.5991	0.6055	**0.4582**
	from 7200	60.29	38.56	0.5773	0.5911	0.4738
	from 8200	61.35	41.46	0.6030	0.6104	0.4612
	from 9800	61.59	**41.63**	0.5940	**0.6108**	0.4700

Table 3: Results for all the experiments over the test set.

where most models achieve a few points less than the baseline. One of the models, though, seems to have some improvement over the baseline: the word+POS model in the *Spanish→LSE*. But the word+DEP model, which was the most promising on dev, did not bring any improvement over test.

In order to understand the big difference in performance achieved by the finetuned models, we measured the vocabulary coverage obtained by the synthetic data corpus created from Ancora. Table 4 shows the main statistics of the Ancora set and the union of Ancora and ID/DL training set, which was the whole set of data used for training.

	Ancora	Ancora+Train
Lines	17345	17611
Total words	481638	484791
Unique words	39705	39785
Total glosses	402539	405491
Unique glosses	26198	26232
Glosses coverage between sets in %		
	Ancora	Ancora+Train
Train coverage	88.3	100
Dev coverage	91.5	99.5
Test coverage	92.3	98.9
Lexicon coverage	62.6	62.7

Table 4: Sizes and coverage statistics for the synthetic data corpus created from Ancora using the rule-based system. We show only the Ancora set, and the union of Ancora and the ID/DL train split.

The dev and test sets coverage obtained using the Ancora and the training split are much higher than using the training split alone. This is because rule 10 in Table 2 is a productive rule that can create any new gloss it needs to accommodate the words seen in the training data. Using this, systems pretrained on the Ancora set will have at least some model for almost all the glosses in the test corpus, which is an advantage over the models that have not seen any of those glosses during training. Note that, as table 1 shows, we had 14.4% out of vocabulary words with the original training corpus, and it dropped to 1.1% with the union of the training and Ancora corpora.

On the other hand, there is no guarantee that the glosses created by rule 10 are indeed valid signs, so this rule is probably fabricating glosses that have no counterpart in LSE. It would be possible to alleviate this problem using some other heuristics. One way of doing this could be obtaining the closest gloss in the embeddings space that is an actual LSE sign, but since the LSE Lexicon coverage is so low, further research is needed to get a larger set of valid glosses and signs that could lead better insights on this process.

6 Conclusions and Future Work

We presented experiments to build machine translation models between Spanish and LSE glosses. Our experiments are based on the ID/DL corpus, a small parallel set of Spanish sentences aligned with their corresponding LSE glosses, about the restricted domain of identity card and driving license renovations. Although glosses are not a full representation of all the complexities of a sign language, they are comprehensive enough and suitable for ML purposes.

First we carried out experiments on infusing linguistic features on a neural model for trying to improve its performance. The results of these experiments were mixed: on dev, the use of words combined with dependency labels seemed to improve performance, but on test the best improvements were achieved using a combination of words and POS labels.

Then we took the Spanish Ancora corpus and transformed it using a rule-based system inspired by the LSE grammar to create a synthetic parallel corpus of Spanish aligned with LSE sequences that is considerably larger than the ID/DL corpus. We found that pretraining on this synthetic corpus, and then finetuning with the original ID/DL training corpus achieves a marked performance improvement (around 20 points on BLEU-char and 15 points BLEU-word) over training using only the ID/DL training corpus. This improvement could be explained in part due to the high coverage of glosses achieved by using the synthetic data, but we have to take in consideration that the process could have also created some glosses that may have no real-world counterpart in LSE. We propose some possible improvements on the process, such as using a heuristic to find appropriate sign glosses when a nonexistent gloss is used.

Furthermore, given that the use of linguistic information showed some potential improvements in some scenarios, we would like to try combining both methods by getting linguistic information for the synthetic data as well for pretraining. Also, as the ID/DL corpus we used is rather small, we would like to see to what extent our approach generalises for other LSE corpora that belong to other domains. We also want to try our approaches on other pairs of spoken and sign languages. Finally, as the dataset is rather small, we could try to use simpler a statistical method, such as phrased-based MT, and combine it with the our rule approach to see if there are also improvements in that scenario.

Acknowledgements

This work has been conducted within the SignON project. SignON is a Horizon 2020 project, funded under the Horizon 2020 program ICT-57-2020 - "An empowering, inclusive, Next Generation Internet" with Grant Agreement number 101017255.

References

Anne Baker. 2015. Sign languages as natural languages. In Anne Baker, Beppie van den Boegarde, Roland Pfau, and Trude Schermer, editors, *Sign Languages of the World: A Comparative Handbook*, chapter 31, pages 729–770. De Gruyter, Berlin.

Danielle Bragg, Oscar Koller, Mary Bellard, Larwan Berke, Patrick Boudreault, Annelies Braffort, Naomi Caselli, Matt Huenerfauth, Hernisa Kacorri, Tessa Verhoef, Christian Vogler, and Meredith Ringel Morris. 2019. Sign Language Recognition, Generation, and Translation: An Interdisciplinary Perspective. In *The 21st International ACM SIGACCESS Conference on Computers and Accessibility*, ASSETS '19, page 16–31, New York, NY, USA. Association for Computing Machinery.

Carmen Cabeza and José M. García-Miguel. 2019. iSignos: Interfaz de datos de Lengua de Signos Española (versión 1.0).

Necati Cihan Camgoz, Oscar Koller, Simon Hadfield, and Richard Bowden. 2020. Sign language transformers: Joint end-to-end sign language recognition and translation. In *CVPR 2020*, pages 10020–10030.

María del Carmen Cabeza-Pereiro, José Mª Garcia-Miguel, Carmen García Mateo, and José Luis Alba Castro. 2016. CORILSE: a Spanish Sign Language repository for linguistic analysis. In *Proceedings of the Tenth International Conference on Language Resources and Evaluation (LREC'16)*, pages 1402–1407, Portorož, Slovenia. European Language Resources Association (ELRA).

Chris Dyer, Victor Chahuneau, and Noah A Smith. 2013. A simple, fast, and effective reparameterization of IBM model 2. In *Proceedings of the 2013 Conference of the North American Chapter of the Association for Computational Linguistics: Human Language Technologies*, pages 644–648.

Santiago Egea Gómez, Luis Chiruzzo, Euan McGill, and Horacio Saggion. 2022. Linguistically enhanced text to sign gloss machine translation. In *Natural Language Processing and Information Systems: 27th International Conference on Applications of Natural Language to Information Systems, NLDB 2022, Valencia, Spain, June 15–17, 2022, Proceedings*, pages 172–183.

Santiago Egea Gómez, Euan McGill, and Horacio Saggion. 2021. Syntax-aware transformers for neural machine translation: The case of text to sign gloss translation. In *14th WS. on BUCC*, pages 18–27, Online.

Fundación CNSE. 2008. Diccionario normativo de la lengua de signos española.

Eva Gutierrez-Sigut, Brendan Costello, Cristina Baus, and Manuel Carreiras. 2016. LSE-Sign: A lexical database for Spanish Sign Language. *Behaviour Research Methods*, 48:123–137.

Thomas Hanke. 2004. Hamnosys—representing sign language data in language resources and language processing contexts. In *LREC 2004, WS on RPSLs*, pages 1–6, Paris, France.

Hany Hassan, Anthony Aue, Chang Chen, Vishal Chowdhary, Jonathan Clark, Christian Federmann, Xuedong Huang, Marcin Junczys-Dowmunt, William Lewis, Mu Li, et al. 2018. Achieving human parity on automatic chinese to english news translation. *ArXiv*, abs/1803.05567.

Ángel Herrero-Blanco. 2009. *Gramática Didáctica de la Lengua de Signos Española*. SM, Madrid.

Ruth Holmes, Ellen Rushe, Frank Fowley, and Anthony Ventresque. 2022. Improving Signer Independent Sign Language Recognition for Low Resource Languages. In *Seventh International Workshop on Sign Language Translation and Avatar Technology: The Junction of the Visual and the Textual*, Marseille, France.

Tommi Jantunen, Rebekah Rousi, Päivi Raino, Markku Turunen, Mohammad Valipoor, and Narciso García. 2021. *Is There Any Hope for Developing Automated Translation Technology for Sign Languages?*, pages 61–73.

Guillaume Klein, Yoon Kim, Yuntian Deng, Jean Senellart, and Alexander Rush. 2017. OpenNMT: Open-source toolkit for neural machine translation. In *Proceedings of ACL 2017, System Demonstrations*, pages 67–72, Vancouver, Canada. Association for Computational Linguistics.

Amit Moryossef, Kayo Yin, Graham Neubig, and Yoav Goldberg. 2021. Data augmentation for sign language gloss translation.

Robert Östling, Carl Börstell, Moa Gärdenfors, and Mats Wirén. 2017. Universal dependencies for swedish sign language. In *Proceedings of the 21st Nordic conference on computational linguistics*, pages 303–308.

Kishore Papineni, Salim Roukos, Todd Ward, and Wei-Jing Zhu. 2002. Bleu: a method for automatic evaluation of machine translation. In *Proceedings of the 40th Annual Meeting of the ACL*, pages 311–318, Philadelphia, Pennsylvania, USA. ACL.

Jordi Porta, Fernando López-Colino, Javier Tejedor, and José Colás. 2014. A rule-based translation from written Spanish to Spanish Sign Language glosses. *Computer Speech & Language*, 28:788–811.

Matt Post. 2018. A call for clarity in reporting BLEU scores. In *3rd Conf. on MT*, pages 186–191, Belgium, Brussels. ACL.

María Ángeles Rodríguez González. 2003. Lenguaje de signos.

Rubén San-Segundo, R Barra, R Córdoba, L Fernando D'Haro, F Fernández, Javier Ferreiros, Juan Manuel Lucas, Javier Macías-Guarasa, Juan Manuel Montero, and José Manuel Pardo. 2008. Speech to sign language translation system for Spanish. *Speech Communication*, 50(11):1009–1020.

Rico Sennrich and Barry Haddow. 2016. Linguistic input features improve neural machine translation. In *1st Conf. on MT*, pages 83–91, Berlin, Germany. ACL.

Matthew Snover, Bonnie Dorr, Rich Schwartz, Linnea Micciulla, and John Makhoul. 2006. A study of translation edit rate with targeted human annotation. pages 223–231.

Mariona Taulé, M Antònia Martí, and Marta Recasens. 2008. Ancora: Multilevel annotated corpora for catalan and spanish. In *Proceedings of the Sixth International Conference on Language Resources and Evaluation (LREC'08)*.

Sara Vegas Cañas, Miguel Rodríguez Cuesta, and Alejandro Torralbo Fuentes. 2020. Text2LSE: Traductor Texto a Lengua de Signos Española (LSE).

Linting Xue, Noah Constant, Adam Roberts, Mihir Kale, Rami Al-Rfou, Aditya Siddhant, Aditya Barua, and Colin Raffel. 2021. mT5: A massively multilingual pre-trained text-to-text transformer. In *NAACL 2021*, pages 483–498, Online. ACL.

Kayo Yin, Amit Moryossef, Julie Hochgesang, Yoav Goldberg, and Malihe Alikhani. 2021. Including signed languages in natural language processing.

Kayo Yin and Jesse Read. 2020. Better sign language translation with STMC-transformer. In *COLING 2020*, pages 5975–5989, Online. ICCL.

Xuan Zhang and Kevin Duh. 2021. Approaching sign language gloss translation as a low-resource machine translation task. In *AT4SSL 2021*, pages 60–70, Online. AMTA.

Hao Zhou, Wengang Zhou, Weizhen Qi, Junfu Pu, and Houqiang Li. 2021. Improving sign language translation with monolingual data by sign back-translation.

Benefiting from Language Similarity in the Multilingual MT Training: Case Study of Indonesian and Malaysian

Alberto Poncelas and **Johanes Effendi**
Rakuten Institute of Technology
Rakuten Group, Inc.
{first.last}@rakuten.com

Abstract

The development of machine translation (MT) has been successful in breaking the language barrier of the world's top 10-20 languages. However, for the rest of it, delivering an acceptable translation quality is still a challenge due to the limited resource. To tackle this problem, most studies focus on augmenting data while overlooking the fact that we can "borrow" high-quality natural data from the closely-related language. In this work, we propose an MT model training strategy by increasing the language directions as a means of augmentation in a multilingual setting. Our experiment result using Indonesian and Malaysian on the state-of-the-art MT model showcases the effectiveness and robustness of our method.

1 Introduction

In machine translation (MT), the definition of "low-resource" is not always tied to the language itself, but also to the pair of which languages we want to translate. For example, although Japanese cannot be classified as a low-resource language, training a Japanese-to-Indonesian (JA→ID) or Japanese-to-Malaysian (JA→MS) MT system can be challenging given that there is a very small number of parallel data for that language pair.

Accordingly, researches on multilingual MT (Liu et al., 2020; Fan et al., 2021) focus on improving translation results in low-resource language with the help of other high-resource languages in a unified singular model. However, such improvements are just significant in the translation directions involving English (EN→XX and XX→EN), while on non-English translation pair (XX→YY) the translation performance significantly decreases (NLLB Team et al., 2022) because the parallel data for those language pairs are not available.

In this work, we propose an MT model training strategy that benefits from the similar language, even when the similar language does not include initially in the model. We showcased the effectiveness of our proposed method using a commonly known similar language family of JA→ID and JA→MS translation pairs.

We use Indonesian and Malaysian as examples of closely-related languages. Both languages are commonly known as such due to their similar geographical and historical contexts, where it was used as the *lingua franca* throughout the Malay archipelago for over a thousand years (Paauw, 2009).

Popular strategies to improve the models that use low-resourced languages are based on data augmentation or transfer learning (Zoph et al., 2016) from a richer-resourced language. However, in this work, we focus on investigating exclusively the impact of including additional language-direction in the training process of a multilingual MT. We present several alternatives in a multilingual context where translation directions of similar languages can be used in combination, and how they can benefit each other. As Malaysian and Indonesian are similar languages, we hypothesize that performing multilingual training from Japanese in these two directions could be mutually beneficial.

We detail our proposal in Section 3. In Section 4 we describe the settings of the data and the models built. The performance of the different models are displayed in Section 5 and an analysis of the outputs in Section 6. Finally, we conclude this paper in Section 7 and propose different experiments that could be carried out in the future.

2 Related Work

In a resource-rich condition, improving an MT model can be done by simply adding more parallel data. This is possible for some European language pairs such as EN-DE, FR-EN, EN-IT and others. However, for most of the languages in the world, such data is more limited, which also yields to a

Proceedings of the 29th International Conference on Computational Linguistic, pages 84–92
October 12–17, 2022.

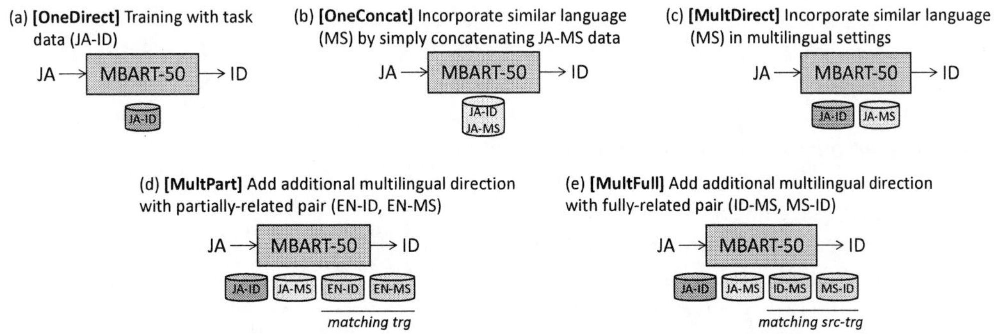

Figure 1: Overview of our proposed training strategy: (a) **[OneDirect]** is the single direction baseline training for JA→ID task, (b) **[OneConcat]** concatenate MS data with ID assuming that it is equivalent, (c) **[MultDirect]** adding JA-MS as additional multilingual direction, (d) **[MultPart]** add additional multilingual direction with partially-related pairs, and (e) **[MultFull]** add additional multilingual direction with fully-related pairs.

more limited performance.

Several method such as mixture-of-experts (Shazeer et al., 2017), data augmentation by paraphrasing (Mehdizadeh Seraj et al., 2015; Sekizawa et al., 2017; Effendi et al., 2018; Zhou et al., 2019) or by backtranslation (Sennrich et al., 2016; Hoang et al., 2018). Unfortunately, augmentation methods looking at the closeness of the language are sometimes overlooked. We argue that before applying an augmentation method that generates synthetic data, we should first focus on using the already available natural data from neighboring similar languages.

Previous studies, such as the work of Aw et al. (2009) and Susanto et al. (2012), focus on developing translation between Indonesian and Malaysian from the perspective of low-resource language. However, we observed that in practice, the translation demand actually comes from high-resource to low-resource language and vice-versa. Given that, the monolingual data will be imbalanced in either source and target of the translation, in addition to the difficulties of looking for parallel data.

Similarly, Zoph et al. (2016) studied transfer learning for NMT, in which a model built on high-resourced language data is used as an initialization for training on a similar low-resource language. While this was developed with data scarcity in mind, this is different from our work as we focus on the benefits of training simultaneously two low-resourced languages rather than transferring the knowledge from one language to another.

Furthermore, Nakov and Ng (2012) proposed a method to paraphrase between Indonesian and Malaysian through a confusion network. The paraphrase between both languages were then used to enrich the phrase table probability in the statistical machine translation (SMT) settings. Unfortunately, such methods are not compatible with the current state-of-the-art MT model, where probabilities are implicit and updated by backpropagation.

3 Extending the Bilingual MT with More Training Directions

In this study, we develop a training strategy that leverages the already available natural data as a means of augmentation, with the closeness of the language in mind, in a multilingual training context. In particular, we use a multilingual pretrained model such as the MBART-50 (Tang et al., 2020) (more information in Section 4). This configuration allows us to explore different approaches to build models. We take advantage of this multilingual setting to propose alternatives to improve the Japanese-to-Indonesian and Japanese-to-Malaysian translations.

The MBART-50 is a sequence-to-sequence model trained on 50 languages (Many-to-Many language directions, pivoting via English).[1] The model is built following the work of Liu et al. (2020). First, a denoising autoencoder on different languages is trained. Then, they performed multilingual training using parallel data where each sentence (both source and target) has a language identifier tag attached in the beginning.

In this work, we refer as "train" to the process of training the MBART-50 model, although in practice

[1] `https://github.com/facebookresearch/fairseq/tree/main/examples/multilingual#mbart50-models`

it corresponds to a fine-tuning task. The term "finetune" is used exclusively to describe the process of further tuning a model that has already been trained with our data.

A summary of our experiments is presented in Figure 1 where we display different configurations of inclusion of language directions. A straightforward approach to address the problem would be to build one MT model in each language direction (**OneDirect**, Figure 1a). We use this setting as the baseline. One common alternative to benefit from both languages is to concatenate the datasets (**OneConcat**, Figure 1b). In our case, we append the training sentence pairs from JA-MS into that of JA-ID. Then we execute the training assuming JA→ID direction (which is preferable to JA→MS because our pretrained model, MBART-50, has not been trained on Malaysian sentences).

This study explores mostly how the translation quality can improve when the MT models of similar languages such as Indonesian and Malaysian are trained together instead as a separate translation direction. Therefore, we build a model where the train consist on a multilingual training using both JA-ID and JA-MS data (**MultDirect**, Figure 1c).

Additionally, we are also interested in exploring the impact of introducing additional similar language pairs. Particularly, we explore increasing the language direction in two cases: **MultPart**, which involves adding EN→ID and EN→MS directions, including therefore an additional language in the source side (Figure 1d); and **MultFull**, which imply adding exclusively sentences on fully-related languages of the target sides, i.e. Indonesian and Malaysian (Figure 1e).

Note that, except for **OneConcat**, in all the experiments we only change the number of language directions in the training process. The training data of each language pair remains always the same.

4 Experimental Settings

To conduct the experiments, we build models based on the pretrained MBART-50 (Tang et al., 2020) model built in Fairseq (Ott et al., 2019). It consists of a transformer (Vaswani et al., 2017) model with 12 layers both in the encoder and the decoder. All the sentences, regardless of the language, are tokenized using the same sentencepiece (Kudo and Richardson, 2018) model. The vocabulary of encoder and decoder is shared.

We use the data from "CCMatrix" (Fan et al., 2021; Schwenk et al., 2021) and "TED2020" (Reimers and Gurevych, 2020) for training and evaluation, respectively. Then, we use "FLORES-101" (Goyal et al., 2022) dataset for evaluation. The size of these datasets can be found in Table 1. The number of sentences of JA-MS is much smaller than JA-ID. In addition, we also calculated the number of shared vocabulary between the Indonesian and Malaysian parts of our training dataset. As can be seen in Table 2, both languages shared a substantial amount of vocabulary in our dataset in particular.

Dataset	JA-ID	JA-MS
train	7.7M	1.7M
dev	156K	11K
test	1K	1K

Table 1: Number of sentences for each dataset.

Language	#Vocab	%Common
ID	485928	21.2%
MS	166682	61.8%
ID ∩ MS	103017	-

Table 2: Number of shared vocabulary between ID and MS in the CCMatrix dataset (Schwenk et al., 2021).

In those experiments were more language direction are added (i.e. **MultPart** and **MultFull**), we also use the datasets from "CCMatrix". The sizes of these are displayed in Table 3.

We use L1-L2 notation to refer to a dataset of pairs of sentences and L1→L2 to specify the translation direction. In the case of multiple translation directions from the same source language, we use L1→{L2,L3} notation. Finally, L1↔L2 implies that the translation directions are both L1→L2 and L2→L1.

5 Experimental Results

The performances of the models are evaluated using both BLEU (Papineni et al., 2002) metric, which is based on the overlap of *n*-grams, and chrF2 (Popovic, 2015) which is a character-based

Dataset	size
EN-ID	15.7M
EN-MS	5.4M
MS-ID	7.8M

Table 3: Number of sentences of the additional datasets.

metric. We present the results in Table 4. Each row shows a different model, in which the dataset shown in the column "Language Directions" is used for the training.

In the first subtable, we show the performance of **OneDirect**, i.e. bilingual MT trained on a single direction, JA→ID (row 1) or JA→MS (row 2). We use these models as baselines.

5.1 Results of Multilingual Settings

In the first set of experiments, we evaluate the models trained in multiple language directions without including additional datasets.

The subtable *"Similar language data multilingual training"* row 4 includes the results of the **MultiDirect**, which is trained in a multilingual setting in both JA→ID and JA→MS direction together. If we compare the results of these models to those of **OneDirect** we observe an increase in performance of 0.2 and 0.4 BLEU points increase.

Note that by following this configuration, the target side is not mixed and there is a clear distinction between Indonesian and Malaysian during the training. Despite that, due to the shared vocabulary, the combination is mutually beneficial. This configuration is also more efficient than simply concatenating both datasets as in **OneConcat**, which underperformed the baselines.

5.2 Results of Augmentation with More Language Directions

In the second set of experiments, we introduced additional language pairs in the training.

In the subtable *"Partially-related language data multilingual training"* we show the results of **MultPart** model. These models include EN→ID and EN→MS directions. Therefore, the set of source languages is extended with a language that is very different from Indonesian or Malaysian (or Japanese). The performance of this configuration increased when compared to those of bilingual models.

We also include the results of **MultFull** model in the subtable *"Fully-related language data multilingual training"*. This consist of three parts as ID-MS data can be integrated in three different ways: (i) ID→MS direction (row 6); (ii) ID→MS direction (row 7); and (iii) both direction ID↔MS (row 8). Although the sentences in these configurations were the same, the biggest impact is observed when both related languages are present in the target. The Inclusion of MS↔IN direction achieves a performance similar to that of **MultPart**. Note that there is some difference in the number of sentences, according to Table 3, the EN→{ID,MS} extension has $15.7M + 5.4M = 21.1M$ sentences and ID↔MS has $2 * 7.8M = 15.6M$.

Interestingly, according to both BLEU and chrF2 metrics, by including only ID→MS or MS→ID directions (rows 6 and 7), the performance is lower than the **OneDirect** baseline. Therefore, simply adding more language directions is not a guarantee of improvement. This effect may be a consequence of the model aiming to find an optimal equilibrium of performance between more language pairs, and therefore it may underperform on those that we are interested in.

5.3 Additional Stage of Fine-tuning

As seen in the previous section, including several languages may harm the quality of the translation of the directions we are evaluating because the training needs to be optimized for more languages.

We suspect that the models could be further optimized for the task on hand. For this reason, we also fine-tune for an additional stage in JA→{ID,MS} directions. The results are shown in the *"+fine-tune"* rows of Table 4.

In these rows, we observe that the performance can increase further. Moreover, some models that underperformed the **OneDirect** baselines, such as **MultFull** where only MS→ID or ID→MS were included, surpassed the baselines after executing an additional fine-tune.

A question that still is left to answer is whether this second stage of fine-tuning should be performed on JA→ID and JA→MS individually or JA→{ID,MS} together. We present in Table 5 the fine-grained results. In this case, the difference in performance is not big. If we compare the *+ fine-tune JA→ID* or *+ fine-tune JA→MS* rows with their corresponding *+ fine-tune JA →{ID, MS}* row in the same subtables, the differences are in the $[-0.2, +0.1]$ BLEU range and $[-0.41, +0.08]$ chrF2 range.

6 Discussion

6.1 Error Analysis of Translation Examples

In Table 6 we show some examples of the translations generated by our models. In particular, we show the outputs of: (i) **OneDirect**, i.e. the baseline models; (ii) **OneConcat**, where training data is concatenated; (iii) **MultPart**, with addition of

No.	Language Directions	JA → ID		JA → MS	
		BLEU	chrF2	BLEU	chrF2
OneDirect - *Single direction training with task data - Fig.1a*					
1.	JA → ID	18.2	49.88	-	-
2.	JA → MS	-	-	15.6	48.86
OneConcat - *Similar language data concatenation - Fig.1b*					
3.	JA → (ID + MS)	17.6	49.15	9.5	41.48
MultDirect - *Similar language data multilingual training - Fig.1c*					
4.	JA →{ID, MS}	18.4	50.14	16.0	49.18
	+ fine-tune JA → ID	18.3	49.40	-	-
	+ fine-tune JA → MS	-	-	16.8	50.13
MultPart - *Partially-related language data multilingual training - Fig.1d*					
5.	JA →{ID, MS}, EN → {ID,MS}	19.3	50.38	16.2	49.20
	+ fine-tune JA →{ID, MS}	20.0	51.69	17.0	50.31
MultFull - *Fully-related language data multilingual training - Fig.1e*					
6.	JA →{ID, MS}, ID → MS	17.0	49.19	15.7	49.16
	+ fine-tune JA →{ID, MS}	18.9	50.49	16.9	49.76
7.	JA →{ID, MS}, MS → ID	17.7	49.67	14.7	48.43
	+ fine-tune JA →{ID, MS}	18.5	49.91	16.6	48.96
8.	JA →{ID, MS}, ID ↔ MS	19.3	50.61	16.6	49.59
	+ fine-tune JA →{ID, MS}	19.9	51.22	16.8	49.94

Table 4: Experiment results.

No.	Language Directions	JA → ID		JA → MS	
		BLEU	chrF2	BLEU	chrF2
OneDirect - *Single direction training with task data - Fig.1a*					
1.	JA → ID	18.2	49.88	-	-
2.	JA → MS	-	-	15.6	48.86
MultPart - *Partially-related language data multilingual training - Fig.1d*					
5.	JA →{ID, MS}, EN → {ID,MS}	19.3	50.38	16.2	49.20
	+ fine-tune JA →{ID, MS}	20.0	51.69	17.0	50.31
	+ fine-tune JA → ID	20.1	51.54	-	-
	+ fine-tune JA → MS	-	-	16.8	50.35
MultFull - *Fully-related language data multilingual training - Fig.1e*					
8.	JA →{ID, MS}, ID ↔ MS	19.3	50.61	16.6	49.59
	+ fine-tune JA →{ID, MS}	19.9	51.22	16.8	49.94
	+ fine-tune JA → ID	20.0	51.30	-	-
	+ fine-tune JA → MS	-	-	16.6	49.53

Table 5: Results of different fine-tuning combination.

#	Direction	System	Text
#1		Source	群島は半島の北120 kmに位置します。最大の島はキングジョージ島で、そこにビジャ・ラス・エストレージャスの集落があります。
		Ref. (EN)	The archipelago lies 120 km north of the Peninsula. The largest is King George Island with the settlement of Villa Las Estrellas.
		OneConcat	島 terletak 120 km di utara Semenanjung, dan pulau terbesar adalah Pulau King George, di mana Anda dapat menemukan permukian di Bija Las Estrellas.
	Japanese to Indonesian	Ref. (ID)	Kepulauan ini terletak 120 km dari utara Semenanjung. Pulau terbesar adalah Pulau King George yang memiliki pemukiman Villa Las Estrellas.
		OneDirect	Pulau ini terletak di 120 km sebelah utara Semenanjung, dan pulau terbesarnya adalah Pulau King George, di mana terdapat permukiman Raja Ruth-Estrajas.
		MultDirect	Kepulauan ini terletak di 120 km sebelah utara semenanjung, dan pulau terbesar adalah Pulau King George, di mana terdapat permukiman Raja Las Straights.
		MultPart	Gugusan ini terletak 120 km sebelah utara semenanjung, pulau terbesar adalah Pulau King George, di mana terdapat permukiman warga Bija Ras Estonia.
	Japanese to Malaysian	Ref. (MS)	Kepulauan itu terbentang 120 km utara di Semenanjung. Pulau yang terbesar adalah King George Island dengan penempatan Villa Las Estrellas.
		OneDirect	Pulau ini terletak 120 km di utara Semenanjung, dan pulau terbesarnya adalah Pulau King George, di mana Anda dapat menemukan permukiman Angkor.
		MultDirect	Kepulauan ini terletak 120 km di utara semenanjung, dan pulau terbesar adalah King George Island, di mana terdapat perkampungan Vijay Rasheed.
		MultPart	Terletak 120 km di utara semenanjung, pulau terbesar adalah Pulau King George, di mana terdapat sebuah pengumpulan Bija Ras Estonia.
#2		Source	最後に、昆虫、げっ歯類、トカゲ、鳥といったはるかに多数の小さい獲物を餌とする小型の猫（野良猫を含む）が数多く生息しています。
		Ref. (EN)	Finally, there are many small cats (including loose pet cats) that eat the far more numerous small prey like insects, rodents, lizards, and birds.
		OneConcat	Akhirnya, banyak kucing-kucing kecil (termasuk kucing liar) yang memberi makan banyak mangsa kecil seperti serangga, gigi betina, kutub, dan burung.
	Japanese to Indonesian	Ref. (ID)	Yang terakhir, ada banyak kucing kecil (termasuk kucing peliharaan yang lepas) yang memakan jauh lebih banyak mangsa kecil seperti serangga, binatang pengerat, kadal, dan burung.
		OneDirect	Akhirnya, ada banyak serangga, jamur, katak, dan burung yang jauh lebih sedikit mangsa (termasuk kucing liar) yang memberi makan kucing-kucing kecil.
		MultDirect	Akhirnya, ada banyak kucing kecil (termasuk kucing liar) yang memberi makan banyak mangsa kecil seperti serangga, belalang, kadal, dan burung.
		MultPart	Akhirnya, ada banyak kucing kecil (termasuk kucing liar) yang memakan banyak mangsa yang lebih kecil, seperti serangga, belalang, kadal, dan burung.
	Japanese to Malaysian	Ref. (MS)	Akhir sekali, terdapat banyak kucing bersaiz kecil (termasuk kucing liar) yang memakan lebih banyak mangsa kecil seperti serangga, tikus, cicak dan burung.
		OneDirect	Akhirnya, banyak kucing-kucing kecil (termasuk kucing liar) yang memakan banyak mangsa yang lebih kecil seperti serangga, gigi betina, topeng, dan burung.
		MultDirect	Akhir sekali, terdapat banyak kucing kecil (termasuk kucing liar) yang memberi makan kepada banyak mangsa kecil seperti serangga, belalang, cicak dan burung.
		MultPart	Akhir sekali, terdapat banyak kucing kecil (termasuk kucing liar) yang memakan banyak mangsa yang lebih kecil, seperti serangga, beruang kutub, cicak dan burung.
#3		Source	科学者たちは、暗黒物質は、通常の物質と同じように他の暗黒物質にも影響を与えていると結論づけました。
		Ref. (EN)	The scientists were able to conclude that the dark matter affect other dark matter in the same way regular matter does.
		OneConcat	: Para ilmuwan menyimpulkan bahwa materi gelap juga mempengaruhi materi gelap lainnya seperti biasa.
	Japanese to Indonesian	Ref. (ID)	Para ilmuwan dapat menyimpulkan bahwa materi gelap mempengaruhi materi gelap lainnya dengan cara yang sama seperti materi biasa.
		OneDirect	Para ilmuwan menyimpulkan bahwa materi gelap juga mempengaruhi materi gelap lainnya seperti materi normal.
		MultDirect	Para ilmuwan menyimpulkan bahwa materi gelap mempengaruhi materi gelap lainnya seperti materi biasa.
		MultPart	Para ilmuwan menyimpulkan bahwa materi gelap juga mempengaruhi materi gelap lainnya, seperti materi biasa.
	Japanese to Malaysian	Ref. (MS)	Para saintis dapat menyimpulkan bahawa jirim gelap menjejaskan jirim gelap yang lain dalam cara yang sama dengan jirim biasa.
		OneDirect	Para ilmuwan menyimpulkan bahwa materi gelap juga mempengaruhi materi gelap lainnya seperti biasa.
		MultDirect	Para saintis menyimpulkan bahawa bahan gelap mempunyai kesan yang sama dengan bahan gelap yang lain seperti bahan biasa.
		MultPart	Para saintis menyimpulkan bahawa bahan gelap juga mempunyai kesan ke atas bahan gelap yang lain, sama seperti bahan biasa

Table 6: Translation examples.

partially-related language data; and (iv) **MultFull** using *ID↔MS* configuration. For (iii) and (iv), we show the output of fine-tuned version (i.e. *+ fine-tune JA* →{*ID, MS*}, which are those that shown the highest performance).

In the first sentence of the table, the translation of "群島" (i.e. "archipelago" in English) is referred as "kepulauan" in the reference. However, the baselines incorrectly generate "pulau" which means "island" and the **OneConcat** method simply copied a Japanese character from the source. The models with additional language directions produced the same word as the reference (i.e. "kepulauan"), or "gugusan", which is also correct.

In this sentence, we can also find an example of the limitation of these systems, which is the translation of proper nouns from katakana (which are the Japanese characters used to transliterate foreign terms into Japanese). For example, the source sentence includes the term "ビジャ・ラス・エストレージャス" which is the transliteration from Spanish of the name of the settlement called "Villa Las Estrellas". In the translations, only **OneConcat** system was partially correct. The other models proposed different incorrect romanizations of the name.

The word 最後に (i.e. "finally") is translated as "akhirnya" by baseline models. Although it is correct, in Malaysian "akhir sekali", is more common. This term is only present in those models with additional data included. Note also that on this models, the term is clearly differentiated in Indonesian and Malaysian. The translation of "cats" (as in "many cats") can be either "banyak kucing" or "kucing-kucing", however some baselines (i.e. JA→MS and JA→(ID+MS)) generate a wrong combination of "banyak kucing-kucing". This is corrected in the models with extra data. A similar outcome happens with the translation of the list "昆虫、げっ歯類、トカゲ、鳥" ("serangga, binatang pengerat, kadal, dan burung", which in English is "insects, rodents, lizards, and birds"). The baselines fail to translate correctly some of these whereas **MultPart** and **MultFull** models translate them accurately.

In the last sentence, the translations of "scientists" (科学者たち), "material" (物質), or "that" are translated into Indonesian as "ilmuwan", "materi" and "bahwa", respectively. In Malaysian, these terms are more commonly translated as "saintis", "jirim" and "bahawa". We can see that in the reference, and also we find more occurrences of them in the JA-MS training data. Despite that, the model trained on JA→MS produced the Indonesian terms instead. This shows that the pretrained MBART-50 model (built only with Indonesian data) has influenced the output. The models with additional data were able to learn this difference, and we see that the Malaysian outputs include the Malaysian terms.

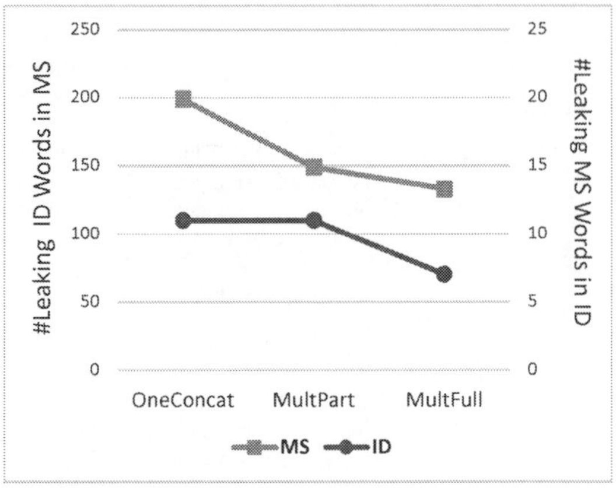

Figure 2: Number of vocabulary that leaks into the other language. Our proposed training strategy successfully decrease the number, which yields better fluency in the generated translation.

6.2 Vocabulary Leak

As seen in the previous subsection, we could find some words that are not present in the training data of their corresponding language in the generated translation. Some of these words, however, can be found in the training data of the counterpart language. This suggests that some terms were unintentionally transferred (i.e. leaked) from one language into another. This might imply that although both languages are similar, the model is mixing the language too much. This will make the model hypotheses becomes unnatural due to decreasing fluency (i.e. sounds like a native Malaysian is speaking Indonesian or vice versa)

For example, in the hypothesis of **OneConcat** model, there were 11 words in the Indonesian output that came from JA-MS data, and 199 words in the Malaysian output that came from JA-ID. Hence, the vocabulary leak is more likely to happen from Indonesian to Malaysian. This is explained by the fact that MBART-50 model is built on Indonesian, and also because the size of JA-ID data is larger (Table 1).

Despite that, **MultPart** and **MultFull** models, which were trained with more sentences, the Indonesian-to-Malaysian vocabulary leak decreased from 199 to 149 (inclusion of EN→{ID,MS}) and to 133 (inclusion of ID↔MS). In the opposite direction, only the **MultFull** caused to decrease from 11 to 7 occurrences. Note that the difference in scale between Indonesian and Malaysian (133 to 7) is due to the dataset size and domain differences.

Nevertheless, the decrease in leaking words number (Figure 2) shows that our proposed method is crucial to let the model better differentiate between the two languages. Although we have shown that the two languages are similar, the model still needs to differentiate between two languages. Therefore, the integrity of the vocabulary is maintained, which increases fluency in the generated translation.

7 Conclusion and Future Work

In this work, we explored different techniques to improve the training of MT models to translate from Japanese into Indonesian and Malaysian. As finding resources in these target languages is not always easy, we focused on how to benefit from their similarities in multilingual conditions.

The results showed how training in both directions jointly boosts the translation quality of each translation. However, an interesting outcome is that simply including additional language pairs alone does not necessarily lead to improvements. In some cases, an additional step of fine-tuning was required so the models achieve higher performances than those built in a single direction.

We believe that the outcomes of these experiments are also applicable to other languages. In the future, we want to explore this approach for other language families, such as Romance or Slavic, or even dialects or variations of the same language. Some of them may also be low-resourced and it may be difficult to find enough data to build competitive MT models. On top of that, the techniques investigated in this study are complementary to other strategies (e.g. data augmentation, zero-shot learning) that are commonly used to increase the performance of low-resourced MT models. Accordingly, we suppose that a combination of them with our proposed training strategy could further improve the translation performance.

References

AiTi Aw, Sharifah Mahani Aljunied, Lianhau Lee, and Haizhou Li. 2009. Piramid: Bahasa Indonesia and Bahasa Malaysia translation system enhanced through comparable corpora. In *TCAST*.

Johanes Effendi, Sakriani Sakti, Katsuhito Sudoh, and Satoshi Nakamura. 2018. Multi-paraphrase augmentation to leverage neural caption translation. In *Proceedings of the 15th International Conference on Spoken Language Translation*, pages 181–188, Brussels.

Angela Fan, Shruti Bhosale, Holger Schwenk, Zhiyi Ma, Ahmed El-Kishky, Siddharth Goyal, Mandeep Baines, Onur Celebi, Guillaume Wenzek, Vishrav Chaudhary, et al. 2021. Beyond english-centric multilingual machine translation. *J. Mach. Learn. Res.*, 22(107):1–48.

Naman Goyal, Cynthia Gao, Vishrav Chaudhary, Peng-Jen Chen, Guillaume Wenzek, Da Ju, Sanjana Krishnan, Marc'Aurelio Ranzato, Francisco Guzman, and Angela Fan. 2022. The flores-101 evaluation benchmark for low-resource and multilingual machine translation. *Transactions of the Association for Computational Linguistics*, 10:522–538.

Vu Cong Duy Hoang, Philipp Koehn, Gholamreza Haffari, and Trevor Cohn. 2018. Iterative back-translation for neural machine translation. In *Proceedings of the 2nd workshop on neural machine translation and generation*, pages 18–24, Melbourne, Australia,.

Taku Kudo and John Richardson. 2018. Sentencepiece: A simple and language independent subword tokenizer and detokenizer for neural text processing. In *Proceedings of the 2018 Conference on Empirical Methods in Natural Language Processing: System Demonstrations*, pages 66–71, Brussels, Belgium.

Yinhan Liu, Jiatao Gu, Naman Goyal, Xian Li, Sergey Edunov, Marjan Ghazvininejad, Mike Lewis, and Luke Zettlemoyer. 2020. Multilingual denoising pre-training for neural machine translation. *Transactions of the Association for Computational Linguistics*, 8:726–742.

Ramtin Mehdizadeh Seraj, Maryam Siahbani, and Anoop Sarkar. 2015. Improving statistical machine translation with a multilingual paraphrase database. In *Proceedings of the 2015 Conference on Empirical Methods in Natural Language Processing*, pages 1379–1390, Lisbon, Portugal. Association for Computational Linguistics.

Preslav Nakov and Hwee Tou Ng. 2012. Improving statistical machine translation for a resource-poor language using related resource-rich languages. *Journal of Artificial Intelligence Research*, 44:179–222.

NLLB Team, Marta R. Costa-jussà, James Cross, Onur Çelebi, Maha Elbayad, Kenneth Heafield, Kevin Heffernan, Elahe Kalbassi, Janice Lam, Daniel Licht,

Jean Maillard, Anna Sun, Skyler Wang, Guillaume Wenzek, Al Youngblood, Bapi Akula, Loic Barrault, Gabriel Mejia Gonzalez, Prangthip Hansanti, John Hoffman, Semarley Jarrett, Kaushik Ram Sadagopan, Dirk Rowe, Shannon Spruit, Chau Tran, Pierre Andrews, Necip Fazil Ayan, Shruti Bhosale, Sergey Edunov, Angela Fan, Cynthia Gao, Vedanuj Goswami, Francisco Guzmán, Philipp Koehn, Alexandre Mourachko, Christophe Ropers, Safiyyah Saleem, Holger Schwenk, and Jeff Wang. 2022. No language left behind: Scaling human-centered machine translation.

Myle Ott, Sergey Edunov, Alexei Baevski, Angela Fan, Sam Gross, Nathan Ng, David Grangier, and Michael Auli. 2019. fairseq: A fast, extensible toolkit for sequence modeling. In *Proceedings of NAACL-HLT 2019: Demonstrations*, Minneapolis, USA.

Scott H Paauw. 2009. *The Malay contact varieties of Eastern Indonesia: A typological comparison*. State University of New York at Buffalo.

Kishore Papineni, Salim Roukos, Todd Ward, and Wei-Jing Zhu. 2002. Bleu: a method for automatic evaluation of machine translation. In *Proceedings of 40th Annual Meeting of the Association for Computational Linguistics*, pages 311–318, Philadelphia, Pennsylvania, USA.

Maja Popovic. 2015. chrF: character n-gram F-score for automatic MT evaluation. In *Proceedings of the Tenth Workshop on Statistical Machine Translation*, pages 392–395, Lisbon, Portugal.

Nils Reimers and Iryna Gurevych. 2020. Making monolingual sentence embeddings multilingual using knowledge distillation. In *Proceedings of the 2020 Conference on Empirical Methods in Natural Language Processing*. Association for Computational Linguistics.

Holger Schwenk, Guillaume Wenzek, Sergey Edunov, Édouard Grave, Armand Joulin, and Angela Fan. 2021. Ccmatrix: Mining billions of high-quality parallel sentences on the web. In *Proceedings of the 59th Annual Meeting of the Association for Computational Linguistics and the 11th International Joint Conference on Natural Language Processing (Volume 1: Long Papers)*, pages 6490–6500, Bangkok, Thailand.

Yuuki Sekizawa, Tomoyuki Kajiwara, and Mamoru Komachi. 2017. Improving Japanese-to-English neural machine translation by paraphrasing the target language. In *Proceedings of the 4th Workshop on Asian Translation (WAT2017)*, pages 64–69, Taipei, Taiwan.

Rico Sennrich, Barry Haddow, and Alexandra Birch. 2016. Improving neural machine translation models with monolingual data. In *Proceedings of the 54th Annual Meeting of the Association for Computational Linguistics (Volume 1: Long Papers)*, pages 86–96, Berlin, Germany.

Noam Shazeer, Azalia Mirhoseini, Krzysztof Maziarz, Andy Davis, Quoc Le, Geoffrey Hinton, and Jeff Dean. 2017. Outrageously large neural networks: The sparsely-gated mixture-of-experts layer. In *The 5th International Conference on Learning Representations, ICLR*, Toulon, France.

Raymond Hendy Susanto, Septina Dian Larasati, and Francis Tyers. 2012. Rule-based machine translation between indonesian and malaysian. In *Proceedings of the 3rd Workshop on South and Southeast Asian Natural Language Processing*, pages 191–200, Mumbai, India.

Yuqing Tang, Chau Tran, Xian Li, Peng-Jen Chen, Naman Goyal, Vishrav Chaudhary, Jiatao Gu, and Angela Fan. 2020. Multilingual translation with extensible multilingual pretraining and finetuning. *arXiv preprint arXiv:2008.00401*.

Ashish Vaswani, Noam Shazeer, Niki Parmar, Jakob Uszkoreit, Llion Jones, Aidan N Gomez, Łukasz Kaiser, and Illia Polosukhin. 2017. Attention is all you need. In *Advances in neural information processing systems*, pages 5998–6008, Long Beach, USA.

Zhong Zhou, Matthias Sperber, and Alexander Waibel. 2019. Paraphrases as foreign languages in multilingual neural machine translation. In *Proceedings of the 57th Annual Meeting of the Association for Computational Linguistics: Student Research Workshop*, pages 113–122, Florence, Italy.

Barret Zoph, Deniz Yuret, Jonathan May, and Kevin Knight. 2016. Transfer learning for low-resource neural machine translation. In *Proceedings of the 2016 Conference on Empirical Methods in Natural Language Processing*, pages 1568–1575, Austin,Texas,USA.

A Preordered RNN Layer Boosts Neural Machine Translation in Low Resource Settings

Mohaddeseh Bastan
Stony Brook University
mbastan@cs.stonybrook.edu

Shahram Khadivi*
Amirkabir University of Technology
khadivi@aut.ac.ir

Abstract

Neural Machine Translation (NMT) models are strong enough to convey semantic and syntactic information from the source language to the target language. However, these models are suffering from the need for a large amount of data to learn the parameters. As a result, for languages with scarce data, these models are at risk of underperforming. We propose to augment attention based neural network with reordering information to alleviate the lack of data. This augmentation improves the translation quality for both English to Persian and Persian to English by up to 6% BLEU absolute over the baseline models.

1 Introduction

NMT has recently shown promising results in machine translation (Wu et al., 2016; Luong et al., 2015; Bastan et al., 2017). In statistical machine translation (SMT), the problem is decomposed into sub-models and each individual model is trained separately, while NMT is capable of training an end-to-end model. For instance, in SMT the reordering model is a feature that is trained separately and is used jointly with other features to improve the translation, while in NMT it is assumed that the model will learn the order of the words and phrases itself.

Sequence-to-sequence NMT models consist of two parts, an encoder to encode the input sequence to the hidden state and a decoder that decodes the hidden state to get the output sequence (Cho et al., 2014; Bahdanau et al., 2014). The encoder model is a bidirectional Recurrent Neural Network (RNN), the source sentence is processed once from the beginning to the end and once in parallel from the end to the beginning. One of the ideas that have not been well-explored in NMT so far is the use of existing reordering models in SMT. We propose to add another layer to the encoder that includes reordering information. The intuition behind our proposal comes from the improvement achieved by bidirectional encoder model. If processing the source sentence in both directions help sequence-to-sequence model to learn better representation of the context in hidden states, adding the order of the input words as they are appearing in the output sequence as another layer may also help the model to learn a better representation in both context vectors and hidden states. In this paper we investigate this hypothesis that another layer in the encoder to process a preordered sentence can outperform both encoder architecture with two or three RNN layers. We empirically show in the experiments that adding the reordering information to NMT can improve the translation quality when we are in shortage of data.

There are a few attempts to improve the SMT using neural reordering models (Cui et al., 2015; Li et al., 2014, 2013; Aghasadeghi and Bastan, 2015). In Zhang et al. (2017), three distortion models have been studied to incorporate the word reordering knowledge into NMT. They used reordering information to mainly improve the attention mechanism.

In this paper, we are using a soft reordering model to improve the bidirectional attention based NMT. This model consists of two different parts. The first part is creating the soft reordering information using the input and output sequence, the second part is using this information in the attention based NMT.

The rest of the paper is as follow, in section 2 a review of sequence-to-sequence NMT is provided, in section 3 the preordered model is proposed, section 4 explains the experiments and results, and section 5 concludes the paper.

* This work is done in 2017 when Shahram Khadivi was with Amirkabir University of Technology.

Proceedings of the 29th International Conference on Computational Linguistic, pages 93–98
October 12–17, 2022.

2 Sequence-to-Sequence NMT

Bahdanau et al. (2014) proposed a joint translation and alignment model which can both learn the translation and the alignment between the source and the target sequence. In this model the decoder at each time step, finds the maximum probability of the output word y_i given the previous output words $y_1, ..., y_{i-1}$ and the input sequence X as follow:

$$p(y_i|y_1, ..., y_{i-1}, X) = softmax(g(y_{i-1}, s_i, c_i)) \quad (1)$$

Where X is the input sequence, g is a nonlinear function, s_i is the hidden state, and c_i the context vector using to predict output i. s_i is the hidden state at the current step which is defined as follow:

$$s_i = f(s_{i-1}, y_{i-1}, c_i) \quad (2)$$

The notation c_i is the context vector for output word y_i. The context vector is the weighted sum of the hidden states as follow:

$$c_i = \sum_{j=1}^{T} \alpha_{ij} h_j \quad (3)$$

The weights in this model are normalized outputs of the alignment model which is a feed-forward neural network. It uses s_{i-1} and h_j as input and outputs a score e_{ij}. This score is then normalized and used as the weight for computing the context vector as follow:

$$\alpha_{ij} = \frac{\exp(e_{ij})}{\sum_{k=1}^{T}(\exp e_{ik})} \quad (4)$$

In the encoder, a bidirectional neural network is used to produce the hidden state h. For each input word x_i there is a forward and a backward hidden state computed as follow respectively:

$$\overrightarrow{h_i} = \overrightarrow{f}(\overrightarrow{h_{i-1}}, x_i) \quad (5)$$

$$\overleftarrow{h_i} = \overleftarrow{f}(\overleftarrow{h_{i-1}}, x_i) \quad (6)$$

Forward and backward hidden states are then concatenated to produce the hidden state h_i as follow:

$$h_i = [\overrightarrow{h_i}, \overleftarrow{h_i}] \quad (7)$$

3 Preordered RNN

The attention-based model is able to address some of the shortcomings of the simple encoder-decoder model for machine translation. It works fine when we have plenty of data. But if we are in lack of data the attention-based model suffers from lack of information for tuning all the parameters. We can use some other information of the input data to inject into the model and get even better results. In this paper, a model is proposed using reordering information of the data set to address the issue of shortage of data. Adding this information to the model, it can improve the attention-based NMT significantly.

3.1 Building Soft Reordered Data

Adding a preordered layer to the encoder of the sequence model boosts the translation quality. This layer add some information to the model which previously hasn't been seen. The preordered data is the source sentence which is reordered using the information in target sentence. The reordered models have been used in statistical machine translation and they could improve the translation quality (Visweswariah et al., 2011; Tromble and Eisner, 2009; Khalilov et al., 2010; Collins et al., 2005; Xia and McCord, 2004).

To obtain the soft reordering model, we first need to have the word alignment between the source and the target sentences, then by using heuristic rules we change the alignment to reordering. The reordered sequence model is built upon the alignment model. First by using GIZA++ (Och and Ney, 2003) the alignment model between the input sequence and output sequence is derived. The main difference between reordering and alignment is that alignment is a many-to-many relation, while the reordering is a one-to-one relation. It means one word in the input sequence can be aligned to many words in the output sequence while it can be reordered to just one position. The other difference is that the alignment is a relation from input sequence space to output sequence space while the reordering is a relation from input sequence space to itself. So we propose some heuristic rules to convert the alignment relation to the reordering relation as follow:

- If a word x in the input sequence is aligned to one and only one word y in the output sequence, the position of x in the reordering model will be the position of y.
- If a word x in the input sequence is aligned to a series of words in the output sequence, the position of x in the reordering model will be

the position of the middle word in the series[1].

- If a word in the input sequence is not aligned to any word in the output sequence, the position for that word is the average positions of the previous and the next word.

These heuristic rules are inspired by the rules which have been proposed in Devlin et al. (2014). The difference is that they are trying to align one and only one input word to all output words, but we are trying to align each word in the input sequence to one and only one position in the same space.
The order of applying these rules is important. We should apply the first rule, then the second rule and finally the third rule to all possible words. If a word is aligned to a position but that position is full, we align it to the nearest empty position. We arbitrarily prioritize the left position to the right position whenever they have the same priority. At the end, each word is aligned with only one position, but there may be some positions which are empty. We just remove the empty positions between words to map the sparse output space to the dense input space. We can build the reordered training data using these rules and use them for training the model. In the next section, we see how the reordered data is used in the bidirectional attention based NMT.

3.2 Three-layer Encoder

The bidirectional encoder has two different layers. The first layer consists of the forward hidden states built by reading the input sequence from left to right and the second layer consists of the backward hidden states, built by reading the input sequence from right to left. We add another hidden layer to the encoder which is built by reading the input sequence in the reordered order. We build the hidden layer of the reordered input as follow:

$$hr_i = f(hr_{i-1}, xr_i) \tag{8}$$

Here xr_i is the word in position i of the reordered data and hr_i is the hidden representation of x_i in reordered set. The function for computing hr is the same as in equation 5 and 6. Then the hidden representation h is computed by concatenating the forward hidden layer, backward hidden layer and reordering hidden layer as follow:

$$h_i = [\overrightarrow{h_i}, \overleftarrow{h_i}, hr_i] \tag{9}$$

[1]We arbitrary round down the even number. For example, the middle position between 1,3,5,7 is the 3rd position.

Corpus	#sents	#words	
		English	Persian
Training	26142	264235	242154
Development	276	3442	3339
Test	250	2856	2668

Table 1: The statistics of data set

4 Experiments

The proposed model has been evaluated on English-Persian translation data set. We believe that adding the reordering information results in a better model in case of low resource data. We evaluate the translation quality based on BLEU (Papineni et al., 2002) and TER (Snover et al., 2006). For implementation we use the Theano (Bergstra et al., 2011) framework.

4.1 Dataset

We use Verbmobil (Bakhshaei et al., 2010), an English-Persian data set, this data set can show the effectiveness of the model on scarce data resources. The detailed information of the data set is provided in 1. In this table, the number of words, shown with #words, number of sentences in each corpus is shown in column #sents.

4.2 Baseline

The baseline model for our experiments is the bidirectional attention based neural network (Bahdanau et al., 2014) as explained in section 1. There are various papers to improve the basic attention based decoder of the baseline, among all we used guided alignment (Chen et al., 2016).

4.3 Reordering Development and Test Set

For building the reordered training set, we use alignment model and heuristic rules. For development and test set, as we don't have access to the target language, we use a preordering algorithm proposed in Nakagawa (2015). This algorithm is the improved version of preordering algorithm based on Bracketing Transduction Grammar (BTG). Briefly, this algorithm builds a tree based on the words, so that each node has a feature vector and a weight vector. Among all possible trees on the data set, the tree with maximum value for the weighted sum of the feature vectors is chosen

Reordering Method

Training Set	Dev/Test Set	BLEU	TER
HG	BI	30.53	53.25
BI	BI	27.91	56.68
BG	BG	25.93	58.1

Table 2: The comparison between different reordering methods on Verbmobil data. HG means the data reordered using alignment model with GDFA and heuristic rules, BI and BG means the data is reordered on intersection alignment and GDFA alignment, respectively, both using (Nakagawa, 2015) algorithm.

as reordering tree. Using a projection function, the tree is converted into the reordered output.
This algorithm also needs part of speech (POS) tagger and word class. For Persian POS tagging we use CMU NLP Farsi tool (Feely et al., 2014) and for the English POS tagging, we use Stanford POS tagger (Toutanova et al., 2003). For word class we use the GIZA ++ word class which is an output of creating alignment.

4.4 Results

We analyzed our model with different configurations. First we use different methods to reorder training, development and test set. The results are shown in 2. In this table, the best results of different combinations for building reordered data is shown. HG means for building the reordered data, heuristic rules and alignment with GDFA (Koehn, 2005) is used. BI means the algorithm in (Nakagawa, 2015) and alignment with intersection method is used to build the reordered data, BG means alignment with GDFA and reordering algorithm in (Nakagawa, 2015) is used. The best possible combinations are shown in Table 2.

In Table 3 we can compare the best 3-layer network with two different 2-layer networks. The 3-layer network has apparently three layers in the encoder, the first two layers are the forward and the backward RNNs, the third layer is again an RNN trained either on the reordered source sentence or the original sentence. The 2-layer network refers to the bidirectional attention based NMT as described in Section 2. This model id trained once with the original sentence, and once with the reordered sentence. As we see, reordering the input can improve the model. It shows that the information we are adding to our model is useful. So using the best 3layer model can use both information of reordering and information of the ordered

Reordering Method

Data set	Model	BLEU	TER
En $\rightarrow$ Pr	Baseline SMT	30.47	–
	Baseline NMT	27.42	50.78
	3-layer RpL	27.58	50.04
	2-layer RI	29.6	50.96
	3-layer RL	31.03	47.5
	Ensemble	**32.74**	**46.4**
Pr $\rightarrow$ En	Baseline SMT	26.91	–
	Baseline NMT	26.12	55.87
	3-layer RpL	26.38	57.42
	2-layer RI	27.52	54.12
	3-layer RL	30.53	53.25
	Ensemble	**32.17**	**52.12**

Table 3: The comparison between different models. base line in SMT is the result of translation in statistical machine translation. The base line NMT is the bidirectional attention based neural network using guided alignment (Bahdanau et al., 2014; Chen et al., 2016). The 2layer RI is the basic model with reordered input. The 3layer RL is the model proposed in this paper. The 3layer RpL is a 3layer model with two forward and one backward layers (No reordering layer). The ensemble model is the combination of different models.

data, so it can improve the translation model significantly. Also we see that adding just a simple repeated layer to bidirectional encoder, can improve the model. But not as much as the reordered layer. Finally, the ensemble of different models has the best results.
There are different interpretations behind this results. Because NMT has too many parameters, it is difficult for scarce data to learn all of the parameters correctly. So adding explicit information using the same data can help the model to learn the parameters better. In addition, although we expect that all the statistical features we use in SMT automatically be trained in NMT, but it can not learn them as well as SMT.

5 Conclusion

In this paper we analyzed adding reordering information to NMTs. NMTs are strong because they can translate the source language into target without breaking the problem into sub problems. In this paper we proposed a model using explicit information which covers the hidden feature like reordering. The improvements is the result of adding extra information to the model, and helping the neural network learn the parameters in case of scarce data better.

References

Amir Pouya Aghasadeghi and Mohadeseh Bastan. 2015. Monolingually derived phrase scores for phrase based smt using neural networks vector representations. *arXiv preprint arXiv:1506.00406*.

Dzmitry Bahdanau, Kyunghyun Cho, and Yoshua Bengio. 2014. Neural machine translation by jointly learning to align and translate. *arXiv preprint arXiv:1409.0473*.

Somayeh Bakhshaei, Shahram Khadivi, and Noushin Riahi. 2010. Farsi-german statistical machine translation through bridge language. In *Telecommunications (IST), 2010 5th International Symposium on*, pages 557–561. IEEE.

Mohaddeseh Bastan, Shahram Khadivi, and Mohammad Mehdi Homayounpour. 2017. Neural machine translation on scarce-resource condition: a case-study on persian-english. In *2017 Iranian Conference on Electrical Engineering (ICEE)*, pages 1485–1490. IEEE.

James Bergstra, Frédéric Bastien, Olivier Breuleux, Pascal Lamblin, Razvan Pascanu, Olivier Delalleau, Guillaume Desjardins, David Warde-Farley, Ian Goodfellow, Arnaud Bergeron, et al. 2011. Theano: Deep learning on gpus with python. In *NIPS 2011, BigLearning Workshop, Granada, Spain*, volume 3. Citeseer.

Wenhu Chen, Evgeny Matusov, Shahram Khadivi, and Jan-Thorsten Peter. 2016. Guided alignment training for topic-aware neural machine translation. *arXiv preprint arXiv:1607.01628*.

Kyunghyun Cho, Bart Van Merriënboer, Dzmitry Bahdanau, and Yoshua Bengio. 2014. On the properties of neural machine translation: Encoder-decoder approaches. *arXiv preprint arXiv:1409.1259*.

Michael Collins, Philipp Koehn, and Ivona Kučerová. 2005. Clause restructuring for statistical machine translation. In *Proceedings of the 43rd annual meeting on association for computational linguistics*, pages 531–540. Association for Computational Linguistics.

Yiming Cui, Shijin Wang, and Jianfeng Li. 2015. Lstm neural reordering feature for statistical machine translation. *arXiv preprint arXiv:1512.00177*.

Jacob Devlin, Rabih Zbib, Zhongqiang Huang, Thomas Lamar, Richard Schwartz, and John Makhoul. 2014. Fast and robust neural network joint models for statistical machine translation. In *Proceedings of the 52nd Annual Meeting of the Association for Computational Linguistics (Volume 1: Long Papers)*, volume 1, pages 1370–1380.

Weston Feely, Mehdi Manshadi, Robert E Frederking, and Lori S Levin. 2014. The cmu metal farsi nlp approach. In *LREC*, pages 4052–4055.

Maxim Khalilov, Khalil Sima'an, et al. 2010. Source reordering using maxent classifiers and supertags. In *Proc. of EAMT*, volume 10, pages 292–299.

Philipp Koehn. 2005. Europarl: A parallel corpus for statistical machine translation. In *MT summit*, volume 5, pages 79–86.

Peng Li, Yang Liu, and Maosong Sun. 2013. Recursive autoencoders for itg-based translation. In *Proceedings of the 2013 Conference on Empirical Methods in Natural Language Processing*, pages 567–577.

Peng Li, Yang Liu, Maosong Sun, Tatsuya Izuha, and Dakun Zhang. 2014. A neural reordering model for phrase-based translation. In *Proceedings of COLING 2014, the 25th International Conference on Computational Linguistics: Technical Papers*, pages 1897–1907.

Minh-Thang Luong, Hieu Pham, and Christopher D Manning. 2015. Effective approaches to attention-based neural machine translation. *arXiv preprint arXiv:1508.04025*.

Tetsuji Nakagawa. 2015. Efficient top-down btg parsing for machine translation preordering. In *Proceedings of the 53rd Annual Meeting of the Association for Computational Linguistics and the 7th International Joint Conference on Natural Language Processing (Volume 1: Long Papers)*, volume 1, pages 208–218.

Franz Josef Och and Hermann Ney. 2003. A systematic comparison of various statistical alignment models. *Computational Linguistics*, 29(1):19–51.

Kishore Papineni, Salim Roukos, Todd Ward, and Wei-Jing Zhu. 2002. Bleu: a method for automatic evaluation of machine translation. In *Proceedings of the 40th annual meeting on association for computational linguistics*, pages 311–318. Association for Computational Linguistics.

Matthew Snover, Bonnie Dorr, Richard Schwartz, Linnea Micciulla, and John Makhoul. 2006. A study of translation edit rate with targeted human annotation. In *Proceedings of association for machine translation in the Americas*, volume 200.

Kristina Toutanova, Dan Klein, Christopher D Manning, and Yoram Singer. 2003. Feature-rich part-of-speech tagging with a cyclic dependency network. In *Proceedings of the 2003 Conference of the North American Chapter of the Association for Computational Linguistics on Human Language Technology-Volume 1*, pages 173–180. Association for Computational Linguistics.

Roy Tromble and Jason Eisner. 2009. Learning linear ordering problems for better translation. In *Proceedings of the 2009 Conference on Empirical Methods in Natural Language Processing: Volume 2-Volume 2*, pages 1007–1016. Association for Computational Linguistics.

Karthik Visweswariah, Rajakrishnan Rajkumar, Ankur Gandhe, Ananthakrishnan Ramanathan, and Jiri Navratil. 2011. A word reordering model for improved machine translation. In *proceedings of the conference on empirical methods in natural language processing*, pages 486–496. Association for Computational Linguistics.

Yonghui Wu, Mike Schuster, Zhifeng Chen, Quoc V Le, Mohammad Norouzi, Wolfgang Macherey, Maxim Krikun, Yuan Cao, Qin Gao, Klaus Macherey, et al. 2016. Google's neural machine translation system: Bridging the gap between human and machine translation. *arXiv preprint arXiv:1609.08144*.

Fei Xia and Michael McCord. 2004. Improving a statistical mt system with automatically learned rewrite patterns. In *Proceedings of the 20th international conference on Computational Linguistics*, page 508. Association for Computational Linguistics.

Jinchao Zhang, Mingxuan Wang, Qun Liu, and Jie Zhou. 2017. Incorporating word reordering knowledge into attention-based neural machine translation. In *Proceedings of the 55th Annual Meeting of the Association for Computational Linguistics (Volume 1: Long Papers)*, volume 1, pages 1524–1534.

Exploring Word Alignment Towards an Efficient Sentence Aligner for Filipino and Cebuano Languages

Jenn Leana Fernandez and Kristine Mae Adlaon
College of Computer Studies
University of the Immaculate Conception
Father Selga Street, Davao City
{jfernandez_190000001847,kadlaon}@uic.edu.ph

Abstract

Building a robust machine translation (MT) system requires a large amount of parallel corpus which is an expensive resource for low-resourced languages. The two major languages being spoken in the Philippines which are Filipino and Cebuano have an abundance in monolingual data that this study took advantage of attempting to find the best way to automatically generate parallel corpus out from monolingual corpora through the use of bitext alignment. Byte-pair encoding was applied in an attempt to optimize the alignment of the source and target texts. Results have shown that alignment was best achieved without segmenting the tokens. Itermax alignment score is best for short-length sentences and match or argmax alignment score are best for long-length sentences.

1 Introduction

Word alignment is the task of discovering the corresponding words or terms in a bilingual sentence pair (Steingrímsson et al., 2021). Word-aligned corpora are a great source of translation-related knowledge. The estimation of translation model parameters usually relies heavily on word-aligned corpora (Liu et al., 2010). Therefore, the alignment of words is a crucial stage in the process of building a machine translation system (McCoy and Frank, 2017).

Sentence alignment is the task of aligning sentences in a document pair (Luo et al., 2021) or in a parallel corpus. In most cases, these sentence pairs share the same meaning or are contextually translated. Abundance of these parallel corpora is very evident for highly resourced languages while the collection and even building of such parallel corpus for low-resourced language is very difficult and is a very tedious task (Callison-Burch et al., 2004). The problem of aligning words in massively parallel texts containing hundreds or thousands of languages remains mostly unexplored (Östling, 2014) and that includes the Filipino and Cebuano languages .

The Philippines has a scarcity of language resources, particularly parallel corpora. Several studies have been conducted in an attempt to build a parallel corpus involving Philippine languages and most of them are paired with the English language (Michel et al., 2020; Ponay and Cheng, 2015; Lazaro et al., 2017). The study of Adlaon and Marcos (2019) had focused on the collection and building of both monolingual and parallel corpus for Filipino and Cebuano to build an NMT System (Adlaon and Marcos, 2018) for the said languages. The abundance of the collected monolingual corpora for the said language pair presents an opportunity for it to be transformed into a parallel corpus using an aligner.

Cebuano and Filipino are the two most spoken languages in the Philippines where the structure of these languages are morphologically-complex. Filipino language is flexible when it comes to word order. In fact, some Filipino sentence can be rearranged up to 6 different ways since sentence structures like SVO, VSO, VOS are accepted. While the Cebuano language, it is said to be predicated which explains why it follows the VSO format (Tariman, 2010). These languages can contribute and get benefits from our existing technology in different aspects, especially for machine translation. Translation studies and contrastive linguistics rely heavily on parallel corpora which are crucial for developing high-quality machine translation systems (Bañón et al., 2020; CLARIN, 2022). The transformation of the available monolingual corpus would be an addition to the existing Filipino-Cebuano parallel corpus. To date, the checking of the translation and the generation of parallel corpus is done manually which is a very laborious and tedious task especially when you have hundreds of thousands of sentences.

To the best of our knowledge, there is still no

Proceedings of the 29th International Conference on Computational Linguistic, pages 99–106
October 12–17, 2022.

word and sentence aligner effective for Cebuano and Filipino. In this paper, the researchers aim to conduct a preliminary investigation on the use of a word aligner for Cebuano and Filipino languages towards the development of an efficient sentence aligner and evaluate its performance in accordance to some ground truth.

2 Related Works

There have been different word alignment approaches that are widely used especially for machine translation. This section discusses the related studies of word and sentence alignment for machine translation.

The study of Kumar et al. (2007) describes a method for improving Statistical Machine Translation (SMT) performance in multiple bridge languages by leveraging multilingual, parallel, sentence-aligned corpora. Their solution includes a simple way for creating a word alignment system using a bridge language and a mechanism for integrating word alignment systems from various bridge languages. The researchers provide studies that show how this framework can be used to improve translation performance on an Arabic-to-English problem by using multilingual, parallel material in Spanish, French, Russian, and Chinese.

The paper goes over the many ways and challenges that come up when it comes to word alignment. Considering Hindi is based on subject object verb "SOV" and English is based on subject verb object "SVO," this study focuses on the major problem that occurs in word alignment. The report gives a survey on word alignment in the application of machine translation for foreign and Indian languages (Mall and Jaiswal, 2019).

Pourdamghani et al. (2018) described a strategy for enhancing word alignments by comparing words. This strategy is based on encouraging semantically comparable words to align in the same way. To estimate similarity, they employ word vectors trained on monolingual data. Additionally, by increasing the alignments of infrequent tokens, the researchers increase word alignments and machine translation in low-resource settings.

To improve the quality of Chinese-Vietnamese word alignment, Tran et al. (2017) incorporate linguistic relationship factors into the word alignment model. These are Sino-Vietnamese and content word linguistic relationships. The results of the experiments demonstrated that their strategy enhanced word alignment as well as machine translation quality.

Beloucif et al. (2016) presents a new statistical machine translation strategy that uses monolingual English semantic parsing to bias Inversion Transduction Grammar (ITG) induction and is specifically oriented to learning translation from low resource languages. The study shows that, in contrast to traditional statistical machine translation (SMT) training methods, which rely heavily on phrase memorization, the approach proposed focuses on learning bilingual correlations that aid in translating low-resource languages, with the output language semantic structure being used to further narrow ITG constraints.

Xiang et al. (2010) presented a novel approach for constructing and merging complementary word alignments for low-resource languages in order to increase word alignment quality and translation performance. In the study, they construct numerous sets of diverse alignments based on different incentives, such as linguistic knowledge, morphology, and heuristics, rather than focused on improving a single set of word alignments. By integrating the alignments acquired from syntactic reordering, stemming, and partial words, they demonstrate their strategy on an English-to-Pashto translation task. With much higher F scores and higher translation performance, the combined alignment surpasses the baseline alignment.

The researchers demonstrate that attention weights do accurately capture word alignments and propose two new word alignment induction methods, SHIFT-ATT and SHIFT-AET. The fundamental idea is to induce alignments when the to-be-aligned target token is the decoder input, rather than the decoder output, as in prior work (Chen et al., 2020).

In the study of Mao et al. (2022), they propose a word-level contrastive objective for many-to-many NMT that takes advantage of word alignments. For various language combinations, empirical studies demonstrate that this results in 0.8 BLEU gains. Analyses show that the encoder's sentence retrieval efficiency in many-to-many NMT is substantially correlated with translation quality, which explains why the suggested method has an impact on translation.

A study where the researchers used HMM-based models that were designed for bitext word and phrase alignment. The models are written in such a way that parameter estimation and alignment can be done quickly. Even with massive training bitexts, it has been founnd that Chinese English word alignment performance is comparable to IBM Model-4 (Deng and Byrne, 2005).

3 Methodology

3.1 Dataset

The parallel corpus that were used in this study come from the curated work of Adlaon and Marcos (2019). Their study aims to build a parallel corpus for Cebuano and Filipino where they used two different sources which is the biblical texts and the web. 500 sentence pairs in total of four domains were used for the experiments where it includes the bible texts, wikipedia, open domain, and news articles.

3.2 Data Cleaning and Transformation

In the dataset, the researchers performed data cleaning. This procedure was necessary in order to convert the data into a format that can be analyzed and be useful for the necessary experiments that will be applied to the corpus. Also, both Cebuano and Filipino texts were converted to lowercase. This is to avoid producing misleading results. Punctuations (i.e..,!?"';:-), numbers (i.e. 123...), and special characters (i.e. &*) were removed from the dataset which the researchers deemed to consider only alpha characters for this experimentation.

3.3 Preprocessing of the Corpus

Data preprocessing is a crucial step in doing an NLP task. This simply means transforming the data into a format that is predictable and easy to analyze (Menzli, 2021). In this experiment, the researchers performed subword tokenization specifically the Byte Pair Encoding to evaluate how tokenization contributes to distinguishing alignment of sentences of two different languages.

Byte Pair Encoding (BPE) or also known as diagram coding is a simple form of data compression in which the most common pair of successive bytes of data is replaced with a byte that does not present within that data (Mao, 2019). The BPE algorithm used in this study was from the work of Sennrich et al. (2016) where we set an average value of 35k merge operations per domain. Table 1 shows the comparison of a sentence without BPE, with BPE, and BPE with Lexicon trained on the corpus mentioned in section 3.1. The combined vocabulary of the four domains used in this study before BPE contains roughly 167k and 171k for Filipino and Cebuano respectively. After BPE, the vocabulary decreased its size to roughly 84k and 83k for Filipino and Cebuano respectively. The disparity of the size of the vocabulary from the set number of merge operations is attributed to the presence of scientific terms in the Wikipedia domain which the researchers supposed to exclude during the preprocessing phase.

In the study of Kudo (2018), they presented that BPE segmentation has the advantage of efficiently balancing vocabulary size and step size (the number of tokens required to encode the sentence). BPE uses a character frequency to train the merged processes. Early joining of frequent substrings will result in common words remaining as a single symbol. Rare character combinations will be broken down into smaller components, such as substrings or characters. As a result, even with a small fixed vocabulary (often 16k to 32k), the amount of symbols necessary to encode a sentence does not grow much, which is a crucial aspect for efficient decoding.

3.4 SimAlign Algorithm

There are different text aligners that are available and perform well on aligning two different languages. However, it requires a parallel data in order to generate great results. Also, the researchers aim to explore an embedding-based language model as several studies have shown that it could better capture both syntactic and semantic alignment(Jalili Sabet et al., 2020; Shen et al., 2017; Thompson and Koehn, 2019). In this paper, SimAlign algorithm which was proposed by Sabet et al. (2020) was utilized. The key concept of SimAlign is to use multilingual word embeddings for word alignment, both static and contextualized. In this study, we have used the pre-trained word embeddings available in the said study. For static embedding, for each language on Wikipedia, they used fastText (Bojanowski et al., 2016) to train monolingual embeddings. The embeddings are then mapped onto a shared multilingual space using VecMap (Artetxe et al., 2018). It must be noted that this algorithm operates without any cross-lingual supervision (e.g., multilingual dictionaries). On the other hand, multilingual BERT model (mBERT) was utilize in the contextualized embedding. It has been pre-trained on the 104 most popu-

Without BPE	**With BPE**
katulong umano ni velasco ang kanyang mga solid supporter sa kamara sa paggapang para maagapan ang inilulutong coup	*katulong umano ni velasco ang kanyang mga solid supporter sa kamara sa pagga@@ pang para maagapan ang inilu@@ lu@@ tong co@@ up*

Table 1: Comparison of a sentence without BPE and with BPE.

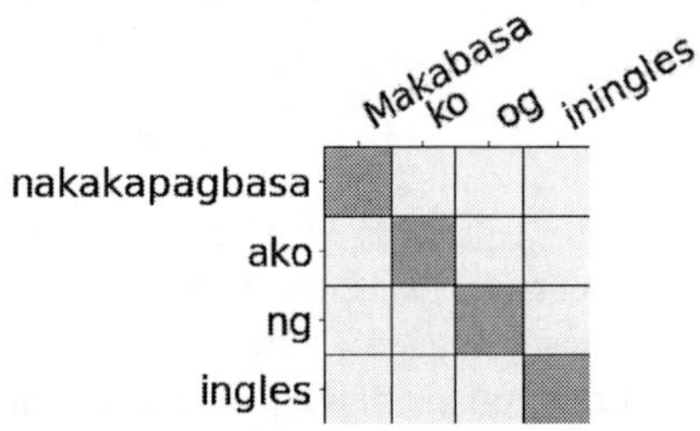

Figure 1: The alignment of Cebuano: Makabasa ko og iningles and Filipino: nakakapagbasa ako ng ingles with 4 words on each sentence. Which translates to *I can read English* in English.

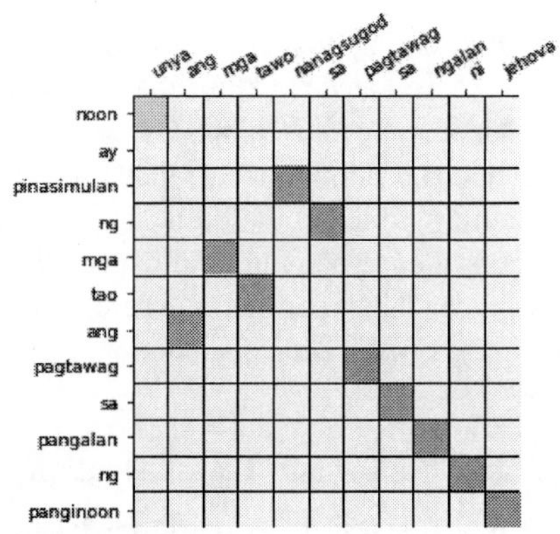

Figure 2: The alignment of Cebuano: unya ang mga tawo nanagsugod sa pagtawag sa ngalan ni jehova and Filipino: noon ay pinasimulan ng mga tao ang pagtawag sa pangalan ng panginoon with 11 and 12 words on each sentence for Cebuano and Filipino respectively. The input translates to *then the people started calling his name lord* in English.

lar Wikipedia languages. Also, only subword-level embeddings are offered by this model. Getting the average vectors of its subwords has been done to obtain a word embedding. Both the concatenation of all levels and word representations from each of the 12 layers are taken into account. It also has to be noted that the model has not been improved or finetuned. The study also proposed three different approaches namely, Itermax, Match, and Argmax to obtain alignments from similarity matrices. Itermax is a cutting-edge iterative approach, Match is a graph-theoretical technique focused on finding matches in a bipartite graph, while Argmax is a straightforward baseline. Figure 1, 2, and 3 shows how the alignment works of Cebuano and Filipino language of different word counts. The darker green shades are the sure links or equivalent translation of words for the both languages while the lighter green shade are the possible links or the translation that might have relation or if its not the exact translation of the word pair.

A gold standard must be created to measure the correctness of the different approaches in automatically aligning words using the SimAlign. The annotated gold standard used in this experiment was manually produced by the researchers where their mother-tongue language was Cebuano and Filipino language as their second language. The automatically generated alignment of Match, Inter, and Itermax will be evaluated using the 4 evaluation measures used for this experiment namely Precision, Recall, F1, and AER. AER requires a carefully annotated gold standard set of "Sure" and "Possible" links (referred to as S and P). Recall is measured using "sure" links, whereas Precision is measured using "possible" links. According to Och and Ney (2003), AER is derived from F-Measure. However, AER lacks one of F-most Measure's crucial features: the penalty for unbalanced precision and recall. The four measures are defined as:

$$Precision = \frac{|A \cap P|}{|A|}$$

$$Recall = \frac{|A \cap S|}{|S|}$$

$$F1 = \frac{2 Precision Recall}{Precision + Recall}$$

$$AER = 1 - \frac{|A \cap S| + |A \cap P|}{|A| + |S|}$$

4 Results and Discussions

In this section, we discussed the results for evaluating the aligned texts of the sentences with BPE and without BPE using the 4 evaluation measures namely Precision, Recall, F1, and AER. To determine the best alignment score, table 2 shows the three basis in choosing the best similarity matrix for each domain.

	Precision	Recall	F1	AER
Open Domain				
Match	0.778	**0.918**	0.842	0.16
Argmax	**0.873**	0.82	0.846	0.154
Itermax	0.813	0.908	**0.858**	**0.144**
Bible				
Match	0.634	**0.86**	0.73	0.273
Argmax	**0.798**	0.677	0.733	0.267
Itermax	0.726	0.817	**0.85**	**0.149**
Wikipedia				
Match	0.7	**0.9**	0.797	0.215
Argmax	**0.879**	0.758	**0.814**	**0.185**
Itermax	0.798	0.831	**0.814**	0.186
News Article				
Match	0.633	**0.858**	0.729	0.274
Argmax	**0.823**	0.688	0.749	0.249
Itermax	0.738	0.786	**0.761**	**0.239**
Applied with Byte-Pair Encoding				
Open Domain				
Match	0.746	0.895	0.814	0.188
Argmax	**0.867**	0.819	0.842	0.157
Itermax	0.816	**0.914**	**0.862**	**0.139**
Bible				
Match	0.515	**0.712**	0.598	0.405
Argmax	**0.649**	0.561	0.602	0.397
Itermax	0.589	0.646	**0.616**	**0.384**
Wikipedia				
Match	0.611	**0.832**	0.705	0.298
Argmax	**0.768**	0.702	0.734	0.266
Itermax	0.704	0.777	**0.739**	**0.262**
News Article				
Match	0.616	**0.836**	0.709	0.294
Argmax	**0.8**	0.669	0.729	0.27
Itermax	0.689	0.82	**0.749**	**0.254**

Table 2: Evaluation results of the aligned sentences with and without embedding. The best results per column on different domains are printed bold.

4.1 Without BPE

The alignments for the source and target texts are by tokens which was separated by white space. The result shows that without implementing BPE, the Open domain gets the highest score for *recall and F1*, with scores **0.918, 0.858** respectively which means the aligner was able to get the most number of matches compared to the other domains. Moreover it also gets the lowest score for AER with 0.144 which indicates that it has the lowest error rate among other domains. This could be attributed to its length that is shortest compared to the other domains.

It can also be observed that News Article domain gets the lowest score for *precision and F1*, with scores **0.633, 0.729** respectively. Additionally, it has the highest *AER* with the score **0.274** which tells us that this domain has the highest error rate. Upon the creation of the gold standard, we observed that the News Article corpus contains a lot of numbers, dates, and figures. However, since the dataset was preprocessed before the aligning of words, these numbers were removed and some necessary punctuations like hyphens which caused segmentation that makes the words incomprehensible and confusing that affects the alignment.

Based on the four domains used in this experiment, the Bible corpus has the most tokens per sentence which contains 1104 and 1507 sentences with number of tokens greater than 50 for Filipino and Cebuano respectively while there were no sentences greater than 50 tokens in the Open Domain. In line with this, we have observed that in short-length domains we acquire best results for Itermax while Match or Argmax are best for long-length domains. Figures 4, 5, 6, and 7 shows the examples of word alignments of Bible and Open Domain with and without BPE.

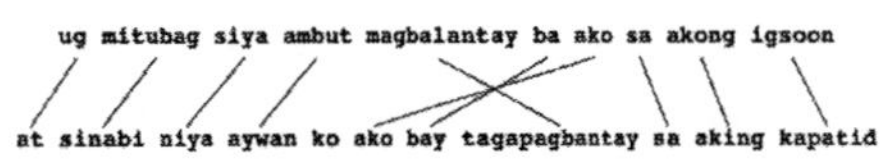

Figure 3: Example word alignment of Bible Text without BPE

4.2 With BPE

We implemented the Byte Pair Encoding on the four domains to evaluate the difference when the tokens are segmented or not. The result shows that with BPE, the Open Domain gets the fore-

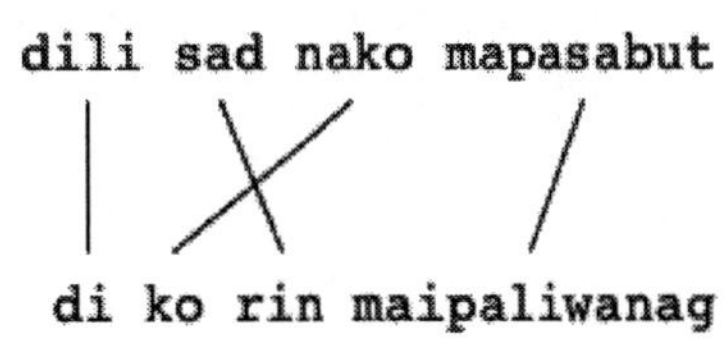

Figure 4: Example word alignment of Open Domain without BPE

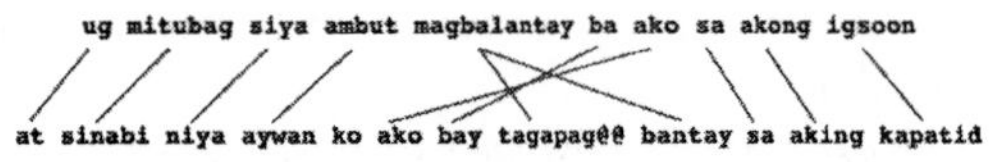

Figure 5: Example word alignment of Bible text with BPE

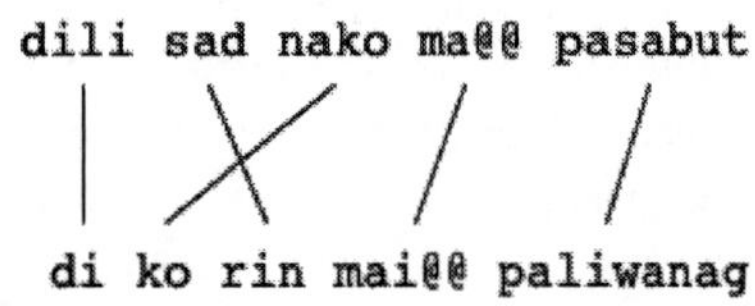

Figure 6: Example word alignment of Open Domain with BPE

most score for *precision, recall, F1, and AER*, with scores **0.867, 0.914, 0.862, 0.139** respectively which means the aligner was able to get the most number of matches compared to the other domains when applied with BPE.

It can be noticed that Bible domain gets the most unsatisfactory results for *precision, recall, F1, and AER*, with scores **0.515, 0.561, 0.602, 0.405** respectively.

Overall, if we compare the results of the dataset without BPE and with BPE, without BPE shows significantly higher scores than the dataset implemented with BPE. As what you have noticed in Table 1, on the 2nd column, the tokens are separated in a way that it is not understandable which also explains why the scores are low.

5 Conclusion

Sentence aligned parallel corpora are crucial in Machine Translation and choosing the most efficient aligner in different languages will be of great help in doing NLP tasks. In this study, we have observed that when aligning words, results are favorable when tokens are not segmented with BPE. Also, in the alignment from similarity matrices Match or Argmax are preferred for long-length sentences and Itermax for short-length sentences.

For future studies, it is recommended to increase the number of sentence pairs in the experimentation of the SimAlign to maximize the performance of algorithm. It is also recommended to explore a different embedding model that is specific to this kind of language to evaluate how embedding models affect the results of the alignment.

References

Kristine Mae M. Adlaon and Nelson Marcos. 2018. Neural machine translation for cebuano to tagalog with subword unit translation. In *2018 International Conference on Asian Language Processing (IALP)*, pages 328–333.

Kristine Mae M. Adlaon and Nelson Marcos. 2019. Building the language resource for a cebuano-filipino neural machine translation system. In *Proceedings of the 2019 3rd International Conference on Natural Language Processing and Information Retrieval*, NLPIR 2019, page 127–132, New York, NY, USA. Association for Computing Machinery.

Mikel Artetxe, Gorka Labaka, and Eneko Agirre. 2018. A robust self-learning method for fully unsupervised cross-lingual mappings of word embeddings. In *Proceedings of the 56th Annual Meeting of the Association for Computational Linguistics (Volume 1: Long Papers)*, pages 789–798, Melbourne, Australia. Association for Computational Linguistics.

Marta Bañón, Pinzhen Chen, Barry Haddow, Kenneth Heafield, Hieu Hoang, Miquel Esplà-Gomis, Mikel L. Forcada, Amir Kamran, Faheem Kirefu, Philipp Koehn, Sergio Ortiz Rojas, Leopoldo Pla Sempere, Gema Ramírez-Sánchez, Elsa Sarrías, Marek Strelec, Brian Thompson, William Waites, Dion Wiggins, and Jaume Zaragoza. 2020. ParaCrawl: Web-scale acquisition of parallel corpora. In *Proceedings of the 58th Annual Meeting of the Association for Computational Linguistics*, pages 4555–4567, Online. Association for Computational Linguistics.

Meriem Beloucif, Markus Saers, and Dekai Wu. 2016. Improving word alignment for low resource languages using English monolingual SRL. In *Proceedings of the Sixth Workshop on Hybrid Approaches to Translation (HyTra6)*, pages 51–60, Osaka, Japan. The COLING 2016 Organizing Committee.

Piotr Bojanowski, Edouard Grave, Armand Joulin, and Tomás Mikolov. 2016. Enriching word vectors with subword information. *CoRR*, abs/1607.04606.

Chris Callison-Burch, David Talbot, and Miles Osborne. 2004. Statistical machine translation with word- and sentence-aligned parallel corpora. In *Proceedings of the 42nd Annual Meeting on Association for Computational Linguistics*, ACL '04, page 175–es, USA. Association for Computational Linguistics.

Yun Chen, Yang Liu, Guanhua Chen, Xin Jiang, and Qun Liu. 2020. Accurate word alignment induction from neural machine translation. In *Proceedings of the 2020 Conference on Empirical Methods in Natural Language Processing (EMNLP)*, pages 566–576, Online. Association for Computational Linguistics.

CLARIN. 2022. Parallel corpora.

Yonggang Deng and William Byrne. 2005. HMM word and phrase alignment for statistical machine translation. In *Proceedings of Human Language Technology*

Conference and Conference on Empirical Methods in Natural Language Processing, pages 169–176, Vancouver, British Columbia, Canada. Association for Computational Linguistics.

Masoud Jalili Sabet, Philipp Dufter, François Yvon, and Hinrich Schütze. 2020. SimAlign: High quality word alignments without parallel training data using static and contextualized embeddings. In *Findings of the Association for Computational Linguistics: EMNLP 2020*, pages 1627–1643, Online. Association for Computational Linguistics.

Taku Kudo. 2018. Subword regularization: Improving neural network translation models with multiple subword candidates. In *Proceedings of the 56th Annual Meeting of the Association for Computational Linguistics (Volume 1: Long Papers)*, pages 66–75, Melbourne, Australia. Association for Computational Linguistics.

Shankar Kumar, Franz J. Och, and Wolfgang Macherey. 2007. Improving word alignment with bridge languages. In *Proceedings of the 2007 Joint Conference on Empirical Methods in Natural Language Processing and Computational Natural Language Learning (EMNLP-CoNLL)*, pages 42–50, Prague, Czech Republic. Association for Computational Linguistics.

A.N. Lazaro, Nathaniel Oco, and Rachel Edita Roxas. 2017. Developing a bidirectional ilocano-english translator for the travel domain: Using domain adaptation techniques on religious parallel corpora. In *11th International Conference of the Asian Association for Lexicography*, Guangzhou, China.

Yang Liu, Qun Liu, and Shouxun Lin. 2010. Discriminative word alignment by linear modeling. *Computational Linguistics*, 36(3):303–339.

Shengxuan Luo, Huaiyuan Ying, and Sheng Yu. 2021. Sentence alignment with parallel documents helps biomedical machine translation. *CoRR*, abs/2104.08588.

Shachi Mall and Umesh Chandra Jaiswal. 2019. Issues in word alignment from hindi-english languages. *International Journal of Engineering and Advanced Technology (IJEAT)*, 8.

Lei Mao. 2019. Byte pair encoding.

Zhuoyuan Mao, Chenhui Chu, Raj Dabre, Haiyue Song, Zhen Wan, and Sadao Kurohashi. 2022. When do contrastive word alignments improve many-to-many neural machine translation? In *Findings of the Association for Computational Linguistics: NAACL 2022*, pages 1766–1775, Seattle, United States. Association for Computational Linguistics.

Tom McCoy and Robert Frank. 2017. Pivot-based word alignment.

Amal Menzli. 2021. Tokenization in nlp: Types, challenges, examples, tools.

Leah Michel, Viktor Hangya, and Alexander Fraser. 2020. Exploring bilingual word embeddings for Hiligaynon, a low-resource language. In *Proceedings of the 12th Language Resources and Evaluation Conference*, pages 2573–2580, Marseille, France. European Language Resources Association.

Franz Josef Och and Hermann Ney. 2003. A systematic comparison of various statistical alignment models. *Computational Linguistics*, 29(1):19–51.

Robert Östling. 2014. Bayesian word alignment for massively parallel texts. In *Proceedings of the 14th Conference of the European Chapter of the Association for Computational Linguistics, volume 2: Short Papers*, pages 123–127, Gothenburg, Sweden. Association for Computational Linguistics.

Charmaine Ponay and Charibeth Cheng. 2015. 23. building an english-filipino tourism corpus and lexicon for an asean language translation system.

Nima Pourdamghani, Marjan Ghazvininejad, and Kevin Knight. 2018. Using word vectors to improve word alignments for low resource machine translation. In *Proceedings of the 2018 Conference of the North American Chapter of the Association for Computational Linguistics: Human Language Technologies, Volume 2 (Short Papers)*, pages 524–528, New Orleans, Louisiana. Association for Computational Linguistics.

Masoud Jalili Sabet, Philipp Dufter, and Hinrich Schütze. 2020. Simalign: High quality word alignments without parallel training data using static and contextualized embeddings. *CoRR*, abs/2004.08728.

Rico Sennrich, Barry Haddow, and Alexandra Birch. 2016. Neural machine translation of rare words with subword units. In *Proceedings of the 54th Annual Meeting of the Association for Computational Linguistics (Volume 1: Long Papers)*, pages 1715–1725, Berlin, Germany. Association for Computational Linguistics.

Gehui Shen, Yunlun Yang, and Zhi-Hong Deng. 2017. Inter-weighted alignment network for sentence pair modeling. In *Proceedings of the 2017 Conference on Empirical Methods in Natural Language Processing*, pages 1179–1189, Copenhagen, Denmark. Association for Computational Linguistics.

Steinþór Steingrímsson, Hrafn Loftsson, and Andy Way. 2021. CombAlign: a tool for obtaining high-quality word alignments. In *Proceedings of the 23rd Nordic Conference on Computational Linguistics (NoDaLiDa)*, pages 64–73, Reykjavik, Iceland (Online). Linköping University Electronic Press, Sweden.

Jun Tariman. 2010. Cebuano 101: The cebuano language sentence structure. pages 22–26.

Brian Thompson and Philipp Koehn. 2019. Vecalign: Improved sentence alignment in linear time and space. In *Proceedings of the 2019 Conference on Empirical Methods in Natural Language Processing and the*

9th International Joint Conference on Natural Language Processing (EMNLP-IJCNLP), pages 1342–1348, Hong Kong, China. Association for Computational Linguistics.

Phuoc Tran, Dien Dinh, Tan Le, and Long H. B. Nguyen. 2017. Linguistic-relationships-based approach for improving word alignment. *ACM Trans. Asian Low-Resour. Lang. Inf. Process.*, 17(1).

Bing Xiang, Yonggang Deng, and Bowen Zhou. 2010. Diversify and combine: Improving word alignment for machine translation on low-resource languages. In *Proceedings of the ACL 2010 Conference Short Papers*.

Aligning Word Vectors on Low-Resource Languages with Wiktionary

Mike Izbicki
Claremont McKenna College
mike@izbicki.me

Abstract

Aligned word embeddings have become a popular technique for low-resource natural language processing. Most existing evaluation datasets are generated automatically from machine translations systems, so they have many errors and exist only for high-resource languages. We introduce the Wiktionary bilingual lexicon collection, which provides high-quality human annotated translations for words in 298 languages to English. We use these lexicons to train and evaluate the largest published collection of aligned word embeddings on 157 different languages. All of our code and data is publicly available at `https://github.com/mikeizbicki/wiktionary_bli`.

1 Introduction

A bilingual lexicon is a mapping of words from a source language into a target language. The *bilingual lexicon induction* (BLI) problem is the task of learning such a mapping from data. Most recent solutions to this problem follow a two step procedure: First, train word vectors on a large monolingual corpus for each language individually using a standard algorithm like word2vec (Mikolov et al., 2013a), GloVe (Pennington et al., 2014), or fastText (Bojanowski et al., 2017). Then, learn a transformation that aligns these two vector spaces into a common space (e.g. Mikolov et al., 2013b; Xing et al., 2015; Joulin et al., 2018; Artetxe et al., 2018a; Zhang et al., 2019; Glavaš et al., 2019; Vulić et al., 2019). The BLI problem is then solved by performing nearest neighbor queries in the common space. The focus of this work is the ground truth bilingual lexicon used to train and evaluate these models.

Recent previous work has relied on the MUSE lexicon collection (Conneau et al., 2017). This collection provides bilingual lexicons between 45 languages and English. This lexicon is generated from a machine translation system, and so suffers from a number of problems. First, many of the mappings in the lexicon do not contain real words in either the source or target language (see Figure 1 for examples from Thai). Second, the distribution of words is inconsistent between languages, with many languages containing only proper nouns in their training and test sets. Due to these problems, Kementchedjhieva et al. (2019) suggest that future research "avoids drawing conclusions from quantitative results on this BLI dataset." Other datasets (described in Section 2 below) have even worse limitations.

This paper introduces a new bilingual lexicon collection based on Wiktionary. Wiktionary contains more than 7 million words in 8166 languages and has been collaboratively edited by 3.9 million users.[1] Our specific contributions are:

1. We use Wiktionary to construct high-quality bilingual lexicons suitable for training and evaluating BLI models from 298 languages into English. Most of these languages are extremely low-resource, and many of them are extinct. We provide the first BLI datasets for 253 of these languages, and for the remaining 45 we improve the quality of existing datasets. Our lexicon collection is the first to allow meaningful cross-lingual performance comparisons on the BLI task.

2. We train the largest collection of BLI models to date. Grave et al. (2018) provide pretrained word vectors in 157 languages, and we train BLI models between each of these languages and English. 112 of these languages had not previously had BLI models trained on them because no training/evaluation data previously existed. Of these 112 previously unstudied languages, we identify 15 as having particularly good performance (Armenian, Austurian,

[1] `https://en.wiktionary.org/wiki/Wiktionary:Statistics`

Proceedings of the 29th International Conference on Computational Linguistic, pages 107–117
October 12–17, 2022.

Thai "Word"	English "Translation"
แคลอรี่	calories
โคมลอย	lanterns
univ	univ
bdfutbol	bdfutbol
efm	efm
พล็อต	plot
getparent	getparent
roca	roca
เป๊ะ	exactly
annie	annie

Figure 1: The last 10 data points for the Thai test files in the widely used MUSE dataset (Conneau et al., 2017). These translation pairs were machine generated without any human input, and this results in bad translation pairs. For example, Thai words should always written in the Thai script, but many words are written in Latin script. Words like `getparent` do not even correspond to words in any natural language and are an artifact of JavaScript code incorrectly included in the original source material. Our Wiktionary dataset contains only high-quality human verified translations and so does not have these problems.

Azerbaijani, Basque, Belarusian, Esperanto, Galician, Georgian, Malayalam, Norwegian Nynorsk, Serbian, Serbo-Croatian, and Welsh) and thus potentially suitable for downstream cross-lingual tasks.

The remainder of this paper is organized as follows. Section 2 discusses related work. Section 3 describes the lexicon construction procedures. Section 4 experimentally demonstrates that the resulting lexicons are of high quality, and trains the new models.

2 Related Work

Applications. Aligned word embeddings have many applications. They are an important component in many document-level translation systems of low-resource languages (Di Gangi and Federico, 2017; Neishi et al., 2017; Artetxe et al., 2017b, 2018b; Qi et al., 2018; Ding and Duh, 2018; Kim et al., 2018; Xia et al., 2019; Font and Costa-Jussa, 2019; Chen and Basirat, 2020). They are also used on non-translation tasks like cross-lingual morphological segmentation (Chimalamarri et al., 2020), dependency parsing (Ahmad et al., 2018), information retrieval (Vulić and Moens, 2015), and document classification (Klementiev et al., 2012; Mogadala and Rettinger, 2016). Our Wiktionary dataset allows better aligned word embeddings to be trained on more languages, allowing all of these "downstream tasks" to be extended into these other languages as well.

Wiktionary. Wiktionary is a valuable resource and widely used by the NLP community. A google scholar search for "Wiktionary" produces 21 000 results on diverse tasks such as synonym detection (Navarro et al., 2009), idiom extraction (Muzny and Zettlemoyer, 2013), and word sense disambiguation (Ben Aouicha et al., 2018). The prior works most closely related to our own are general purpose information extractors (e.g. Acs, 2014; Sérasset, 2015; Nastase and Strapparava, 2015; Kirov et al., 2016; Sajous et al., 2020; Wu and Yarowsky, 2020). Although these extractors can be used to extract translation information, they have not been used explicitly for the purpose of generating datasets for machine translation problems like the BLI problem.

Alternative Datasets. Many datasets have been proposed for the training and evaluation of word vectors. Prior to the MUSE lexicons (Conneau et al., 2017), papers studying BLI all used their own ad-hoc datasets. For example: Mikolov et al. (2013b) introduce Spanish-English and Czech-English lexicons; Dinu and Baroni (2014) introduce an Italian-English lexicon; Artetxe et al. (2017a) introduce German-English and Finish-English lexicons; and Zhang et al. (2017) introduce Spanish-English and Chinese-English lexicons. Since the introduction of MUSE, Glavaš et al. (2019) followed a similar procedure to create an additional 28 bilingual lexicons for high-resource non-English language pairs. Using a machine translation system makes it impossible to create lexicons for low-resource languages without introducing serious mistakes as seen in Figure 1. Furthermore, inter-language comparisons should not be done because the topics covered by the languages' test sets vary considerably (Kementchedjhieva et al., 2019). Our Wiktionary dataset fixes all of these problems.

3 Dataset Overview

In this section, We first describe the data extraction process, then we describe how we split the data into training and test sets. Both steps use language-agnostic approaches. Our goal is to make the data for each language as similar as possible so that cross-lingual evaluations can be made in a fair and consistent manner.

Category	Small	Full
Adjective	50	350
Adverb	25	150
Conjunction	–	25
Determiner	–	25
Interjection	–	25
Noun	125	500
Number	–	50
Pronoun	–	25
Proper noun	–	50
Verb	50	300
Total	250	1500

Table 1: The number of source words of each part of speech for the small and full test sets.

3.1 Data Extraction

Users enter all their data into Wiktionary using the MediaWiki Markdown language. This language is designed primarily for human editors, but contains sufficient semantic annotations to enable machine parsing of entries. We extract all words, also storing the associated language, part of speech, and English-language definition.

Table 2 summarizes the total number of words extracted for selected languages, including a breakdown by part of speech. Many of the languages for which we provide BLI data are now extinct. For example, Ancient Greek has 11381 data points, Old English has 7362, and Tocharian B has 1807.

3.2 Train/Test Splits

In order to train BLI models, we need to split the data extracted above into training and testing sets for each language. We follow the precedent of the MUSE dataset and have the "full test set" contain 1500 words. To facilitate comparison between low resource languages for which it will be difficult to find 1500 meaningful words, we also create a "small test set", which is a subset of the full test set containing 250 words.

We take particular care to construct these test sets so that fair comparisons can be made between languages. In particular, we use the part of speech information extracted from Wiktionary to ensure that each test set has the same number of words in each part of speech. Table 1 shows the number of words. The small test set includes only the "semantic" parts of speech (Adjective, Adverb, Noun, Verb) and not the "syntactic" parts of speech because many low-resource languages lack entries for the syntactic parts of speech and we believe the semantic parts of speech to be more intuitively meaningful.

To populate the small test set, we select the most frequent words from each category. A sampling strategy could result in a harder test set for languages with more words to choose from because they might select less-frequently used words. The remaining words in the large test set are sampled uniformly from the 10 000 most common words for each category. In practice, this allows ranked as high as 20 000 to be included in the test set. This choice makes the Wiktionary test sets significantly harder than the MUSE test sets, which use the 5000-6500 most frequent words regardless of their part of speech.

Finally, we note that not all languages will be able to fully construct test sets according to the procedures above. For example, the Finish lexicon is large (76 375 words), but it only has 17 determiners, and so the final full test set cannot contain 1500 words. This is not due to a defect of the Wiktionary dataset in this language, but just due to the fact that Finish naturally has fewer determiners than other languages. We do not resolve this conflict by adding more words of a different part of speech to the test set, as this would distort the proportions of each part of speech, making the results less comparable. Instead, we simply use a smaller test set. Most languages have a truncated test set due to this effect. Table 3 shows the number of languages with different size test sets. We suggest that meaningful inter-lingual comparisons can be made with models evaluated on 80% of a complete small test set, and so there are 298 languages that can be evaluated using our Wiktionary dataset. Of course many of these languages will have essentially no training data available, and so these languages represent an extreme test-case for unsupervised vector alignment algorithms.

4 Experiments

We perform three experiments. The first experiment measures the importance of the size of the BLI training dataset on model performance. The second experiment compares the quality of the MUSE and Wiktionary lexicons. The final experiment trains BLI models on 112 new, previously unstudied languages.

For all experiments, we align the common crawl vectors provided by Grave et al. (2018) to the English-language vectors trained on the common crawl provided by Mikolov et al. (2018). We use

Rank	Language	Total	Parts of Speech									
			Adj	Adv	Conj	Det	Interj	Noun	Num	Pron	PN	Verb
1	Italian	82 948	22 045	3 799	91	49	123	45 264	108	118	2 809	8 542
2	Finnish	76 375	11 832	3 843	48	17	298	46 631	145	123	1 381	12 057
3	Chinese	75 750	7 142	1 813	192	18	199	43 472	111	387	9 892	12 524
4	Spanish	69 086	17 827	2 605	37	54	201	39 353	53	93	2 488	6 375
5	French	60 692	15 613	2 857	26	25	183	33 444	94	100	2 492	5 858
6	Romanian	54 068	11 873	545	25	38	118	29 537	44	89	7 310	4 489
7	Japanese	47 965	3 052	1 029	94	0	231	32 936	67	225	3 330	7 001
8	German	47 128	11 385	1 071	60	37	141	25 004	242	96	3 116	5 976
9	Serbo-Croatian	47 040	8 793	3 606	92	3	106	24 579	84	231	1 524	8 022
10	Portuguese	41 621	9 428	1 458	33	6	213	22 579	55	75	3 592	4 182
11	Polish	40 096	7 427	1 855	81	0	181	20 939	123	97	1 106	8 287
12	Russian	38 799	7 258	1 467	45	13	215	18 876	52	93	1 680	9 100
13	Dutch	34 716	4 952	792	49	59	161	16 415	105	110	7 539	4 534
14	Macedonian	30 149	7 356	2 681	30	26	91	13 382	53	69	578	5 883
15	Czech	26 958	6 557	702	65	0	133	14 972	45	83	849	3 552
16	Latin	23 155	6 545	1 112	58	19	47	10 074	97	56	2 004	3 143
17	Korean	22 796	790	511	2	97	89	17 814	161	89	1 276	1 967
18	Catalan	22 024	4 528	965	14	19	48	12 266	104	81	1 033	2 966
19	Hungarian	21 660	4 735	967	69	27	143	11 605	215	138	677	3 084
20	Swedish	18 933	3 543	1 002	45	13	88	10 461	145	111	781	2 744
⋮												
101	Zulu	2 208	24	35	15	1	9	1 346	0	42	3	733
102	Volapük	2 194	198	72	20	18	8	1 454	42	48	119	215
103	Basque	2 168	210	59	14	9	18	1 487	31	36	114	190
104	Yoruba	2 165	62	33	10	13	11	1 503	73	38	170	252
105	Westrobothnian	2 107	410	111	15	5	9	879	10	26	5	637
106	Northern Kurdish	2 079	255	42	8	0	5	1 536	21	17	58	137
107	Cimbrian	2 020	199	106	24	13	9	1 095	49	67	23	435
108	Interlingua	2 017	430	60	8	19	7	1 072	24	29	67	301
109	Old Irish	2 013	322	33	33	18	3	1 033	22	42	57	450
110	Egyptian	2 001	67	34	1	25	12	991	21	74	110	666
⋮												
201	Laz	688	20	4	0	0	3	641	7	1	9	3
202	Chechen	686	74	14	3	0	0	498	25	6	17	49
203	Karelian	683	69	13	0	9	0	484	16	29	14	49
204	Tuvan	683	109	27	8	6	4	363	20	27	7	112
205	Low German	683	82	20	8	1	2	487	22	12	10	39
206	Romagnol	683	102	13	3	2	1	415	12	6	12	117
207	Piedmontese	674	118	2	0	0	1	389	28	11	9	116
208	Kavalan	669	63	7	1	0	1	568	11	14	0	4
209	Maquiritari	654	0	72	0	0	3	347	7	27	6	192
210	Zazaki	648	51	15	6	0	3	463	27	21	19	43
⋮												
501	Khaling	127	2	9	1	0	0	76	0	19	1	19
502	Muong	127	17	2	0	0	0	77	11	4	0	16
503	Western Lawa	126	11	1	0	0	1	77	2	1	0	33
504	Picard	126	6	3	0	1	0	77	0	5	3	31
505	Old Marathi	125	17	5	0	0	0	88	0	0	2	13
506	Pohnpeian	125	17	1	1	4	3	70	1	1	1	26
507	Saaroa	123	1	0	0	0	0	121	1	0	0	0
508	Jingpho	121	6	1	0	0	0	81	9	2	0	22
509	Sierra Miwok	120	6	8	1	3	0	88	0	0	0	14
510	Khorezmian Turkic	120	1	1	0	0	0	1	0	0	0	117
⋮												

Table 2: Number of words in the Wiktionary Dataset broken down by their part of speech. Nouns form the bulk every language's vocabulary. The column abbreviations are Adj: Adjective, Adv: Adverb, Conj: Conjunction, Det: Determiner, Interj: Interjection, Num: Number, Pron: Pronoun, PN: Proper Noun.

Percent	Small	Full
100	164	8
90	236	81
80	298	104
70	356	124
60	412	153
50	478	185

Table 3: The "Small" and "Large" columns indicate the number of languages whose completed test set is "Percent" the size that it is supposed to be. For example, only 8 languages can construct a proper full test set with 1500 source words, but 104 languages can construct a full test set with $(80\%)(1500) = 1120$ words.

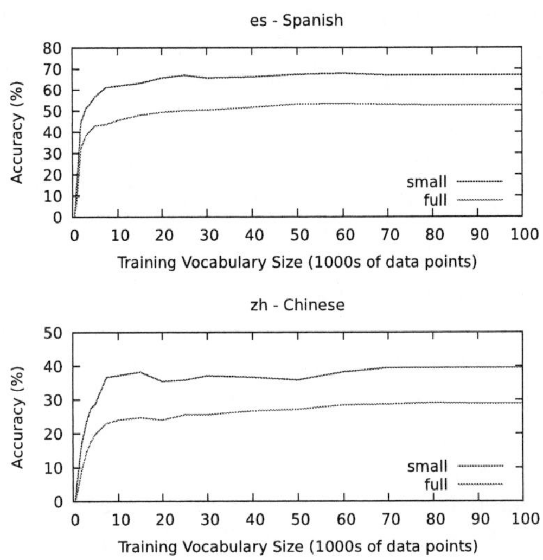

Figure 2: BLI accuracy as a function of dataset size.

the iterative normalization preprocessing procedure (Zhang et al., 2019) to transform both the source and target language vectors before learning. This is different than the most common evaluation setup in the literature, which aligns vectors trained on wikipedia provided by Bojanowski et al. (2017). We use this non-standard setting because our preliminary tests (not shown) found it to give significantly better results for the low-resource languages that we study in Section 4.3 and equivalent results for the high-resource languages.

4.1 Training Dictionary Size

The goal of this experiment is to measure the effect of training dataset size on the performance of supervised BLI models. There are two reasons for performing this experiment. The first is computational. The runtime and memory usage of most BLI training algorithms is proportional to the input training set size. So for languages with large training sets, we want to learn at what size should we truncate the dataset in order to speed up training without sacrificing performance. The second reason is statistical. The size of the training sets we extracted from Wiktionary follow a power law distribution, with a small number of high-resource languages having many translations, but most languages having few translations. We want to understand how having a small training set will effect the BLI performance of these datasets.

To perform the experiment, we construct modified training sets by taking the first n samples from the Wiktionary training set, where n ranges from 0 to 100 000. For each truncated training set, we train the supervised VecMap model (Artetxe et al., 2018a), and evaluate on both the small and full test sets. Results are shown in Figure 2 for the Spanish-English and Chinese-English language pairs. In both cases, BLI accuracy rapidly increases as the number of training samples reaches 5k, and then tapers off. After 20k training points, there is minimal improvement and the performance occasionally decreases due to statistical randomness.[2] This is consistent with previous findings on the effect of training dataset size using the MUSE dataset (Vulić and Korhonen, 2016; Qiu et al., 2018; Glavaš et al., 2019).

In the experiments below, we will train many models. For computational reasons, we truncate the training set size to 20k and expect not to lose any accuracy. We also know that if we observe extremely poor BLI performance in an experiment with at least (about) 5k entries in the BLI training set, then the poor performance is likely not explained by the size of the BLI training set but by some other cause.

4.2 MUSE Corpus vs Wiktionary Corpus

Our next experiment attempts to measure the quality of the MUSE and Wiktionary datasets for the 45 language pairs supported by both datasets. The first three columns of Table 4 show summary statistics of both datasets (details are provided in the table caption). The fourth column is the most interesting, and is the focus of our explanation here.

We train the VecMap (Artetxe et al., 2018a) BLI

[2]Other language pairs are not shown for space reasons, but all had similar results.

model on each language pair, once on the MUSE dataset and once on the Wiktionary dataset. Then for both models, we evaluate on the Wiktionary dataset. The results are shown in the rightmost column of Table 4. Surprisingly, the MUSE training set outperforms the Wiktionary training set for 22/45 of the languages despite coming from a seemingly different distribution. This suggests that despite the high quality nature of the Wiktionary test set data, it is not complete, and more data from more data sources could still be used to improve the alignment of vector spaces.

We hypothesize two reasons to explain this effect. First, the effect only happens when the MUSE training set is much larger than the Wiktionary training set. For example, in the case of Slovak, the MUSE training set has 36 891 data points and the Wiktionary set has only 5 396. The experiments in Section 4.1 above suggest that our Wiktionary dataset's size of about 5k words is large enough to get meaningful results, but that a larger dictionary would still improve performance. Second, Wiktionary is naturally biased towards containing the "dictionary" (i.e. unconjugated) forms of words. Slovak is a fusional language with many inflected forms for each word, and this helps explain the smaller size of the wiktionary dataset.

4.3 The Grave et al. (2018) Languages

Grave et al. (2018) released word vectors in 157 languages trained on the common crawl corpus (a multi-petabyte collection of webpages). All 45 of the languages in the MUSE corpus studied above appear in the Grave et al. (2018) corpus; so in this section we focus on the 112 languages that do not. As far as we are aware, no one has previously attempted to align these embeddings, and there are no previously published datasets of bilingual lexicons suitable for training or evaluation. The Wiktionary corpus is therefore the first publicly available dataset for training and testing alignment models in these languages. The size of each language's dataset and the accuracy for each model on the small and full test set are shown in Table 5.

We train 3 alignment models on each language: the Procrustes (Xing et al., 2015) and Bootstrap Procrustes (Glavaš et al., 2019; Vulić et al., 2019) as implemented by the MUSE project, and VecMap (Artetxe et al., 2018a). There are many other supervised methods and unsupervised methods that would be interesting to train on these datasets, but we did not have the computational resources to do so. Thirteen languages achieve an accuracy on the full test set greater than 30: Esperanto (50.00), Galician (46.62), Armenian (39.15), Azerbaijani (37.38), Georgian (37.30), Austurian (36.92), Basque (36.32), Belarusian (35.75), Welsh (34.84), Malayalam (33.62), Serbo-Croatian (33.17), Norwegian Nynorsk (32.35), and Serbian (30.76). An additional 2 languages achieve an accuracy on the small test set greater than 30: Urdu (37.08) and Mongolian (31.38). We call out the 30% threshold in particular because these languages achieve competitive performance with the languages from the widely used MUSE test set (Table 4), and therefore are good candidates for downstream applications. Because of the careful construction of the test set, as described in Section 3.2 above, it is reasonable to compare the absolute performance between languages. Such comparisons were not recommended for the MUSE dataset (Kementchedjhieva et al., 2019) due to the high variability in quality and content between languages.

We observe that the higher-resource languages (top of table) tend to have better BLI performance than the lower resource languages (bottom of table). We suggest that this difference is not due to a lower quality of the Wiktionary lexicons, but to the lower quality of the Grave et al. (2018) word vectors trained on smaller datasets. We note that in our dictionary size experiment from Section 4.1 above, training lexicons as small as 5k examples give strong performance when the monolingual word vectors are high quality. In Table 5, however, we see performance drop off long before this 5k mark. This is particularly notable in the Latin and Sanskrit languages. Both languages have a large Wiktionary dataset (41 278 and 11 363), but poor BLI performance (13.03 and 2.98 on the full test set). We attribute this to the fact that these languages are of particular interest to the Wiktionary community for their historical importance, and thus have a lot of entries; but their historical nature also means there are few webpages written in these languages, and so the word vectors trained on the common crawl corpus will be of low quality. Word vectors trained on small corpuses are known to be less stable (Pierrejean and Tanguy, 2018; Wendlandt et al., 2018; Leszczynski et al., 2020; Burdick et al., 2021) and therefore difficult to align even with large BLI training data (Vulić et al., 2020).

Source Language		Full Vocab Size		Fraction Distinct		Distinct Vocab Size		BLI Accuracy	
		MUSE	Wikt	MUSE	Wikt	MUSE	Wikt	MUSE	Wikt
af	Afrikaans	**37 421**	4 848	0.30	**0.95**	**11 226**	4 605	**42.13**	35.08
ar	Arabic	**31 355**	26 361	**1.00**	**1.00**	**31 355**	26 361	**31.94**	30.35
bg	Bulgarian	**55 170**	13 827	**1.00**	**1.00**	**55 170**	13 827	48.91	**52.84**
bn	Bengali	**23 829**	5 712	**1.00**	**1.00**	**23 829**	5 712	**28.34**	26.68
bs	Bosnian	43 318	**73 449**	0.38	**0.99**	16 460	**72 714**	**35.95**	29.49
ca	Catalan	78 081	**116 348**	0.30	**0.99**	23 424	**115 184**	**49.79**	49.53
cs	Czech	**64 211**	35 879	0.55	**0.98**	**35 316**	35 161	47.78	**49.67**
da	Danish	**81 959**	16 680	0.46	**0.94**	**37 701**	15 679	49.79	**53.56**
de	German	**101 997**	68 029	0.52	**0.94**	53 038	**63 947**	47.46	**48.88**
el	Greek	**45 515**	32 519	**1.00**	**1.00**	**45 515**	32 519	53.02	**55.45**
es	Spanish	**112 583**	91 066	0.45	**0.95**	50 662	**86 512**	54.40	**54.67**
et	Estonian	**32 776**	6 901	0.64	**0.98**	**20 976**	6 762	**50.04**	48.07
fa	Persian	**41 321**	14 238	**1.00**	**1.00**	**41 321**	14 238	37.39	**39.40**
fi	Finnish	43 102	**105 030**	0.62	**0.99**	26 723	**103 979**	**43.90**	43.11
fr	French	**113 324**	78 837	0.35	**0.90**	39 663	**70 953**	**53.92**	53.57
he	Hebrew	**45 679**	12 234	**1.00**	**1.00**	**45 679**	12 234	33.47	**35.32**
hi	Hindi	**31 046**	21 887	**1.00**	**1.00**	**31 046**	21 887	33.99	**38.28**
hr	Croatian	56 424	**73 449**	0.49	**0.99**	27 647	**72 714**	**47.57**	45.21
hu	Hungarian	**42 823**	34 569	0.62	**0.99**	26 550	**34 223**	45.48	**49.29**
id	Indonesian	**96 518**	12 269	0.30	**0.97**	**28 955**	11 900	35.20	**40.15**
it	Italian	103 613	**119 697**	0.40	**0.98**	41 445	**117 303**	**46.43**	45.47
ja	Japanese	25 969	**73 669**	**1.00**	**1.00**	25 969	**73 669**	**24.96**	24.96
ko	Korean	20 549	**34 739**	**1.00**	**1.00**	20 549	**34 739**	23.84	**31.64**
lt	Lithuanian	**33 435**	6 270	0.55	**1.00**	**18 389**	6 270	**51.22**	49.86
lv	Latvian	**46 385**	14 428	0.72	**1.00**	**33 397**	14 428	50.11	**52.12**
mk	Macedonian	**43 935**	41 054	**1.00**	**1.00**	**43 935**	41 054	37.97	**40.23**
ms	Malay	**73 092**	5 821	0.23	**0.97**	**16 811**	5 646	27.60	**28.56**
nl	Dutch	**93 853**	67 309	0.38	**0.97**	35 664	**65 289**	**39.78**	36.57
no	Norwegian Bokmål	**75 171**	21 386	0.37	**0.95**	**27 813**	20 316	**54.24**	43.96
pl	Polish	**73 901**	66 225	0.48	**0.98**	35 472	**64 900**	**44.18**	41.11
pt	Portuguese	**108 686**	55 927	0.42	**0.95**	45 648	**53 130**	58.42	**58.68**
ro	Romanian	**80 821**	65 122	0.39	**0.93**	31 520	**60 563**	**48.96**	48.58
ru	Russian	48 714	**70 740**	**1.00**	**1.00**	48 714	**70 740**	**46.99**	39.86
sk	Slovak	**65 878**	5 681	0.56	**0.95**	**36 891**	5 396	**54.29**	53.27
sl	Slovene	**62 890**	4 401	0.53	**0.99**	**33 331**	4 356	**49.40**	40.86
sq	Albanian	**52 090**	8 628	0.53	**1.00**	**27 607**	8 628	**36.97**	33.47
sv	Swedish	**82 348**	27 724	0.42	**0.95**	**34 586**	26 337	49.12	**52.82**
ta	Tamil	**21 230**	8 376	**1.00**	**1.00**	**21 230**	8 376	**29.11**	21.20
th	Thai	**25 332**	19 988	0.38	**1.00**	9 626	**19 988**	19.70	**23.33**
tl	Tagalog	**34 984**	17 817	0.28	**0.98**	9 795	**17 460**	28.24	**30.14**
tr	Turkish	**68 611**	15 271	0.42	**0.98**	**28 816**	14 965	34.51	**40.49**
uk	Ukrainian	**40 723**	16 910	**1.00**	**1.00**	**40 723**	16 910	59.10	**59.18**
vi	Vietnamese	**76 364**	9 708	0.08	**1.00**	6 109	**9 708**	11.34	**12.34**
zh	Chinese	21 597	**119 459**	**1.00**	**1.00**	21 597	**119 459**	24.66	**27.78**
Total Best		35	10	14	45	24	21	22	23

Table 4: A comparison of the MUSE and Wiktionary datasets. The "Full Vocab Size" measures the total number of source/target word pairs in each dataset. Recall, however, that the MUSE dataset is machine translated, and has many artifacts from this process. One such artifact is the presence of many duplicate entries where the source and target words are the same, and frequently not valid words in either language (See Figure 1 for examples in Thai). The "Fraction Distinct" column measures the fraction of source/target word pairs where the source value does not equal the target. This number is extremely low for many of the MUSE lexicons (e.g. 0.38 for Thai and 0.08 for Vietnamese) due to the machine translation generation process. This number is high for all of the Wiktionary lexicons because they are sourced from high quality human generated translations. All of the duplicate entries are the result of true cognate words between the source language and English. The "Distinct Vocab Size" column computes the total number of distinct source/target pairs in each lexicon, and is equal to the Full Vocab Size column times the Fraction Distinct column. We see that many of the MUSE lexicons are still larger than the Wiktionary lexicons because they allow conjugates of words to appear in a lexicon multiple times, but this does not happen in the Wiktionary lexicon. Finally the "BLI Accuracy" column presents the result of a MUSE-trained model and a Wiktionary trained model on the Wiktionary test set. See Section 4.2 for details.

				Small Test Set			Full Test Set		
Rank	Source Language		Vocab Size	Proc	Proc-B	VecMap	Proc	Proc-B	VecMap
1	`sr`	Serbian	73 449	28.51	**47.79**	42.57	19.43	**30.76**	29.27
2	`sh`	Serbo-Croatian	73 449	42.34	**52.42**	46.37	28.64	**33.17**	31.78
3	`la`	Latin	41 278	14.11	14.11	**21.37**	9.65	9.65	**13.03**
4	`ga`	Irish	26 579	24.79	24.79	**29.75**	16.20	16.20	**18.81**
5	`hy`	Armenian	22 748	50.00	**52.02**	50.40	37.91	38.10	**39.15**
6	`nn`	Norwegian Nynorsk	19 881	26.53	26.53	**28.98**	30.17	30.17	**33.25**
7	`is`	Icelandic	19 570	32.52	36.59	**39.43**	29.82	29.91	**34.59**
8	`gl`	Galician	19 155	47.77	**52.63**	51.82	45.06	45.32	**46.62**
9	`ka`	Georgian	18 898	36.71	36.71	**42.19**	34.14	34.14	**37.30**
10	`eo`	Esperanto	18 534	49.36	49.36	**54.94**	47.14	47.14	**50.00**
11	`te`	Telugu	13 289	14.11	14.11	**15.77**	13.81	13.81	**16.19**
12	`gd`	Scottish Gaelic	12 443	9.80	9.80	**11.84**	8.32	8.32	**8.53**
13	`km`	Khmer	11 378	21.54	**26.42**	22.76	16.28	17.56	**18.50**
14	`sa`	Sanskrit	11 363	**4.08**	4.08	1.22	**2.98**	2.98	1.56
15	`kk`	Kazakh	11 323	**26.67**	26.67	23.33	27.11	27.11	**27.20**
16	`ceb`	Cebuano	10 853	**5.88**	5.88	5.88	**8.22**	8.22	3.88
17	`az`	Azerbaijani	10 713	37.65	**39.27**	38.46	36.09	**37.38**	37.12
18	`azb`	Southern Azerbaijani	10 713	**2.10**	2.10	1.40	**2.91**	2.91	1.82
19	`cy`	Welsh	10 459	40.57	**46.31**	44.26	30.98	34.34	**34.84**
20	`io`	Ido	8 127	**14.00**	14.00	14.00	12.30	12.30	**12.75**
21	`gv`	Manx	8 105	**5.93**	5.93	3.39	**6.39**	6.39	3.27
22	`mt`	Maltese	8 089	**0.00**	0.00	0.00	**0.00**	0.00	0.00
23	`ml`	Malayalam	7 465	27.78	28.63	**30.34**	29.60	32.47	**33.62**
24	`lb`	Luxembourgish	7 438	4.88	**8.54**	5.69	10.89	**11.99**	6.13
25	`sw`	Swahili	7 324	12.45	12.86	**15.35**	15.94	**18.01**	17.49
26	`ur`	Urdu	7 013	26.25	**37.08**	26.25	23.64	**29.73**	24.81
27	`yi`	Yiddish	6 869	4.86	4.86	**5.26**	7.79	7.79	**9.79**
28	`my`	Burmese	5 902	13.52	**16.80**	13.11	13.77	**15.90**	15.26
29	`ast`	Asturian	5 645	27.98	30.86	**33.33**	30.12	33.65	**36.92**
30	`bcl`	Bikol Central	5 069	**6.22**	6.22	4.98	**5.16**	5.16	3.53
31	`be`	Belarusian	4 598	27.92	**30.00**	27.92	32.81	**35.75**	33.92
32	`mn`	Mongolian	4 470	21.34	**31.38**	19.67	21.10	**27.97**	19.14
33	`as`	Assamese	4 341	1.28	1.28	**1.70**	4.49	4.49	**4.72**
34	`oc`	Occitan	4 317	16.96	18.70	**20.87**	20.26	**22.23**	22.23
35	`gu`	Gujarati	4 068	10.78	**18.53**	10.34	10.85	**16.81**	12.51
36	`ba`	Bashkir	4 053	7.00	7.00	**9.47**	9.03	9.03	**9.54**
37	`sco`	Scots	3 734	**9.09**	9.09	3.54	**10.82**	10.82	8.19
38	`mg`	Malagasy	3 634	**5.26**	5.26	4.78	**4.05**	4.05	3.64
39	`vec`	Venetian	3 570	**3.24**	3.24	2.43	**3.94**	3.94	3.48
40	`yo`	Yoruba	3 536	**1.34**	1.34	0.00	**0.87**	0.87	0.00
41	`bo`	Tibetan	3 438	**1.02**	1.02	0.00	**1.48**	1.48	0.00
42	`sah`	Yakut	3 265	**2.87**	2.87	0.82	**4.00**	4.00	2.83
43	`qu`	Quechua	3 190	**4.13**	4.13	0.00	**3.60**	3.60	0.00
44	`eu`	Basque	3 117	20.89	**38.67**	23.56	25.42	**36.32**	23.48
45	`mr`	Marathi	3 016	11.02	**22.88**	13.98	13.73	**19.82**	12.85
46	`pnb`	Western Punjabi	2 692	0.00	**0.52**	0.00	0.00	**0.37**	0.00
47	`pa`	Punjabi	2 692	**4.66**	4.66	2.54	**5.35**	5.35	3.36
48	`vo`	Volapük	2 673	**2.98**	2.98	0.85	**3.92**	3.92	2.04
49	`ku`	Northern Kurdish	2 658	**2.87**	1.64	2.87	5.52	**5.79**	3.77
50	`rm`	Romansch	2 479	**2.03**	2.03	1.22	**5.64**	5.64	4.05
51	`ia`	Interlingua	2 397	7.29	**10.12**	4.45	8.25	**9.68**	5.22
52	`ne`	Nepali	2 185	7.88	**10.37**	2.07	10.11	**10.51**	4.65
53	`fy`	West Frisian	2 137	7.50	**10.83**	4.17	10.48	**14.06**	5.41
54	`scn`	Sicilian	2 050	**2.86**	2.86	1.63	**5.41**	5.41	2.85
55	`ug`	Uyghur	1 919	**1.72**	1.72	0.00	**3.78**	3.78	0.15
56	`als`	Alemannic German	1 888	**0.50**	0.50	0.00	**2.64**	2.64	0.00
57	`uz`	Uzbek	1 845	**8.06**	8.06	7.11	**12.64**	12.64	8.58
58	`kn`	Kannada	1 837	6.19	**20.00**	8.10	9.12	**21.40**	7.19
59	`tg`	Tajik	1 725	11.79	**18.34**	14.69	**16.25**	0.00	0.00
60	`jv`	Javanese	1 641	**0.00**	0.00	0.00	**0.00**	0.00	0.00

Table 5: Results of the experiment described in Section 4.3. Displayed are results on the languages with the 60 largest lexicons from the Grave et al. (2018) corpus that are not also included in the MUSE corpus.

References

Judit Acs. 2014. Pivot-based multilingual dictionary building using wiktionary. *LREC*.

Wasi Uddin Ahmad, Zhisong Zhang, Xuezhe Ma, Eduard Hovy, Kai-Wei Chang, and Nanyun Peng. 2018. On difficulties of cross-lingual transfer with order differences: A case study on dependency parsing. *arXiv preprint arXiv:1811.00570*.

Maria Antoniak and David Mimno. 2018. Evaluating the stability of embedding-based word similarities. *Transactions of the Association for Computational Linguistics*, 6:107–119.

Mikel Artetxe, Gorka Labaka, and Eneko Agirre. 2017a. Learning bilingual word embeddings with (almost) no bilingual data. In *Proceedings of the 55th Annual Meeting of the Association for Computational Linguistics (Volume 1: Long Papers)*, pages 451–462.

Mikel Artetxe, Gorka Labaka, and Eneko Agirre. 2018a. Generalizing and improving bilingual word embedding mappings with a multi-step framework of linear transformations. In *Proceedings of the AAAI Conference on Artificial Intelligence*, volume 32.

Mikel Artetxe, Gorka Labaka, and Eneko Agirre. 2018b. Unsupervised statistical machine translation. *arXiv preprint arXiv:1809.01272*.

Mikel Artetxe, Gorka Labaka, Eneko Agirre, and Kyunghyun Cho. 2017b. Unsupervised neural machine translation. *arXiv preprint arXiv:1710.11041*.

Mohamed Ben Aouicha, Mohamed Ali Hadj Taieb, and Hania Ibn Marai. 2018. Wordnet and wiktionary-based approach for word sense disambiguation. In *Transactions on Computational Collective Intelligence XXIX*, pages 123–143. Springer.

Piotr Bojanowski, Edouard Grave, Armand Joulin, and Tomas Mikolov. 2017. Enriching word vectors with subword information. *Transactions of the Association for Computational Linguistics*, 5:135–146.

Laura Burdick, Jonathan K Kummerfeld, and Rada Mihalcea. 2021. Analyzing the surprising variability in word embedding stability across languages. *EMNLP*.

Shifei Chen and Ali Basirat. 2020. Cross-lingual word embeddings beyond zero-shot machine translation. *Swedish Language Technology Conference (SLTC-2020)*.

Santwana Chimalamarri, Dinkar Sitaram, and Ashritha Jain. 2020. Morphological segmentation to improve crosslingual word embeddings for low resource languages. *ACM Transactions on Asian and Low-Resource Language Information Processing (TALLIP)*, 19(5):1–15.

Alexis Conneau, Guillaume Lample, Marc'Aurelio Ranzato, Ludovic Denoyer, and Hervé Jégou. 2017. Word translation without parallel data. *arXiv preprint arXiv:1710.04087*.

Mattia Antonino Di Gangi and Marcello Federico. 2017. Monolingual embeddings for low resourced neural machine translation. In *Proceedings of the 14th International Conference on Spoken Language Translation*, pages 97–104.

Shuoyang Ding and Kevin Duh. 2018. How do source-side monolingual word embeddings impact neural machine translation? *arXiv preprint arXiv:1806.01515*.

Georgiana Dinu and Marco Baroni. 2014. How to make words with vectors: Phrase generation in distributional semantics. In *Proceedings of the 52nd Annual Meeting of the Association for Computational Linguistics (Volume 1: Long Papers)*, pages 624–633.

Joel Escudé Font and Marta R Costa-Jussa. 2019. Equalizing gender biases in neural machine translation with word embeddings techniques. *arXiv preprint arXiv:1901.03116*.

Goran Glavaš, Robert Litschko, Sebastian Ruder, and Ivan Vulic. 2019. How to (properly) evaluate cross-lingual word embeddings: On strong baselines, comparative analyses, and some misconceptions. *arXiv preprint arXiv:1902.00508*.

Edouard Grave, Piotr Bojanowski, Prakhar Gupta, Armand Joulin, and Tomas Mikolov. 2018. Learning word vectors for 157 languages. In *Proceedings of the International Conference on Language Resources and Evaluation (LREC 2018)*.

Armand Joulin, Piotr Bojanowski, Tomas Mikolov, Hervé Jégou, and Edouard Grave. 2018. Loss in translation: Learning bilingual word mapping with a retrieval criterion. In *Proceedings of the 2018 Conference on Empirical Methods in Natural Language Processing*.

Yova Kementchedjhieva, Mareike Hartmann, and Anders Søgaard. 2019. Lost in evaluation: Misleading benchmarks for bilingual dictionary induction. *EMNLP/IJCNLP*.

Yunsu Kim, Jiahui Geng, and Hermann Ney. 2018. Improving unsupervised word-by-word translation with language model and denoising autoencoder. *Empirical Methods in Natural Language Processing (EMNLP)*.

Christo Kirov, John Sylak-Glassman, Roger Que, and David Yarowsky. 2016. Very-large scale parsing and normalization of wiktionary morphological paradigms. In *Proceedings of the Tenth International Conference on Language Resources and Evaluation (LREC'16)*, pages 3121–3126.

Alexandre Klementiev, Ivan Titov, and Binod Bhattarai. 2012. Inducing crosslingual distributed representations of words. In *Proceedings of COLING 2012*, pages 1459–1474.

Megan Leszczynski, Avner May, Jian Zhang, Sen Wu, Christopher Aberger, and Christopher Ré. 2020. Understanding the downstream instability of word embeddings. *Proceedings of Machine Learning and Systems*, 2:262–290.

Tomas Mikolov, Kai Chen, Greg Corrado, and Jeffrey Dean. 2013a. Efficient estimation of word representations in vector space. *arXiv preprint arXiv:1301.3781*.

Tomas Mikolov, Edouard Grave, Piotr Bojanowski, Christian Puhrsch, and Armand Joulin. 2018. Advances in pre-training distributed word representations. In *Proceedings of the International Conference on Language Resources and Evaluation (LREC 2018)*.

Tomas Mikolov, Quoc V Le, and Ilya Sutskever. 2013b. Exploiting similarities among languages for machine translation. *arXiv preprint arXiv:1309.4168*.

Aditya Mogadala and Achim Rettinger. 2016. Bilingual word embeddings from parallel and non-parallel corpora for cross-language text classification. In *Proceedings of the 2016 Conference of the North American Chapter of the Association for Computational Linguistics: Human Language Technologies*, pages 692–702.

Grace Muzny and Luke Zettlemoyer. 2013. Automatic idiom identification in wiktionary. In *Proceedings of the 2013 Conference on Empirical Methods in Natural Language Processing*, pages 1417–1421.

Vivi Nastase and Carlo Strapparava. 2015. knowitiary: A machine readable incarnation of wiktionary. *Int. J. Comput. Linguistics Appl.*, 6(2):61–82.

Emmanuel Navarro, Franck Sajous, Bruno Gaume, Laurent Prévot, Hsieh ShuKai, Kuo Tzu-Yi, Pierre Magistry, and Huang Chu-Ren. 2009. Wiktionary and nlp: Improving synonymy networks. In *ACL Workshop on The People's Web Meets NLP: Collaboratively Constructed Semantic Resources*, pages 19–27.

Masato Neishi, Jin Sakuma, Satoshi Tohda, Shonosuke Ishiwatari, Naoki Yoshinaga, and Masashi Toyoda. 2017. A bag of useful tricks for practical neural machine translation: Embedding layer initialization and large batch size. In *Proceedings of the 4th Workshop on Asian Translation (WAT2017)*, pages 99–109.

Jeffrey Pennington, Richard Socher, and Christopher D. Manning. 2014. Glove: Global vectors for word representation. In *Empirical Methods in Natural Language Processing (EMNLP)*, pages 1532–1543.

Bénédicte Pierrejean and Ludovic Tanguy. 2018. Towards qualitative word embeddings evaluation: Measuring neighbors variation. In *Conference of the North American Chapter of the Association for Computational Linguistics: Student Research Workshop*, pages 32–39.

Ye Qi, Devendra Singh Sachan, Matthieu Felix, Sarguna Janani Padmanabhan, and Graham Neubig. 2018. When and why are pre-trained word embeddings useful for neural machine translation? *arXiv preprint arXiv:1804.06323*.

Yuanyuan Qiu, Hongzheng Li, Shen Li, Yingdi Jiang, Renfen Hu, and Lijiao Yang. 2018. Revisiting correlations between intrinsic and extrinsic evaluations of word embeddings. In *Chinese computational linguistics and natural language processing based on naturally annotated big data*, pages 209–221. Springer.

Franck Sajous, Basilio Calderone, and Nabil Hathout. 2020. Englawi: From human-to machine-readable wiktionary. In *12th Conference on Language Resources and Evaluation (LREC 2020)*, pages 3016–3026.

Gilles Sérasset. 2015. Dbnary: Wiktionary as a lemon-based multilingual lexical resource in rdf. *Semantic Web*, 6(4):355–361.

Ivan Vulić, Goran Glavaš, Roi Reichart, and Anna Korhonen. 2019. Do we really need fully unsupervised cross-lingual embeddings? *EMNLP-IJCNLP*.

Ivan Vulić and Anna-Leena Korhonen. 2016. On the role of seed lexicons in learning bilingual word embeddings. *Proceedings of ACL*.

Ivan Vulić and Marie-Francine Moens. 2015. Monolingual and cross-lingual information retrieval models based on (bilingual) word embeddings. In *Proceedings of the 38th international ACM SIGIR conference on research and development in information retrieval*, pages 363–372.

Ivan Vulić, Sebastian Ruder, and Anders Søgaard. 2020. Are all good word vector spaces isomorphic? *arXiv preprint arXiv:2004.04070*.

Laura Wendlandt, Jonathan K Kummerfeld, and Rada Mihalcea. 2018. Factors influencing the surprising instability of word embeddings. *NAACL HLT*.

Winston Wu and David Yarowsky. 2020. Wiktionary normalization of translations and morphological information. In *Proceedings of the 28th International Conference on Computational Linguistics*, pages 4683–4692.

Mengzhou Xia, Xiang Kong, Antonios Anastasopoulos, and Graham Neubig. 2019. Generalized data augmentation for low-resource translation. *arXiv preprint arXiv:1906.03785*.

Chao Xing, Dong Wang, Chao Liu, and Yiye Lin. 2015. Normalized word embedding and orthogonal transform for bilingual word translation. In *Proceedings of the 2015 conference of the North American chapter of the association for computational linguistics: human language technologies*, pages 1006–1011.

Meng Zhang, Yang Liu, Huanbo Luan, and Maosong Sun. 2017. Adversarial training for unsupervised bilingual lexicon induction. In *Proceedings of the 55th Annual Meeting of the Association for Computational Linguistics (Volume 1: Long Papers)*, pages 1959–1970.

Mozhi Zhang, Keyulu Xu, Ken-ichi Kawarabayashi, Stefanie Jegelka, and Jordan Boyd-Graber. 2019. Are girls neko or sh\= ojo? cross-lingual alignment of non-isomorphic embeddings with iterative normalization. *arXiv preprint arXiv:1906.01622*.

Author Index

Association for Computational Linguistics
209 N. Eighth Street
Stroudsburg, Pennsylvania 18360

ISBN 978-1-7138-6191-1

CURRAN ASSOCIATES INC.
proceedings
.com